OXFORD THEOLOGY AND RELIGION MONOGRAPHS

Schelling's Theory of Symbolic Language

Forming the System of Identity

DANIEL WHISTLER

OXFORD

UNIVERSITY PRESS

OXFORD
UNIVERSITY PRESS

Great Clarendon Street, Oxford, OX2 6DP,
United Kingdom

Oxford University Press is a department of the University of Oxford.
It furthers the University's objective of excellence in research, scholarship,
and education by publishing worldwide. Oxford is a registered trade mark of
Oxford University Press in the UK and in certain other countries

First Edition published in 2013

Impression: 1

British Library Cataloguing in Publication Data

Data available

ISBN 978-0-19-967373-5

Printed in Great Britain by
the MPG Printgroup, UK

Preface

F. W. J. Schelling's construction of symbolic language in §73 of his *Philosophie der Kunst* sheds much-needed light on both the history of the emergence of the symbol in the *Goethezeit* and Schelling's own philosophical practice of the time.[1] Such is the thesis defended in this book. As my argument progresses, it will become clear that both the peculiar theory of language Schelling lays out in §73 and the distinctive manner in which he so lays it out contribute to a new ideal of systematization. My argument therefore needs to be situated in terms of two critical debates: first, historical reconstructions of the symbol; second, philosophical reconstructions of Schelling's project.

The fate of the symbol in the twentieth century has been far from propitious. In Musil's *Der Mann ohne Eigenschaften*, for instance, the legacy of 'the romantic symbol'[2] is characterized as follows by Ulrich, the novel's protagonist:

> What they meant by 'symbol' was the great images of grace, which made everything that is confused and dwarfed in life . . . clear and great, images that suppress the noise of the senses and dip the forehead into the stream of transcendence. Such symbols were the Isenheim Altar, the Egyptian pyramids, and Novalis . . . But they did not state, in so many words, what a symbol was: first, because a symbol cannot be expressed in so many words; second, because Aryans do not deal in dry formulas, which is why they achieved only approximations of symbols during the last century; and third, because some centuries only rarely produce the transcendent moment of grace in the transcendent human being. (Musil 1995, 338)

Ulrich's reflections on the nationalist and racist appropriation of the idea of the symbol act out our post-Romantic unease over the concept. It is a mysterious means of accessing the transcendent, a way of escaping this world into an other-worldly realm of perfection; it is ineffable and so escapes rational criticism; it is bestowed upon a few world-historical individuals, thereby feeding into early twentieth-century fascistic and proto-fascistic discourse. The implication is not just that the symbol is a conservative relic from

---

[1] I use the underdetermined term, *Goethezeit*, to describe this period of German thought, since the labels 'Idealism', 'Romanticism', and 'Classicism' all suggest an artificial separation between Schelling and (for instance) Goethe or A. W. Schlegel.

[2] As I will make clear in Chapter 1, I place quotation marks around 'romantic' in this context to indicate the fact that for the most part the Romantics were not involved in the development of the symbol.

a reactionary era; it is also pernicious—both theoretically and politically. Such is the legacy of the symbol in the twentieth century.

In what follows, I make the case for a fresh recovery of the symbol. We need to re-attend to the emergence of the symbol in *Goethezeit* Germany to uncover the diversity at its root. Not all theories of the symbol possessed the properties listed above, not all theories of the symbol could be appropriated by the political worldview Ulrich intimates. In fact, during the first few years of the nineteenth century the symbol was a site of experimentation: it was theorized and re-theorized in radically conflicting ways for radically different ends. What we remember as the monolithic 'romantic' symbol did not exist; it is a fiction instituted by our cultural memory at the expense of divergent, even antithetical formulations of the symbol.

I set about provisionally demonstrating these claims by focusing on Schelling's theory of symbolic language. Schelling's theory is suited to this role because it has been so carelessly treated in the past by both historians of the symbol and Schelling scholars alike. Schelling is consistently (and falsely) taken to be a proponent of 'the romantic symbol'—and a particularly poor proponent at that. Indeed, it is rare that the Schellingian symbol is mentioned without accompanying accusations of plagiarism or, at least, unoriginality. Yet, a study of the place of the symbol (and, in particular, symbolic language) in his philosophical system of the time (the *Identitätssystem*) very quickly reveals its irreducible difference from traditional accounts of the symbol. Schellingian symbolic language is distinctive—peculiar, even—and this puts into question any unitary account of 'the romantic symbol' and its development. Schelling's theory is illustrative of the multiple experiments undertaken in the name of the symbol in the first few years of the nineteenth century.

The second critical debate in which this book intervenes concerns interpretations of Schelling's philosophy, for my concentration on Schelling's theory of symbolic language is not merely for the sake of historical accounts of the symbol alone, but is also intended as a way-in to Schelling's philosophical system. This book is, therefore, an attempt to reconstruct Schelling's philosophy of the time, the *Identitätssystem*, by means of a focus on the role the symbol plays therein. This period of Schelling's philosophical output has been seriously neglected over the last thirty years and stands in need of critical attention. To begin to remedy this situation, I provide a detailed reconstruction of the system which Schelling developed in his writings between 1801 and 1805. Moreover, I go on to argue that the concept of symbolic language illuminates Schelling's metaphilosophical practice. Unlike Hegel, Fichte, and Maimon, Schelling is often reticent about what he is doing when he writes philosophy; the concept of symbolic language, however, sheds light on this underexplored area of Schelling's thought by drawing attention to his conception of the work done by the words on the page of a philosophy text in forming a system.

The contribution that an analysis of §73 of the *Philosophie der Kunst* can make to these two critical debates (understanding the history of the symbol and understanding Schelling's *Identitätssystem*) explains why I place so much emphasis in what follows on this short, unassuming paragraph from a set of posthumously published lecture notes. When read in the context of the emergence of the symbol and the monistic rigour of the *Identitätssystem*, §73 of the *Philosophie der Kunst* is a hidden gem in Schelling's output. And while one should not make too much of it (it is, after all, sketchy on details and sometimes carelessly phrased), I hope that by the end of the book readers will agree that it deserves the central position I have given it.

Over the course of the book, I approach Schelling's construction of symbolic language in §73 of his *Philosophie der Kunst* in three ways. First, I compare Schellingian symbolic language to other contemporary theories of the symbol and language (in particular, those of Goethe, Kant, and A. W. Schlegel). While Schelling's theory of symbolic language possesses properties similar to these other theories (the identity of being and meaning, organic wholeness, the co-existence of opposites), I show that it differs in how those properties are interpreted. Second, I excavate the metaphysical and epistemological principles from Schelling's philosophy of the period which underlie this theory of language. Three tenets from the *Identitätssystem* are crucial: formation, quantitative differentiation, and construction. They illuminate why Schelling interprets symbolic language very differently to his contemporaries. Third, I consider the metaphilosophical significance of Schellingian symbolic language. This significance is twofold. First, his theory gives rise to a conception of discourse without reference, and so to the notion of a science without reference.[3] On this basis, Schelling criticizes current practices of science for remaining too concerned with referring to reality, when what is at stake is rather the degree of intensity to which they produce reality. Science therefore stands in need of reformation. Second, the way in which the science of theology (in particular) is utilized by Schelling in order to construct symbolic language in §73 of the *Philosophie der Kunst* itself provides a model for reformed scientific practice. I argue that Schelling conceives of the sciences as material for intensifying the production of reality. In this way, an absolute system is engendered which has no concern for reference or for the integrity of particular scientific pursuits.

Part I of the book therefore focuses on other theories of language and the symbol formulated in the years leading up to Schelling's construction of symbolic language in late 1802. Chapter 1 considers Kant, Goethe, and A. W. Schlegel's theories of the symbol, so as to delineate an interpretation

---

[3] 'Science' is here used to refer to any knowledge-orientated discourse, in line with the German *Wissenschaft*.

of this concept which was dominant then and since (what I call, the 'romantic' interpretation) against which Schelling vehemently reacts. In Chapter 2, I turn to the other element of symbolic language—language—and I outline the various traditions of linguistic thought which provide the context for Schelling's construction. For the most part my focus rests on other accounts of (or failures to account for) *symbolic* language in the *Goethezeit*.[4]

In Part II, I examine Schelling's *Identitätssystem*, and so the metaphysical and epistemological principles underlying his construction of symbolic language. Chapter 3 provides a brief introduction to the *Identitätssystem*. Chapter 4 looks in detail at its metaphysical foundations by rehearsing Schelling's answer to the fundamental metaphysical question, 'in what does reality consist?' Chapter 5 concentrates on a much-neglected but central tenet of the *Identitätssystem*—quantitative differentiation. I use quantitative differentiation to elucidate the doctrine of the potencies (the *Potenzlehre*). In Chapter 6, I turn to Schellingian epistemology and in particular his notion of construction.

Part III explores the key sections from the *Philosophie der Kunst* in which Schelling constructs first the symbol in general and second symbolic language in particular. Chapter 7 is a detailed commentary on §39 of the *Philosophie der Kunst* where Schelling constructs his notion of the symbol; I show how he subverts and mutates previous theories of the symbol. In Chapter 8, I turn to some of the more general questions concerning the status and role of language in Schelling's *Identitätssystem*. This chapter is preliminary to my more sustained engagement with Schellingian symbolic language in Chapter 9. Chapter 9 itself is another detailed commentary, this time on §73 of the *Philosophie der Kunst*. I bring all the preceding arguments to bear in an attempt to fully describe the meaning, role, and significance of the construction of symbolic language.

Part IV argues for the metaphilosophical import of this construction. In Chapter 10, I draw some general conclusions from Schelling's philosophy of language and transpose them into the domain of systematic practice. Employing the example of the science of theology in particular, I argue that (a) Schelling's views on language compel him to critique theology both past and present and consequently (b) Schelling sets about reforming theology (and so science in general). Finally, Chapter 11 takes up the metaphilosophical

---

[4] It is worth pointing out at this point a lacuna in my argument. I do not discuss Coleridge's theory of the symbol, for example, or Humboldt's theory of language, nor in Part II do I consider Hegel's criticisms of Schelling's *Identitätssystem* in any detail. In fact, philosophical, theological, and linguistic developments after 1805 are not discussed here at all. The reader may find this a somewhat frustrating lack, since the question 'how does this relate to X?' seems extremely pressing at many points. However, understanding Schelling's own thought (and the sources on which he drew) is the prime objective of my argument, rather than complex comparisons with later thought.

significance of Schellingian symbolic language from another perspective, concentrating on a specific strategy Schelling practises to make scientific language symbolic: systematic eclecticism. All scientific forms are materials to be plundered in the formation of the system of identity.

We are living through a Schelling renaissance. Markus Gabriel, Iain Hamilton Grant, Joseph Lawrence, Bruce Matthews, Sean McGrath, Dalia Nassar, and Jason Wirth, among others, are reviving his legacy and, in so doing, building on the ground-breaking writings of a decade ago (by Bowie, Courtine, Fischbach, Frank, Hogrebe, Vater, and Žižek). This book is thoroughly indebted to such innovative Schelling scholarship, even if I take issue with the continual and pathological neglect of the *Identitätssystem*. Indeed, one has to look back to Hermann Zeltner or Klaus Düsing's work from the 1970s to find the last focused reconstruction of this stage of Schelling's philosophy.

The arguments which follow were forged in conversation with numerous teachers, friends, and colleagues: Pamela Sue Anderson, Jenny Bunker, Nick Bunin, Michael Burns, James Carter, Kirill Chepurin, Rocco Gangle, Douglas Hedley, Tobias Hübner, Judith Kahl, A. W. Moore, Karin Nisenbaum, Joel Rasmussen, Anthony Paul Smith, Sebastian Stein, and Johannes Zachhuber. Crucial to its genesis was the funding of the Arts and Humanities Research Council and the support (in very different ways) of my family, colleagues at the University of Liverpool, support staff at the University of Oxford, Diarmaid MacCulloch, Tom Perridge, and Elizabeth Robottom. Nick Adams' comments on a draft manuscript were extraordinarily helpful. Most of all, the patience, attention, and advice of George Pattison made it all possible. I am extremely grateful for his wisdom. This book is dedicated to Jenny, *sine qua non*.

Contents

Note to Reader

Schelling Citations of Schelling's works will include two references: the first to the German original; the second to the English translation (where available). Two abbreviations will be used for the German editions:

SB   F. W. J. Schelling, *Briefe und Dokumente*. 3 volumes. Edited by Horst Fuhrmans. Bonn: Bouvier, 1962–75.

SW   F. W. J. Schelling, *Werke*. 14 volumes. Edited by K. F. A. Schelling. Stuttgart: Cotta, 1856–61.

Goethe Citations of Goethe's works are likewise twofold: the first to the German original; the second to the English translation (where available). The exception is for citations from Goethe's *Maximen und Reflectionen* where the aphorism number alone will be given. Two abbreviations will be used:

M J. W.   Goethe, *Maxims and Reflections*. Edited by Peter Hutchinson. Translated by Elisabeth Stopp. London: Penguin, 1998.

WA J. W.   Goethe, *Werke: Weimarer Ausgabe*. Edited by Sophie von Sachsen. 5 Reihen, 133 volumes. Weimar: Böhlau, 1887–1919.

Kant All citations will be to English translations of Kant's works. However, page references (as is conventional) will be to the German *Akademie* edition, except in the case of the *Kritik der reinen Vernunft* where they will be to the A and B editions.

All translations are my own whenever the sole reference for a work is a non-English language publication.

I have not yet succeeded in unravelling the idea of the symbolical in poetry, but it seems to me that a great deal is contained in it.

(Schiller in Goethe and Schiller 1914, 1:458–9)

Those who carry on combining—they can be called the systematic eclectics.

(Diderot 2011, 283)

Part I

Context

1

The Symbol in the *Goethezeit*

'Symbol' is one of the most polysemic words in theoretical discourse. Its connotations can be logico-mathematical, Lacanian, Peircean, anthropological, liturgical, or romantic—and more often than not the symbol plays on a mixture of more than one of these discursive frameworks. What is more, the symbol takes on divergent, often opposed, forms depending on the connotations one has in mind: the slippage and deferral constitutive of the Lacanian symbolic realm stand opposed to the unity of meaning and being in 'the romantic symbol'. Nevertheless, the following is not a *Begriffsgeschichte* of the symbol, but a study of its fate in the hands of F. W. J. Schelling alone. What matters is not how we understand the term 'symbol' today, but how Schelling did: the contexts on which he drew and the conversations into which he entered when forming his theory of the symbol. In what follows, therefore, I will be almost entirely concerned with 'the romantic symbol' which emerged in German aesthetics and philosophy at the turn of the nineteenth century—even if one of my aims is to problematize the very existence of one, monolithic 'romantic' symbol.

Part I of this book is devoted to the context in which Schelling's construction of symbolic language takes place. The present chapter considers theories of the symbol written during the *Goethezeit*, prior to Schelling's own. I initially consider them historically, then from a synchronic viewpoint, examining in particular the essential properties of a symbol and the typical ways in which it was interpreted. It is the interplay between 'the romantic symbol' and the Schellingian symbol in which I am most interested: to what extent is Schelling to be positioned unproblematically in a genealogy of 'the romantic symbol' and to what extent does his theory in fact react against such an interpretation of the symbol?

A BRIEF HISTORY OF THE SYMBOL

This initial section takes the form of a history of the term 'symbol' as it developed during the late eighteenth century. I am concerned in particular with Kant, Goethe, and A. W. Schlegel's theories and how they may have influenced Schelling's own thought.[1]

Meanings of 'Symbol' Prior to 1790

Before 1790, the 'romantic' notion of a symbol had yet to emerge. There are five pre-1790 resonances the term possessed.

1. Neoplatonism: In Neoplatonism and early Christian theology, 'symbol' refers to a cipher for the divine. This usage remained entrenched within much Christian discourse, both mainstream theology and esoteric mysticism. In eighteenth-century Germany, the mystical use of 'symbol' can be found in the works of Franz Baader and J. G. Hamann,[2] but—as we shall see—it can also be easily discerned in most theories of the symbol during the *Goethezeit*. In all such theories, there is (directly or indirectly) an influence from early Christian theologians, such as Pseudo-Dionysius, as well as pagan Neoplatonists, like Iamblichus. Passed down through the centuries was a conception of the symbol as providing a point of mediation between the created world and what transcends it. Proclus, for example, defined symbols as 'heavenly things on earth in a terrestrial form';[3] Pseudo-Dionysius, in a similar manner, speaks of material objects as 'symbolic veils' (1987, 1108b) or 'revealing signs' (1109a) which lift us beyond the finite into a higher, immaterial realm.

2. Allegory: 'Symbol' was also employed within eighteenth-century aesthetics to refer to the attributes accompanying an emblematic figure. For example, the lamb with which St John the Evangelist is portrayed was designated a 'symbol' by which the saint could be recognized. Also relevant here is the fact that the English 'symbol' has two German equivalents, *Symbol* and *Sinnbild*. *Sinnbild* was the term used in the early modern era to designate this emblematic symbol, whereas *Symbol* was reserved more for the epistemological usage discussed below. In the late eighteenth century, when the emblematic symbol came under attack, it was criticized under the name of *Sinnbild*. As a consequence, theorists of the symbol initially employed the term *Symbol* to distinguish their theories from the emblematic symbol. Indeed (as we shall see), Schelling was the first theorist of the symbol to redeploy the term *Sinnbild*.[4]

3. Epistemology: 'Symbol' (this time, *Symbol* not *Sinnbild*) was also a key term in the Leibniz–Wolffian tradition which dominated German

---

[1] Sørensen 1963, 1972 remain the standard histories on which I draw.
[2] See Sørensen 1972, 72–4, 101–2.
[3] Quoted in Halmi 2007, 107.   [4] See further Marache 1960, 20.

philosophy during the eighteenth century. At the heart of Leibniz–
Wolffian epistemology lies a distinction between intuitive and symbolic
cognition. Here is Christian Wolff's seminal pronouncement on the
issue:

It should be noted that words are the basis of a special type of cognition which we
call symbolic cognition. For we represent things to ourselves either in themselves
or through words or other signs. The first type of cognition is called *intuitive*
cognition, the second is symbolic cognition.[5]

Intuitive knowledge is immediate, indubitable knowledge that grasps
things as they actually are, without aid from artificial conventions. It
has two properties: immediacy and particularity. There is, however, a
second inferior mode of gaining knowledge which is dependent on the
sign rather than the thing itself—symbolic cognition. The sign is the
vehicle which the mind passes through on the way to the thing itself,
when that thing cannot be immediate intuited. It is a means to an end.
Symbolic cognition is attenuated knowledge, distanced from the thing
itself by the mediation of the sign.

4. Theology: 'Symbol' was occasionally used (following the Greek and
   Latin) to designate the Christian creeds or denominational confessions.
   As was also the case in eighteenth-century English, 'Nicene symbol'
   commonly designated the Nicene Creed. Schleiermacher, for one, speaks
   in *The Christian Faith* of 'Confessions or Symbols' of the Church which
   ensure 'the individual shall conform to the original utterances of
   the Spirit' (1999, 618). Indeed, this use of 'symbol' (more than any
   other) foreshadows the performativity of later employments, for to recite
   a creed or confession was both to declaratively assert the truth of the
   statements contained therein, but also to performatively assert one's
   participation in and belonging to a specific community. Symbols in
   this sense were speech-acts.

5. Mathematics: Mathematical symbols are those signs used in algebra and
   arithmetic to represent quantities ('7' and 'x') and operations ('+'). To a
   limited extent, the logic of the time also employed symbols in this
   manner, for (although modern 'symbolic logic' is a product of the late
   nineteenth century) Leibniz' call for the creation of an *ars characteris-
   tica*—an algebrization of all ideas—was still a live option at the end
   of the eighteenth century.[6] In both mathematics and logic, symbols
   were abstractions from the given which allowed a greater freedom
   of thought and simplicity of representation when dealing with

---

[5] Quoted in Wellbery 1984, 22; translation modified.
[6] See *SW* 8:439–54.

complicated problems. As such, the connection of this usage of 'symbol'
to Leibniz–Wolffian 'symbolic cognition' should be obvious: 'symbol' in
both traditions meant a reliance on abstract signs.

All five of these meanings were relatively insignificant compared with the role
the symbol went on to have. In 1809, Friedrich Creuzer could write, 'Today
the term "symbol" is mentioned by everyone in various guises as if there
were some deep-seated need to employ only this term.'[7] It is now my task to
understand whence this sudden popularity came.

The Kantian Symbol

The pre-history of the symbol (in its 'romantic' usage) begins in the 1760s with
the critique of allegory launched by Lessing and Mendelssohn. In the late
1770s and 1780s (as a consequence of this attack), a new participative and
expressive ideal for art emerged in the writings of Herder and Moritz that
would go on to influence theories of the symbol. However, it is in 1790, in §59
of his *Kritik der Urteilskraft*, that Kant first explicitly sets forth a new theory
of the symbol. The revolutionary importance of this theory can be seen from
a remark Kant makes in the middle of his exposition: 'The more recent
logicians have come to use the word *symbolic* in another sense that is wrong
and runs counter to the meaning of the word' (1987, 5:352). That is, previous
philosophical usage of 'symbol' has been incorrect; instead, the term has
a completely different theoretical role and significance, so a new definition is
required.

   The concept of the symbol presented in §59 of the *Kritik der Urteilskraft* is
a key component of Kant's overall task in this work to bridge the 'immense
gulf... fixed between the domain of the concept of nature, the sensible,
and the domain of the concept of freedom, the supersensible' (1987, 5:175).
At stake is the ability of judgements about the sensible world to exhibit
that realm's compatibility with the supersensible, and symbolic judgements
achieve precisely this to the extent that they establish an analogous relation
between a sensible object and a supersensible idea. Or, in Kant's words:

> In symbolic hypotyposis there is a concept which only reason can think and
> to which no symbolic intuition can be adequate, and this concept is supplied with
> an intuition that judgment treats in a way merely analogous to the procedure
> it follows in schematising. (5:351)

Central, therefore, to the idea of the symbol from 1790 onwards is its capacity
to reconcile dualisms and its method of achieving this through an operation

---

[7] Quoted in Sørensen 1963, 16.

of analogy.[8] Added to Kant's vehement rejection of symbolic cognition, his understanding of the symbol in terms of *Darstellung* (presentation or exhibition), and his foregrounding of perception in regard to the symbol, many of the key features of 'the romantic symbol' here emerge for the first time.[9] Indeed, I will return to them at length both in this chapter and in subsequent ones.

Furthermore, there is no doubting the Kantian symbol's influence. In Sørensen's words, 'A worth and meaning was given to "symbol" that it had never before possessed' (1963, 92). One could thus repeat of Kant in respect to the symbol what Schelling later claimed of his philosophy in general: it was 'herald and prophet' to what was to come (*SW* 6:4). For example, Schelling himself was noticeably influenced by Kant's theory: the majority of his pre-1801 uses of 'symbol' are patently Kantian in inspiration.[10]

The Goethean Symbol

On 17 August 1797, Johann Wolfgang von Goethe wrote a letter to Friedrich Schiller that speaks of 'symbolic objects' in a new way. Commentators frequently ascribe to this letter the first new use of the concept.[11] Goethe writes:

> A thought has struck me which, as it may be important for the rest of my journey, I will at once communicate to you . . . In following the calm and cold path of an observer, nay of mere onlooker, I very soon remarked that the accounts which I had given of certain objects were in some measure sentimental, and this struck me so forcibly that I was instantly induced to reflect upon the cause . . . I have carefully observed the objects which produce this effect and have found to my astonishment that in fact they are symbolic, that is (as I scarcely need say), they are eminent cases which in characteristic variety, stand as the representative of many others, embrace a certain totality in themselves, demand a certain succession, excite similar and foreign subjects in my mind, and thus, from within as well as from without, lay claim to a certain oneness and universality. (*WA* IV/ 12, 243–4; Goethe and Schiller 1914, 1:372–3)

One of the strangest elements of Goethe's letter is the throwaway phrase, 'as I scarcely need say', by which he prefaces his definition of the symbol. If his use of 'symbol' here were as radically new a departure as some critics maintain,

---

[8] On the symbol's role in the *Kritik der Urteilskraft* as a whole, see Nuzzo 2005; Guyer 2006.

[9] Nevertheless, Kant's own theory does not totally anticipate the notion which was to fully emerge in the late 1790s on all points: there are some traits of the later usage which are absent from Kant's account and others which are muted. See A. W. Schlegel's criticisms (1997, 205–6). Indeed, Schlegel claims, 'The symbolic nature of the beautiful [is] a concept that unfortunately eludes Kant entirely' (200).

[10] See *SW* 1:405–6; 1994b, 105–6—*SW* 3:510; 1978, 138—559; 176.

[11] Sørensen 1979, 638; Gadamer 2004, 66.

then surely Goethe would not excuse himself for repeating what is self-evident? Goethe must be drawing on some common source he and Schiller share, and such a source is, of course, Kant's 1790 *Kritik der Urteilskraft*. Kant's first exposition of the concept remained definitive for all subsequent theorists.

Goethe's attempt to articulate this new experience is (as is to be expected) slightly confused; however, a number of elements require note. First, Goethe defines the symbol as an 'eminent case' which represents many others, but also 'embraces a certain totality in itself'—the symbol both refers beyond itself but is also self-sufficient. We will see this tension repeated throughout the *Goethezeit*. Second, Goethe claims, the symbol brings about 'a certain oneness and universality': it does not just represent others; it is, Goethe implies, the paradigmatic or archetypical case. These characteristics will go on to be fundamental to the *Goethezeit* definition of the symbol.

Goethe continues:

> The matter is an important one, for it annuls the contradiction which lies between my nature and direct experience, and which in former years I was never able to solve immediately and happily. For I confess that I would rather have turned straight home again, in order to work out of my inmost being phantoms of every kind, than to have again, as hitherto, to buffet with the million-faced Hydra of Empiricism. (246–7; 1:375)

Again, Goethe here puts his finger on a property of the symbol that will go on to play a crucial role in its later history. The symbol mediates between mind and world. Goethe describes himself as, prior to this experience, beset by dualisms between thought and the empirical world: each subsisted in an independent realm and reconciliation seemed impossible. However, the symbol achieves this seemingly impossible task: a symbolic experience is one in which the empirical object becomes imbued with, and so commensurate to, thought.

Goethe, having identified this new form of symbolic experience in August 1797, continued discussing it with his close friend Friedrich Meyer, and later that year they both began drafting articles (both entitled *Über die Gegenstände der bildenden Kunst*) which define the 'symbol' in this new way. Goethe's essay, however, never got beyond draft form, and indeed—and this is significant—none of his claims about the symbol were published until the 1820s.

Goethe was certainly extremely influential on Schelling's employment of the term 'symbol'.[12] This is certain because in November 1803 after Schelling had moved to Würzburg, Goethe wrote him a letter which ends as follows:

[12] Goethe's influence on Schelling more generally is also becoming increasingly better recognized. See Adler 1998; Richards 2002; Nassar 2010.

This year [in the annual Weimar art competition] we have bestowed our whole prize of 60 Ducats on a Würzburg artist, Martin Wagner... Could you make comprehensible to him the difference between allegorical and symbolic treatment; in this you would be his benefactor, since so much turns on this axis. (*WA* IV/16 367; *SB* 3:32)

On the basis of this letter, we can be sure that Schelling and Goethe discussed the notion of the symbol at length while Schelling still lived in Jena. *That* Goethe and Schelling discussed the symbol is thereby proven and so it most likely follows that Goethe played a crucial role in the genesis of Schelling's theory of symbolic language.

However, Sørensen—commenting on this passage—goes further to suggest that Schelling must have been in complete agreement with Goethe on the topic of symbolic and allegorical presentation at this period (1963, 249). For Sørensen the implication is that Schelling takes up Goethe's concept of the symbol unchanged: Schelling displays 'a *verbatim* dependence on Goethe' (264). However, we should be wary of jumping to such a conclusion. Krueger has shown, *pace* Sørensen, how Goethe distances himself from Schelling's exposition of the symbol in the *Philosophie der Kunst*. In a discussion of two of Goethe's most famous assertions concerning the symbol (*M* §1112–3—which she dates as early as 1807), Krueger observes how they 'might in fact be understood as Goethe's reply to Schelling, not least as a rejection of Schelling's *Indifferenz* in favour of two reciprocal and utterly mediated figurative strategies' (Krueger 1990, 65).[13] Presumably, if Schelling were reproducing Goethe's thought *verbatim*, there would have been no need to respond critically. Krueger's example shows that there may have been some disagreement on the details of how the symbol was to be conceived. For similar reasons, Titzmann directly disputes Sørensen's claim. He criticizes histories of the symbol, like Sørensen's, 'based on a common and unfounded overestimation of Goethe, not only as a theoretician, but also as a historical source, making as many other authors as possible dependent on this one writer'. Such historical dependence, Titzmann claims, 'is certainly false in the case of Schelling' (1979, 642). Be that as it may, the evidence is certainly clear that Goethe was one of the major stimuli to Schelling's own theory of the symbol.

Jena Romanticism

The fact that Goethe's statements concerning the symbol remained unpublished until a much later date makes it difficult to assess his influence on the

---

[13] Although Krueger's argument has a problem of its own: how could Goethe reply to an unpublished lecture course he did not attend?

rise of the symbol. It is certain from the above example that he discussed the concept with his friends in Jena and Weimar; however, what exactly was discussed—or even whether he let others read his draft essay, *Über die Gegenstände der bildenden Kunst*—will never be known.[14] However, we can be sure that Goethe must have had some influence, because the similarities between Goethe's initial use and later uses are too great to be merely coincidental. The various properties Goethe identifies in his letter to Schiller remain entrenched throughout the *Goethezeit*.

There is therefore some kind of oral transmission from Goethe to later adherents of the symbol. Indeed, much aesthetics in Jena and Weimar during the 1790s did take place verbally. Out of this climate of verbal exchange emerged a series of employments of the term 'symbol' identical to the way in which Goethe had already used it; employments which would ultimately lead to the term becoming a popular new addition to German critical vocabulary.

It is worth pausing here to see if any sign of this oral discussion is evident in the texts written by the inhabitants of Jena and Weimar during the last few years of the 1790s. This is a particularly significant question because, at this time in Jena, Romanticism was born; it is thus natural to wonder whether the notion of the symbol played any role here. The question becomes even more pressing when we realize that the next theory of the symbol to be written after Goethe was by a member of the Jena Romantic group—A. W. Schlegel. The question therefore becomes: what were the sources for Schlegel's theory of the symbol? Was there a precedent within Jena Romanticism itself? Or was A. W. Schlegel exceptional among the Jena Romantics in the influence Goethe had upon him?

Two cases are worth brief consideration: Friedrich Schlegel and Novalis. These two thinkers more than any other have been considered in recent years to define early German Romanticism.

The term 'symbol' is a frequent one in Novalis' fragments from the late 1790s.[15] While their appearance is cryptic, they do hint at some fuller theory of the symbol lying behind them—a theory which, like so much of Novalis' thought, remains implicit. This does not, however, mean that Novalis esoterically subscribed to a theory of the symbol in line with Goethe, Schelling, or A. W. Schlegel; instead, the reader can only guess what Novalis meant.

---

[14] Heinrich Meyer's essay was published in a journal in 1798, so this suggests at least one possible means of dissemination (although none of his contemporaries discuss Meyer's work in this respect, and critics often write off him off (Sørensen 1963, 111; Todorov 1982, 212–13)).

[15] See Novalis 1997, 26, 57, 67, 71, 87, 102, 105, 117, 121, 132, 165. The frequency of these examples certainly belies the usual critical prejudice that they 'present a relatively rare slip by Hardenberg [Novalis] into the terminology and ideology of the symbol' (O'Brien 1995, 347).

Like Novalis, Friedrich Schlegel employs the term in his writings of the late 1790s. He even claims, 'All knowledge is symbolic' (1997, 246).[16] However, despite these occurrences, we can be confident that Schlegel did not subscribe to a theory of the symbol (or at least a theory of the symbol comparable to his contemporaries) at this time. This is because in the 1820s—influenced by later theories of the symbol—Schlegel corrected his publications from the late 1790s. This is nowhere more apparent than in the revised version of his *Gespräch über die Poesie*. To quote Dieckmann's study of the relevant 'corrections' made to this work:

> Very consistently the term 'symbol' has been added, a term which is rare and quite unimportant in the 1800 version. Thus the title of the third part of the *Gespräch* is changed from *Rede über Mythologie* to *Rede über Mythologie und symbolische Anschauung*. At least six times in this very short *Discourse on Mythology* we find added to the word 'mythology' such expressions as: 'symbolic art, symbolic legend, symbolic world of ideas, symbolic knowledge, a symbolic science of the whole universe'. Moreover, there are several insertions of some length in the second version, some of which deal exclusively with problems of symbolism. The revision goes consistently through the entire *Gespräch* and is not limited to Part Three. (1959, 276)

It is, Dieckmann goes on to suggest, the influence of Creuzer and Goethe's theories of the symbol which accounts for these revisions (283). As she insists, this implies that in the original 1800 version of the work, 'Schlegel disregarded or ignored these discussions' (277). Perhaps the most notorious change was to alter the famous statement in the *Gespräch* that 'all beauty is allegory' to 'all beauty is symbolic'.[17] Paul de Man in his influential critique of the symbol, 'The Rhetoric of Temporality' (to which I will return repeatedly throughout this book), makes much of this alteration. For de Man, the fact that Schlegel uses allegory, rather than symbol, in the original edition is representative of the manner in which Schlegel's thought as a whole is opposed to all the symbol represents (1983, 190–1).

The above perhaps tells us more about critical prejudice than it does Novalis and Friedrich Schlegel themselves. Since de Man, it has become customary to oppose theories of the symbol to an alternative mode of thinking during the *Goethezeit*. This alternative thoroughly repudiated any notion of the symbol in the name of 'discontinuity, rupture and reversal' (Seyhan 1992, 3).[18] Crudely put, it is claimed that, in opposition to the 'Idealists' (Schelling, Hegel, and even Goethe) who made 'totalitarian' claims for the coincidence of meaning

[16] See also 1957, §1171, §2013.
[17] See de Man 1983, 190.
[18] As well as in de Man and Seyhan, this position can be found in Behler 1993, O'Brien 1995, and Frank 2004.

and being,[19] the Jena Romantics (of whom only Friedrich Schlegel and Novalis are consistently cited in this regard) refused to synthesize meaning and being, but instead insisted on the arbitrariness of language and the open-endedness of philosophy. There is, indeed, much in Friedrich Schlegel's and Novalis' work that does sit uncomfortably with a metaphysics of the symbol (irony and allegory, for example); yet, as we have also seen, this tendency to oppose Jena Romanticism to the symbol is simplistic. A. W. Schlegel *did* propose a highly influential theory of the symbol as early as 1801 (as I will discuss below). Moreover, Novalis' position is not clear-cut: his constant use of 'symbol' suggests he did hold to some kind of theory of the symbol, although this never comes to full expression in his extant writings. Therefore, while it is disingenuous to draw so clear a boundary between Jena Romanticism and the symbol, it remains true that these two case studies (Novalis, F. Schlegel) reach inconclusive results in pinning down the transmission of the concept of the symbol in the late 1790s. Hence, the scare quotes with which I speak of 'the romantic symbol': in Germany at least, the contribution of Romantics to the development of this concept was not decisive.

1801 and Beyond

A. W. Schlegel's theory of the symbol is definitively expounded in his 1801 *Vorlesungen über schöne Literatur und Kunst*, given in Berlin to a private audience. Schlegel did more than any other to (as Sørensen puts it) 'popularise and communicate' the concept of the symbol to a new generation of students (1972, 168).

The passage in which Schlegel introduces the notion of the symbol occurs at a key juncture in his argument, at the beginning of the eighth lecture. The previous seven lectures had taken the form of a critical survey of all previous attempts at aesthetics. Schlegel now tries his hand at proposing his own aesthetic theory, and begins thus:

> According to Schelling, the beautiful is *the infinite represented in finite form* ...
> I entirely agree with this definition, but I would prefer to define the expression in the following manner: the beautiful is a symbolic presentation of the infinite. Stated in this way, it becomes clear at the same time how the infinite can appear in the finite. (1997, 209)

Obviously for my argument, Schlegel's reference to Schelling's 1800 *System des transzendentalen Idealismus* (in which, as Schlegel implies, 'symbol' is not used) is intriguing. Schlegel uses Schelling's pre-*Identitätssystem* aesthetics as the springboard for developing a new theory of the symbol; in so doing, he

---

[19] See O'Brien 1995, 73, 114.

designates the symbol as the hidden key to the whole *System des transzenden-talen Idealismus*.

While Schlegel's definition of beauty as symbolic may not seem surprising to a reader today, for his audience (to whom 'symbol' denoted either a technical Leibnizian term or a reference to unfashionable emblematic painting) it was radically new. Nevertheless, what was developed here became the benchmark for later Romantic theory. Schlegel defines the symbol (following Goethe) as that which 'bind[s] together and merge[s] even what is most distant' (210). He also cements the intimate relation between the symbol and mythology already suggested by Goethe and Meyer (1989, 440–60). Moreover, not only does Schlegel use the term 'symbol' in a sustained manner and as part of a system of aesthetics, he gives it pride of place in his definition of beauty—the crux of a series of lectures devoted to '*schöne Literatur und Kunst*'. The mystery of beauty, Schlegel claims, can only be satisfactorily explained by means of the symbol, and further, 'Poesy (taken in the most general sense as that which underlies all the arts) is nothing but an eternal act of symbolisation' (1997, 210). All art is a process of symboliza-tion—such is Schlegel's radically new claim. It is no wonder Schlegel concludes that what is now needed not only in aesthetics but also in science in general is 'research into the symbolic in our cognition' (211). Such an investigation, he states, will lead to 'the most surprising discoveries' (212)—an unsurprising conclusion if this neglected concept does really form the basis of all artistic activity.

On 3 September 1802, Schelling wrote to A. W. Schlegel in reference to the latter's Berlin lectures. Schelling (as Fuhrman points out) would have encoun-tered the manuscript to these lectures when he visited Schlegel in Berlin in May 1802 (*SB* 2:436); now, he requests a copy to help him write his own lecture course on the philosophy of art:

> Your manuscript would be of excellent service to me, so as to provide me with some orientation [in aesthetics] . . . Could you let me have your manuscript copied in Berlin at my own cost and send it here towards the middle of next month, or even leave it with me until then to get a copy of it here, in which case I would be highly indebted to you . . . I will make use of your work with thanks as long as my power of assimilation allows. (*SB* 2:436–7)

Schelling borrows Schlegel's manuscript to help him draft the *Philosophie der Kunst*. That is, he uses the work in which Schlegel puts forth his theory of the symbol to write his own theory of the symbol. Thus, just as with Goethe, we can be fairly certain that A. W. Schlegel's theory of the symbol was a crucial stimulus to Schelling's own. Indeed, Schelling even writes to Schlegel a month later, having received the manuscript:

Your manuscript on aesthetics gives me unnameable pleasure; it delights me to read it. Part of it I am in the process of having completely copied, another part I read with feather in hand. (*SB* 2:449)

Since Schelling admits here to writing his own lectures with Schlegel's open in front of him, there is no doubting that his theory of the symbol was written in direct conversation with Schlegel's. However, just as with Goethe, we should not conclude from this that Schelling merely reproduced Schlegel's theory. In fact, in their correspondence, Schelling is at pains to point out that he does not intend merely to 'plagiarize' Schlegel's thought, but to creatively transform it. I return to this issue at length in Chapter 3.

In Winter 1802, F. W. J. Schelling lectured on the *Philosophie der Kunst* and proposed his own theory of the symbol. As with Schlegel, Schelling's fullest exposition of the symbol occurred in a series of lectures that was only published posthumously. Therefore, despite introducing the term to many students of philosophy, neither Schlegel's nor Schelling's lectures on the symbol can be called popularizations as such. In 1805, however, a former student of Schelling, Friedrich Ast, published his *System der Kunstlehre*, a work heavily dependent on his former teacher's theory of the symbol. Solger, another of Schelling's former students, also proposed an influential theory of the symbol later in the decade. By means of such publications, 'symbol' became firmly established as a term of aesthetic criticism. Such later developments (including most prominently Hegel's and Coleridge's theories) come after Schelling's own thoughts on the symbol had long been formed. They lie outside the scope of this work.

Such then are the major sources of Schelling's theory of the symbol. In this section, I have merely been concerned with charting the genesis of these early theories of the symbol and their relation to Schelling's in regard to the history of ideas. In what follows, I consider the content of these theories. Schelling's divergence from, rather than continuity with, his predecessors will thus become increasingly clear. Indeed, all I have demonstrated so far is that some influence from Kant, Goethe, and A. W. Schlegel was likely; what precisely this influence was has yet to be determined.

ELEMENTS OF THE SYMBOL

In the previous section I considered the development of the symbol historically. In this section I switch to considering the symbol analytically. More specifically, I will delineate the three basic structural features that defined a symbol during the *Goethezeit*. Of course, these features should not be considered as boxes into which everything needs to be fitted, but windows through which clusters of themes become evident. There are two 'first-order' properties which apply to the symbol in all media (that is, to linguistic, pictorial, musical symbols, etc.) and one additional property that applies specifically to symbolic *language*. I label these features 'first-order' because, I contend, they are the necessary and universal structures by which a symbol becomes a symbol; yet, as I will argue, on their own and in the form in which I expound them below, they do not form a complete theory of the symbol. There is therefore always a second-level of interpretation required to theorize the symbol fully: it is here that theorists diverge significantly.[20]

Heautonomy

The symbol is an image which need not look outside itself for meaning. Unlike the sign or allegory, its referent is not external to it. It is thus self-contained or heautonomous. A number of different terms could have served just as well to describe this property. One such name, as we shall see, is organicism, but one could equally speak of the 'absoluteness' of the symbol, if one bears in mind (as many theorists of the period did) that *ab-solutum* has the etymological sense of something dissolved from all relations.[21]

'Heautonomy' is a term Kant employs in the third *Kritik* to designate a form of autonomous judgement that legislates only to itself (1987, 5:185). While a merely autonomous being governs itself with a law that need not be peculiar to itself (like the categorical imperative, for example, which applies to all rational beings), a 'heautonomous' being governs itself by means of a law specific to itself. The term was later appropriated by Schiller, where it becomes central to his aesthetics—indeed, it is the basic property of beauty. In this book, I employ the term (taking my cue from Schiller) as one of the defining features of the symbol. The symbol is therefore an autonomous image whose determining rule applies to itself alone. Schiller writes of heautonomous beauty that it does not 'require anything outside of itself, but commands and obeys itself for the sake of its own law' (2003, 167): it is a completely self-sufficient, autarchic whole. This characteristic is basic to early elucidations of the symbol. Heinrich Meyer writes in his initial 1797 essay, *Über die Gegenstände der bildenden Kunst*: 'It must be demanded of every artwork that it composes a whole . . . [that] it expresses itself wholly. It must be independent . . . The object must be essentially grasped and understood without external assistance or auxiliary

---

[20] Obviously, there are other ways to break down the symbol than what follows. See Todorov 1982, 221; Sørensen 1972, 264.

[21] See Lacoue-Labarthe and Nancy 1988, 56.

explanations.'[22] Or as he puts it in a later work, symbols should aim to be 'perfectly self-sufficient'.[23]

The symbol is therefore a whole. What is more, it is an organic whole, in particular. Schiller again provides the precedent: in explaining the holism of the beautiful image, he resorts to the framework Kant introduced in his discussion of the organism in the *Kritik der Urteilskraft*. In §§64–6, Kant argues that the organism is judged to 'relate to itself in such a way that it is both cause and effect of itself' (1987, 5:372): it both acts and is acted on without any reference to what is outside of it. It is causally self-contained. Its purpose is not imposed upon it by an external concept but lies 'within itself and its inner possibility' (5:373). Its original cause, its form, and its telos are immanent to its own being. The organism therefore exemplifies heautonomy. Schiller's appropriation of Kant's vocabulary in his aesthetics is based on the realization that both the organism and the beautiful object are heautonomous in this sense. Theorists of the symbol, especially Schelling (as we shall see), followed Schiller on this point.

Syntheticism

The second first-order property by which the symbol is universally defined is 'syntheticism'—the bringing together of contraries, or, as Todorov puts it, the symbol's 'capacity to absorb and resolve the incompatibility of contraries' (1982, 159). Although Todorov goes on to contend that 'Schelling contributed more than any other romantic author to the establishment of syntheticism' (184), we will in fact find that the term 'syntheticism' is extremely problematic in reference to Schelling. However, the basic idea of the unity of opposites must still be acknowledged as a universal first-order property of the symbol during this period.

Fundamental to the constitution of the symbol is its ability to gather into itself opposing principles; in it, what is usually distinct and hard to reconcile is thrown into unity.[24] The symbol achieved what for Novalis was 'the highest task of the higher logic'—'to annihilate the principle of contradiction'.[25] There are many different oppositions that theorists see united within the symbol; for example, in Schelling's *Philosophie der Kunst* alone, there are references to the symbol as the unity of particular and universal, finite and infinite, and schema and allegory.[26] Nor is Schelling alone in emphasizing this aspect of the symbol:

---

[22] Meyer in Sørensen 1972, 145.

[23] Meyer in Sørensen 1972, 145. See also Moritz in Sørensen 1972, 113–19.

[24] This is suggested by the etymology of the word, if nothing else: σύμβολον means a 'contract' or 'pledge' binding together individuals into a community (Gadamer 2004, 63).

[25] Quoted in Todorov 1982, 184.

[26] All discussed further in Chapter 7.

Solger also notes the symbol's ability to unify universal and particular (1984, 128), idea and appearance (130), and imagination and reality (129).

Despite, however, the plethora of terms that the symbol is meant to unify, there is one general synthesis to which they all refer. The symbol unifies the real, particular, and concrete symbolic image and the ideal, universal, and abstract meaning which that image evokes. It is this basic synthesis of empirical being and intellectual meaning which describes most fully the reconciliation the symbol performs. As Gadamer and de Man note, theorists of the symbol 'refuse to distinguish between experience and the representation of this experience', between empirical fact and intellectual reflection upon it (de Man 1983, 188; Gadamer 2004, 69–70). Meaning and being become one in the symbol. Such is the import of Schelling's statement: 'Meaning here [in the symbol] is simultaneously being itself, passed over into the object itself and one with it' (*SW* 5:411; 1989, 49). This identity of meaning and being is ultimately what is meant by 'symbol' during the *Goethezeit*. In this book, I reserve the term 'syntheticism' for the symbol's capacity to unify opposites *in general*, while I dub the unity of meaning and being in particular 'tautegory'. I will explore tautegory at far greater length in the next chapter, since it is especially problematic in respect to the phenomenon of symbolic language. Heautonomy, syntheticism, and tautegory are therefore the three first-order properties of the symbol during the *Goethezeit*.

INTERPRETING THE SYMBOL

Heautonomy, syntheticism, and tautegory are the three principles basic to the symbol during the *Goethezeit*; however, these three principles do *not* constitute a theory of the symbol by themselves. In fact, I now want to argue, they underdetermine the symbol.

Absolute and Partial Tautegory

Take, for example, Schelling's statement that in the symbol 'meaning is simultaneously being itself'—how is this to be understood? The first-order properties themselves give no clue to the type or manner of unity the symbol should display; they merely require that there should be some kind of unity of being and meaning. Indeed, there are at least three different ways of interpreting such unity which each imply very different theories of the symbol. First, meaning and being could be said to really exist in separation, but merely be identified as one by the subject. This is a subjective, rather than real, unity: the subject judges *as if* meaning and being are one, whereas objectively this is not the case. Kant's theory of the symbol as well as Schiller's early aesthetics operate in something like this manner.

Furthermore, even when theorists assert that meaning and being are objectively unified, this assertion can be made in a number of ways. For example, many adherents to this view during the *Goethezeit* conceived of this union only partially—as a form of synecdoche, in which the being of the symbol is a part participating in the ideal meaning (the whole). On the one hand, the part (the symbolic image) is continuous with its meaning and actually unified with it, but, on the other hand, the two are not absolutely identical—meaning still transcends being: the whole is still greater than the part. Yet, this is not even the only way to understand the objective unity of meaning and being. Schelling's interpretation of this principle, for example, conceives of meaning as utterly immanent to being, and not at all exceeding it. His is a commitment to absolute tautegory. Here, the statement 'meaning is simultaneous with being' is interpreted as an absolute identity between the two, not as a synecdoche. Meaning is being and being is meaning, according to Schelling.

The two latter ways of interpreting the unity of being and meaning objectively are discussed fruitfully in Adams' *Philosophy of the Literary Symbolic*. The same structural properties of the symbol can be interpreted, Adams contends, in two opposed ways.[27] There is, on the one hand, a 'miraculous' symbol, equivalent to the synecdochical symbol described above. This symbol, Adams writes, 'is not identical with its [meaning] but a sort of fallen form of it' (1983, 18). It exhibits a broadly Platonic structure in which the symbol participates in the intelligible realm, but still remains caught in the worldly sensuousness of the image. Meaning here exceeds being and so points beyond it.

However, Adams is at pains to stress, there is 'a second type of romantic symbol' (1983, 18) which has far more affinities with Schelling's interpretation. Adams writes, 'In [this version of the] symbol, the universal becomes not something previously there to be contained but something *generated by* the particular, as the seed generates the plant' (19). The universal is produced out of the particular, rather than pre-existing it; the movement of the symbol is no longer a fall inward, but a productive development outwards. The emphasis in this second type is not so much on an artefact which bears traces of meaning beyond it, but rather on 'symbolic activity' producing the infinite meaning it carries (20). The productive symbol constitutes its own meaning: meaning 'is created in the image' and as such is 'fully there' (57). Two-world Platonism is here rebuked in favour of a this-worldly conception of the symbol. Symbolic meaning does not point us beyond the world, but is part of our activity within it.[28] It is, I will argue, Schelling who breaks with the 'two-world' conception of the symbol most fully so as to claim that the symbol is productive.

---

[27] See also Frenzel 1963, 96.
[28] See A. W. Schlegel (1997, 28) for a version of this sentiment.

The Kantian subjective symbol, the 'miraculous' synecdochical symbol, and the productive symbol: these are three very different interpretations that can be given to the same first-order properties. They are conflicting models used to flesh out an identical symbolic structure.

The Birth of 'the Romantic Symbol' in the Twentieth Century

Despite the potential variety in theories of the symbol, much of the scholarly work on this topic fails to acknowledge such capacity for diversity at all. The label, 'the romantic symbol', has come to represent a monolithic, totalizing tendency in modern scholarship: histories of the symbol during the *Goethezeit* are histories of how far some figures prefigure 'the romantic symbol' and how far others corrupt it. There is *one* interpretation of the symbol worthy of discussion, it is assumed, and this is '*the* romantic symbol'.

In this regard, it is difficult to escape the long shadow cast by de Man's 'The Rhetoric of Temporality' (dubbed by Jonathan Culler 'the most photocopied essay in literary criticism'[29]). The criticisms of the symbol contained in this essay have dominated theory ever since; yet, what is most striking about this essay is its disregard for particular theories of the symbol. De Man fails to engage with the notion of the symbol in any of its concrete details—he ignores the history of its development and barely mentions German thinkers at all. Thus, the essay begins by rejecting the usual procedure of 'retrac[ing] the itinerary that led German writers of the age of Goethe to consider symbol and allegory as antithetical' (1983, 188). De Man does then proceed to name-check Goethe, Schiller, and Schelling who 'stand out' as exemplars of the symbolic tradition (189), but this is as much as he is inclined to write about these crucial figures. Instead, having catalogued a few figures who do not so easily fit into a history of 'the romantic symbol' (Goethe again, Hölderlin, and Friedrich Schlegel) (189–91), de Man concludes with the following:

> To make some headway in this difficult question [concerning the validity of the symbol in literary theory], it may be useful to leave the field of German literature and see how the same problem appears in English and French writers of the same period. Some help may be gained from a broader perspective. (191)

At this point, de Man abandons Germany altogether to concentrate on Coleridge's notion of symbol and Rousseau's practice of allegory. Of course, de Man is right to seek 'a broader perspective' to his question, but it must be asked at what cost does he largely ignore (let alone analyse) German theories of the symbol. Germany was the ground on which the symbol developed; it is

---

[29] Quoted in Godzich 1983, xvi.

also from earlier German manifestations that Coleridge developed his own theory.

De Man claims that the issues surrounding the theorization of the symbol during this period 'have [already] been treated at length [and so] we do not have to return to them here' (189). It is on the basis of this prior treatment that de Man feels able to write off German theories of the symbol. The only text, however, that he cites in this regard is Gadamer's *Wahrheit und Methode*. Yet, this is a work which itself devotes only a few pages to the question of the symbol in the *Goethezeit* (2004, 62–70). Indeed, just like de Man, Gadamer too relies heavily on a previous study—in this case, Curt Müller's *Die Geschichtlichen Voraussetzungen des Symbolbegriffs in Goethes Kunstanschauung* (98).

It is worth pausing over Müller's work, for it marks one of the origins of twentieth-century fascination with the notion of the symbol and is (directly and indirectly) the source for much subsequent scholarship. One significant fact about Müller's book is its date, 1937, and the text does indeed bear traces of being written during the Nazi regime. For example, it stresses the symbol's power in forming communities that are to be privileged over all others and whose 'bearer' embodies the general will (1937, 17). Indeed, this concept of the irrational grace (or 'cosmic feeling' (17)) bestowed on the privileged orients the whole outlook of the book. Moreover, it is precisely this aspect which is subsequently taken up (in a critical mode) both by Gadamer and de Man. Thus, when de Man criticizes the 'tenacious self-mystification' and 'regressive' nature of the symbol (1983, 208), it is from Müller's original study that this view is ultimately derived. It is little wonder then that de Man denounces the symbol as fascistic!

This is not to deny that there are irrational and mystifying elements present in theories of the symbol during the *Goethezeit*—little research would be necessary to establish this fact. Rather, I am disputing the way in which these elements have been made *constitutive* of the symbol at this time, and so one form of the symbol is thereby considered to the exclusion of all others. A different model for critical discourse is required, a model that sees this one interpretation of the symbol for what it is—merely one, non-exclusive way in which it was conceived during the *Goethezeit*. This monopoly on the symbol running from Müller through Gadamer and de Man (but also through Sørensen and, most recently, Halmi) has reduced into a single, determinate form what was in fact an atmosphere of plural, competing understandings of the symbol. What the twentieth century has forgotten is that the symbol was, during the *Goethezeit*, a site of radical experimentation.

Let me try to develop these criticisms of recent studies further through considering the case of Todorov's two studies of the symbol (1982, 1983). In many ways, Todorov attempts to escape the monopolizing heritage outlined above and he explicitly makes clear that his basic methodological tenet is plurality:

I have tried to establish a framework that makes it possible to understand how so many different theories, so many irreconcilable subdivisions, so many contradictory definitions, can have existed—each one including (this is my hypothesis) a measure of the truth. (1983, 22)

Yet, when Todorov turns to the *Goethezeit*, such good intentions are forgotten:

It is not possible here, nor would it be interesting, to present in succession . . . the theses upheld by each member of the [Romantic] group. There is one doctrine and one author, even if their names are several: not that each one repeats the others; but each one formulates, better than any other, some part of the same single doctrine. (1982, 165)

Todorov does recognize the artificiality of this method ('Instead of "finding" the past, I am constructing it'); he also acknowledges problems that arise out of homogenizing these very different thinkers (for example, treating Goethe as a Romantic[30]) (167). Nevertheless, he remains resolute in bringing together all these figures under one interpretation of the symbol. Again therefore, what Goethe (for example) claims about the symbol becomes constitutive of the symbol as such. No room is permitted for competing conceptions. While Todorov at least tries to stay open-minded and non-prescriptive, in the end he—like so many of the other twentieth-century critics of the symbol— homogenizes. It is for these reasons that the symbol in Romanticism has been transformed into '*the* romantic symbol'. Nicholas Halmi's recent *The Genealogy of the Romantic Symbol* (2007) is only the last in a series of studies presupposing one, monolithic theory of the symbol during the *Goethezeit*.

However, my contention is that this is an artificial imposition of twentieth-century critical theory onto the past. Of course, there are figures for whom 'the romantic symbol' of the twentieth century was the way they understood the symbol. However, for the most part and especially prior to 1810, 'the romantic symbol' of twentieth-century critical theory is merely one interpretative strand of theorizing the symbol.

AN INTRODUCTION TO 'THE ROMANTIC SYMBOL'

Having said all this, 'the romantic symbol' will be employed in this book as a convenient fiction, for it will be useful in what follows to show the ways in which Schelling's theory departs from this conventional interpretation. I will therefore retain a reference to 'the romantic symbol' in order to show more clearly how the Schellingian symbol is radically different from it. My purpose

---

[30] Halmi follows Todorov in lumping Goethe in with the Romantics (2007, 10), but this move has been severely criticized (Nygaard 1988, 58, 74).

in employing the concept of 'the romantic symbol' in what follows is therefore to undermine it: to show preliminarily, by focusing on Schelling's work, that no such single entity exists. In order to achieve this end, in the final section of this chapter I provide an initial analysis of 'the romantic symbol' insofar as it is possible to isolate certain 'second-order' features of it. After this analysis, it will be easier to mark the ways in which the Schellingian symbol differs. The 'romantic symbol' is therefore (for the purposes of this book) one specific interpretation given to the three properties of heautonomy, syntheticism, and tautegory.[31]

Modes of Signification in 'the Romantic Symbol'

Goethe's early pronouncements are a good place to begin. He writes in his 1797 letter to Schiller:

> [Symbols] are eminent cases which in characteristic variety, stand as the representative of many others, embrace a certain totality in themselves . . . and thus, from within as well as from without, lay claim to a certain oneness and universality. (*WA* IV/12, 243–4; Goethe and Schiller 1914, 1:372–3)

Goethe outlines three ways in which the symbol gives rise to meaning: first, the symbol is an 'eminent case' and 'stands as the representative of many others'; second, it 'embraces a certain totality in itself'; and third, it 'lays claim to a certain oneness and universality'. First, therefore, the symbol acts like a conventional sign; such signs are substitutes for a class of objects: they can be used as a token (or 'representative') to refer to all other members of the same class. Signs are used to bring to mind all the objects which this sign represents. Thus (in a rather convoluted manner), Goethe initially considers symbolic objects as a form of sign. Second, Goethe states that the symbol 'embraces a certain totality in itself': as opposed to a conventional sign, it has its own intrinsic worth and forms a whole. It is heautonomous. Third, Goethe speaks of the universality of the symbol—that is, the symbol participates in the universal, animating idea which informs all particular phenomena. Thus, as well as representing the meaning of a class of objects like the conventional sign, the symbol participates in this meaning immediately, and so exhibits it as directly as it exhibits itself. The symbol is its own meaning, and so is tautegorical. These, then, are the three modes of signification Goethe initially identifies in the symbol. My contention is that they are more than this: they are the

---

[31] The fictional status of this 'romantic symbol' needs also to be emphasized within the corpus of thinkers whom I cite but whose work I do not explore fully. For example, Goethe is often alluded to in what follows as an exponent of 'the romantic symbol', yet it would not take much critical attention to show that there is no *one* theory of the symbol in Goethe's writings, but a plurality of heterodox symbols.

three modes by which 'the romantic symbol' as such signifies—as representative, as heautonomous and as participative or evocative.

The same three aspects are to be found a month later in Goethe's draft, *Über die Gegenstände der bildenden Kunst*:

> Subjects presented in this [symbolic] way appear merely to stand for themselves, but do, in fact, always signify what is deepest [*im Tiefsten bedeutend*], and do this on account of the ideal, which always carries a form of universality with it. When the symbolic refers to anything still outside of the presentation, it always does so in an indirect manner. (*WA* I/47, 94; 1983, 396; translation modified)

In the essay as a whole, Goethe concentrates extensively on the proper subjects of artistic representation and he delimits a number of subjects whose representations are to be dubbed 'symbolic'. These representations are all mythological in nature, giving rise to an association between symbolism and mythology that will persist for at least the next twenty years. In the above quotation, he proceeds to discuss the manner in which such symbolic representations operate. Symbolic representations, he claims, give rise to the appearance of heautonomy (such representations 'appear merely to stand for themselves'). However, despite this, symbols still do signify and they signify 'what is deepest'. What does Goethe mean here? He continues that symbols signify 'on account of' the ideal, which possesses 'a form of universality' that it brings to appearance. My reading of such an elliptical sentence (this was, of course, only a draft) is that symbols evoke the ideal form of what they represent (for example, symbolic sculptures of Jupiter *are* already the ideal representation of Jupiter).[32] Moreover, by so relating themselves to the ideal in this second (participative) manner, they possess their own meaning: they possess a universality that mere conventional representation cannot access directly.

These two forms of positive signification—representation and evocation— are quite different. The first is a conventional mimetic relation in which the symbolic representation faithfully imitates its object. Evocation, on the other hand, requires a close ontological relation between the symbol and the 'deep' meaning it signifies; here the symbol participates in universal meaning and brings it immediately to the surface. This is the Platonic aspect of 'the romantic symbol', manifesting another, 'deeper' realm.

Thus, again, three moments are present in Goethe's description of the symbol: an initial moment of mere representation—in which the symbol cannot really be differentiated from a conventional sign; a second moment of heautonomy, the self-sufficiency of which stands in contrast to attempts at signification; and finally, a moment when a deeper evocation of universal meaning occurs. In this final moment, the symbol gains an ontological relation

---

[32] See Sørensen 1963, 120–1, for a similar reading.

to the universal which takes the onlooker beyond mere representation. It is these three moments which form the basis of the 'romantic' interpretation of the symbol.

Double Intentionality

Ricoeur has defined this dual capacity to both represent and evoke meaning as the 'double intentionality' of the symbol (1974, 289).[33] Ricoeur claims that the symbol 'presents a first or literal intentionality that, like every significant expression, supposes the triumph of the conventional sign over the natural sign . . . But upon this first intentionality there is erected a second intentionality' (289). He writes elsewhere:

> Contrary to perfectly transparent technical signs, which say only what they want to say in positing that which they signify, symbolic signs are opaque, because the first, literal, obvious meaning itself points analogically to a second meaning which is not given otherwise than in it. (1967, 15)

This notion of a 'second meaning' is, I think, crucial for understanding the operation of 'the romantic symbol'. Indeed, here is how A. W. Schlegel speaks of symbolic signification: 'A second, non-sensible intuition is built into language on the basis of the first representation of the sensible world' (1989, 211).

The Kantian symbol provides the template for 'double intentionality'. In §59 of the *Kritik der Urteilskraft*, Kant argues that the symbol ultimately overcomes representation in favour of a deeper form of signification. The very title of §59, 'Beauty as a Symbol of Morality', is significant in this regard, for it boldly states the claim that Kant will go on to elucidate: beautiful representations, as well as obviously *representing* 'beautiful' objects, also *symbolize* an aspect of morality. The Kantian symbol has a 'double intentionality': while, on the one hand, beauty is predicated of the object of representation, on the other: 'we refer the beautiful to the morally good' (1987, 5:351–3). Thus, added to a process of representation, there is also a process of evoking the moral, supersensible realm.[34]

This double intentionality can clearly be seen in the examples Kant gives in §59 of the symbolic character of metaphysical terms. First, he points to the German *Grund* (cause, reason) which has its origins in the more prosaic meaning of foundation; second, *abhängen* the German for 'to depend' which has a primary meaning of 'to be held from above'. In both cases, the initial

---

[33] See also Müller 1937, 14; Todorov 1982, 203. One should more accurately speak of 'triple intentionality', since as well as representation and evocation, there is also 'the romantic symbol's refusal to signify at all (heautonomy).

[34] See further Zammito 1992, 289.

representative meaning of a sensible object is sublated in favour of a symbolic expression of something more abstract. As Marty puts it, 'The first meaning of a word concerns what can be given in intuition. This term is then transposed symbolically to serve as a concept which cannot find a corresponding intuition' (1980, 362). It is this process of symbolization which allows intuitive exhibitions to exhibit the supersensible as well as the sensible, to signify in two ways simultaneously.

Partial Tautegory

'The romantic symbol' represents *and* evokes—the rest of this chapter is devoted to exploring how each moment of signification operates in isolation and how both fit together. First, it is necessary to consider what is meant by 'evocation'. Goethe's early theory of the symbol is, as we have seen, obscure on this point—the symbol somehow is (or participates in) its own meaning. To get to the heart of what is going on, one needs to return to a distinction made earlier in the chapter (drawing on Adams' work) between partial and absolute tautegory. My thesis is as follows: 'the romantic symbol' is characterized by its commitment to partial tautegory—that is, being is meaning but meaning is more than being. Out of this partial identity almost all the defining features of 'the romantic symbol' emerge.

(a) Synecdoche

While for proponents of absolute tautegory (like Schelling) meaning and being are in utter identity, theorists of 'the romantic symbol' understand them in unity but only with the added qualification that meaning also exceeds being. There is a synecdochical structure at work here, and what is absolutely crucial about such a model is that it allows both a partial identification of being and meaning without in any way problematizing the superiority and transcendence of meaning. Thus Galland-Szymkowiak defines the 'paradox of the symbol' thus, 'A particular thing or image should make fully visible a universal idea which still remains transcendent—and it can only ever make it wholly visible to the extent that it remains transcendent' (2007, 326).[35] Being is meaning without thereby impacting on meaning's transcendence. The symbol still points beyond itself to a transcendent meaning (the Neoplatonic employment of 'symbol' introduced at the beginning of the chapter is obviously a key influence here). Many German theorists interpret the symbol along these lines.

---

[35] Significantly for this book: although she tries to read the Schellingian symbol through the lens of this paradox, Galland-Szymkowiak concludes that they are ultimately incommensurable, because Schelling denies transcendence (342).

Solger speaks of the sensible 'clothing' of meaning the symbol provides (1984, 129), of meaning 'actively lowering itself into existence' (132), or even of symbolic meaning 'emanat[ing] out into reality as a divine energy' (131). Explicit theological terminology is common. Ast speaks of the symbol as 'the revelation and incarnation of God'[36]—that is, the descent of meaning into the sensible world.

This emphasis on descent gives rise to the model of *revelation* which is central to Goethe's theory. His definitions of the symbol make much of the idea of the descent of a universal idea into finite particularity:

> This is true symbolism, where the particular represents the universal, not as dream and shadow, but as a live and immediate revelation of the unfathomable. (*M* §314)

The universal descends into the particular and is revealed therein. In other words, the universal is both fully embedded in reality (fully unified with the particular) and also exceeds all particulars as their prior cause and archetype. This is synecdoche once more.

Moreover, a crucial consequence of such a synecdochical structure is that, in Sørensen's words, 'the universal outweighs the particular' (1963, 111).[37] This is particularly evident in Goethe's maxim, §569, 'The universal and the particular coincide; the particular is the universal made manifest under different conditions.' The two halves of this sentence express different truths: the first half affirms the identity of universal and particular. However, the second half of the sentence suggests a different view: universal is given priority over particular; the particular is the subsequent manifestation of a prior universal idea. The particular is little more than a copy of this archetype. Such is Goethe's Platonic model for reality: the particular participates in the universal, but the universal still exceeds the particular.

Tautegory—the union of image and meaning—is thus made possible through the participatory metaphysics on which 'the romantic symbol' is based. Yet, even this metaphysical backdrop cannot conceal the paradoxes in which partial tautegory results. Meaning is and is not being—from this initial contradiction flows a rhetoric of paradox in theories of 'the romantic symbol'. I have already introduced Galland-Szymkowiak's 'paradox of the symbol'; Goethe, moreover, contends:

> We are right to call such presentations symbolic . . . It is the thing itself, without being the thing, and yet the thing; an image summarised in the mirror of the spirit and nevertheless identical with the object. (*WA* I/41, 142; translated in Todorov 1982, 203)

---

[36] Ast in Sørensen 1972, 199.
[37] Todorov similarly speaks of 'a superabundance of meaning' (1982, 191).

Symbolic presentations are, are not, and then are again what they present. This is a direct result of Goethe's synecdochical interpretation of the symbol. Goethe subscribes to partial tautegory, even if it means that the logic of his sentences is stretched to its limit and he hovers on the verge of nonsense. Partial tautegory leads to tensions, convolutions, and even flat-out contradictions. Such problems are typical of 'the romantic symbol' in general.

(b) Occasionality

There is a further consequence of this commitment to partial tautegory. 'Partial' is temporalized into 'occasional'—that is, the ambiguity of the identity of meaning and being is conceived temporally: meaning is *sometimes* equivalent to being. Tautegory only applies on occasion. Artistic media sometimes attain the level of the symbol, even if mostly such media are non-symbolic (residing merely at the level of the sign). Symbolism is a state occasionally attained by artworks; it is by no means universal.

In consequence, theorists of 'the romantic symbol' do not rethink the nature of the sign—but merely sometimes add symbolic properties onto it. Signs occasionally deviate to become 'more than signs' (symbols). The conventional sign remains intact, for the symbol is at bottom a sign—but with extra modes of signifying added onto it (the result of a synthesis). I dub this method of describing the symbol as *additive*—on top of a conventional sign whose basic structure is left unchanged, there are grafted symbolic properties.

The Ineffable

Evocation is a consequence of partial tautegory and, as such, meaning both is and is more than being. The symbolic image refers to something which transcends it. In fact, theorists of 'the romantic symbol' go much further and claim that the symbol refers to (or participates in) something ineffable. 'The romantic symbol' evokes the ineffable.

For example, Kant conceives the symbol—as opposed to the schema—as exhibiting ideas of reason (the element of Kantian epistemology which cannot be attended to in determinate cognition and so can never be directly exhibited in intuition). It is Goethe, however, who emphasizes this ineffability most, when, for example, he defines the symbol as 'the momentary living revelation of the ungraspable' (*M* §314) or again as that wherein 'the idea always remains infinitely operative and unattainable so that even if it is put into words in all languages, it still remains inexpressible' (*M* §1113). The symbol is conceived as that which makes present what ineluctably escapes the grasp of our understanding. The meaning revealed in the symbol remains simultaneously concealed.

Henn has drawn attention to Goethe's persistent stress on a meaning beyond language—a sublimity that words are unable to capture (1994, 252). This leads Goethe, according to Henn, to a validation of speechless awe in the face of the mysterious: 'Silence allows Goethe to go beyond language and allude to that which is infinitely challenging' (252).[38] Moreover, Henn also points out, this silence which preserves the ineffability of the transcendent is precisely what the symbol achieves: 'It was this ultimate effectiveness to express the mysterious and ineffable which attracted Goethe to the symbolic mode' (262). In this manner, Goethe writes of the symbol that 'it determines and esteems nothing through words; it merely provides an indication so as to arouse the object in the imagination' (*WA* II/3, 202). The symbol is the form of discourse which, according to Goethe, retains the required mystery that silence otherwise provides.

Analogy

'The romantic symbol' evokes the ineffable. How? The answer for Goethe, Kant, and others is always—analogy. The relation between image and meaning is always analogous. Kant, for example, defines the symbol as 'a *Darstellung* in accordance with mere *analogy*' (1987, 5:352); in fact, at times, analogy and symbol are employed interchangeably (5:354). Goethe also turns straight to the concept of analogy as the means to understand symbols while still pre-serving their mystery (1988, 145). As Marache has put it, 'The rule by which the symbol operates [is] analogy' (1960, 116).[39]

There are two basic reasons analogy is appropriate here. First, analogy preserves the ineffability of what is referred to. Kant is especially insistent on this point: the object of the analogy 'remains unknown to me in its intrinsic character, and hence I cannot exhibit it, but can exhibit only that relation' (2002, 20:280). To think analogously is to preserve the mystery of the object of one's thought. Second, analogy mirrors (and is even a result of[40]) the paradoxes that hold between being and meaning when interpreted synecdo-chically. Analogy is defined by the very dialectic of being and non-being (of identity and difference) which characterizes the partial tautegory of 'the romantic symbol'. Meaning is being and is more than being, just as the *analogatum* is and is more than the analogous image. Therefore, 'the romantic

---

[38] See *WA* IV/2, 289, IV/6, 36.

[39] This emphasis on analogy as a key concept in the *Goethezeit* may seem contentious, especially within theology—due to the near monopoly of Thomist thought on all discussions of analogy. It is important, however, to emphasize that the spectre of Thomism is not relevant here, even though the concept of analogy is.

[40] That is, the epistemological employment of analogy is often a direct result of the participa-tory metaphysics on which 'the romantic symbol' is erected.

symbol' is interpreted as evoking the ineffable by means of an operation of analogy. Occasionally, conventional signs are transformed: they participate in their meaning—a meaning which is identified with the symbolic image but also exceeds it. This excess is the ineffable that can only be experienced analogously.

Indeed, analogy is important to Christian theology for these two reasons as well: it preserves transcendence and is also a product of the broadly Platonic metaphysics Christianity inherited. Christian theology traditionally has a synecdochical structure and it was precisely this tradition that theorists of 'the romantic symbol' tapped into when they too began to interpret the symbol synecdochically. It is for such reasons that Blumenberg has written, 'Probably nothing in the terminology of aesthetics is as instructive in regard to the problematic of secularisation as is the concept of a "symbol"' (1983, 111). The symbol is an extremely visible example of how theorists of the *Goethezeit* recovered many of the thought structures of pre-modernity and redeployed them. Again, we see the impact of the Neoplatonic tradition and its employment of 'symbol' for theorists of 'the romantic symbol'. Of course, there are many forms of analogy, and these conclusions cannot be applied to all of them;[41] however, Goethe, for example, directly cites and imitates Plotinus in formulating his own analogical metaphysics.[42] Thus, when Marache claims that the Goethean symbol is grounded in 'a completely new sense of analogy' (1960, 321), he could easily have written that it 'is grounded in a completely ancient sense of analogy'.

The foregoing is a schematic description of the operation of 'the romantic symbol': on top of a conventional, representational mode of signification, a special, participatory mode is grafted. This participation depends on a partial interpretation of tautegory or (in other words) a synecdochical relation between meaning and being. It must be remembered, however, that this is only one of many competing interpretations of the symbol at the turn of the nineteenth century. Schelling, for example, interprets the three first-order properties (heautonomy, syntheticism, tautegory) in a very different way, and in consequence the Schellingian symbol is extremely different to 'the romantic symbol'—as we shall see.

---

[41] Kant's employment of analogy, especially, does not fit into this picture. For a detailed discussion of the role of analogy in Kant's philosophy in general and his theory of the symbol in particular, see Whistler 2012c.

[42] Invocations of Plotinus' *Enneads* appear most famously at the beginning of the *Farbenlehre* (*WA* II/1, xxxi) and *Wilhelm Meisters Wanderjahre* (*WA* I/48, 196). Goethe also writes in a draft of his autobiography, *Dichtung und Wahrheit*, 'All at once [in 1782]—and as if by inspiration— Neoplatonic philosophers and especially Plotinus emotionally appealed to me in a quite extraordinary way ... [and] for a long time [afterwards] Plotinus still clung to me' (*WA* I/27, 382). In the *Farbenlehre* especially, Goethe utilizes Plotinus as an aid for developing his concept of analogy.

2

Language in the *Goethezeit*

The previous chapter examined theories of the symbol in the years leading up to the *Philosophie der Kunst*; this chapter explores in a parallel fashion theories of language which may have had some impact on Schelling as he drafted his lectures. Together these two chapters describe the contemporary context of Schelling's construction of symbolic language. The first section of this chapter sketches three lines of linguistic thought in the late eighteenth century which were important for Schelling's own understanding of language. However, the vast majority of the chapter is concerned with the more specific issue of how (or even whether) language is reconcilable with the notion of the symbol. The basic problem is whether tautegory is a suitable (or even possible) ideal for language. My concern is both with late eighteenth-century theorists (Kant, Goethe) who grappled with this issue and also with recent critics (de Man, Titzmann) who have attacked the very idea of a symbolic language by means of the simple criticism—'language is just not like that'.

TRENDS IN LINGUISTIC THOUGHT BEFORE 1800

To begin, therefore, I consider tendencies in German philosophy of language in the late eighteenth century.

The Lockean Tradition

Recent work in the history of linguistics has emphasized the dominance of Locke's philosophy for eighteenth-century understandings of language.[1] While such contentions could be seen as problematic to the extent they downplay strands of eighteenth-century linguistic speculation that do not sit

---

[1] See Aarsleff 1982, 2006; Keach 1993.

so happily with twentieth-century presuppositions, there is obviously much truth to them. In movements as diverse as the French Enlightenment, British Romanticism, and Leibniz–Wolffian rationalism, Lockean linguistics was a common element. And the central feature of Locke's philosophy of language was the arbitrariness of the sign: 'Sounds have no natural connexion with our *ideas*, but have all their signification from the arbitrary imposition of men' (1993, 3.9.4).[2] Linguistic signs are formed when a subject chooses to use a set of sounds (or graphic marks) as the representative for another object. There is no pre-existing or natural connection between word and referent which determines the decision; the choice is completely conventional.

Acknowledgement of the arbitrariness of language was not particularly new in Western linguistic thought. Locke's novelty was to assert that language is essentially and originally arbitrary. The arbitrary sign, Locke contended, is not a corruption of an original, motivated relation between signifier and signified, and so in consequence there is no radical distinction between prelapsarian and postlapsarian language, since language is defined as arbitrary—even Adamic language consisted in unmotivated signs (1993, 3.6.51).

The *Essay on Human Understanding* therefore marks a watershed.[3] Seventeenth-century philosophy of language prior to Locke conceived language as fundamentally motivated and merely presently in a corrupt state of unmotivation. The task for the philosopher was then to reform this inheritance of corrupt language so as to return it to its natural condition. While traces of this view remained in the eighteenth century (as we shall soon see), the vast majority of post-Lockean philosophy of language accepted the arbitrary sign as a fact of human existence. Wolff, for example, defines the sign in a Lockean manner,[4] and this definition also orientates every quest for the origin of language in late eighteenth-century Europe (whether Condillac's, Rousseau's, Süssmilch's, or Herder's). Indeed, it is precisely this common presupposition of arbitrariness that Schelling will question in §73 of the *Philosophie der Kunst*.

What is more, the arbitrary sign formed the basis of philosophy of language in late 1790s Jena. Novalis' *Fichte-Studien* reveal this clearly. In 'the relationship of the sign to the signified', Novalis insists 'the signifying [agent] is *completely free* in the choice of the sign...In *this* agent, both [sign and signified] are freely posited' (2003, §11). The subject is free to designate a meaning with whatever sound is desired; as such, the sign is completely unmotivated—a 'voluntary imposition' as Locke had put it (1993, 3.2.1).[5] This broadly Lockean outlook was given its fullest elucidation within German

---

[2] The eighteenth-century conception of the arbitrary sign must be kept separate from the post-Saussurean version. For the eighteenth century, language 'depend[s] on the free choice of intelligent beings' (Wolff, quoted in Wellbery 1984, 19).

[3] See further Aarsleff 2006, 451.

[4] See Wellbery 1984, 18–19.

[5] For a similar insistence in Friedrich Schlegel, see Behler 1993, 90, 106–7.

Idealism by Fichte. In *Von dem Sprachfähigkeit und dem Ursprung der Sprache*, Fichte attempts to 'deduce the use of arbitrary signs from the essential constitution of human nature' (1996, 120)—that is, he provides a transcendental account of the genesis of the arbitrary sign.[6] Language operates with a type of 'sign which has no resemblance whatsoever to the object it is supposed to express' (120).

Fichte and Novalis are therefore to be located within a very different tradition of linguistic thought than theorists of the symbol. The former reject tautegory (the coincidence of meaning and being) in all its forms. Novalis and Fichte celebrate precisely the lack of an ontological connection between meaning and being. Friedrich Schlegel's very unsymbolic appeals to irony and allegory are ultimately grounded in the arbitrariness of the sign.[7] The symbol, on the contrary, is premised on a critique of the arbitrary sign to which Fichte, Novalis, and Friedrich Schlegel cling. Theorizing symbolic language was a marginal, critical enterprise, even in the *Goethezeit*. While the symbol has received most attention in twentieth-century critical theory, the Lockean arbitrary sign was the norm for understandings of language at that time.

Natural Signs

Despite the widespread dominance of the Lockean tradition in late eighteenth-century philosophy of language, traces of non-arbitrary language did remain. In what follows, I describe three such traces: the natural sign, the *Logosmystik* conception of language, and of course symbolic language.

'Cratylism', a term coined by Genette (1976),[8] characterizes those theories of language which make the signifier/signified relation a *motivated* one, as does the eponymous hero of Plato's *Cratylus*.[9] Such a conception of language is extremely problematic: it suggests, for example, that the word 'state' has a natural, objective relation to one specific form of state (monarchy, for example). Such is the basis of ideology: one form of political structure is privileged as the evident, obvious manifestation of politics. 'State' just means monarchy, because 'that is how the world is'. In consequence, in much late twentieth-century theory, the critique of ideology has presupposed the critique of Cratylism and this has led recent theory to stress unmotivated language (drawing heavily on concepts

---

[6] O'Brien concludes, 'Fichte inverts the typical eighteenth century hierarchy of natural over arbitrary signs by viewing arbitrariness as the hallmark of "true" language' (1995, 92). On the contrary, as we have just seen, Fichte is here typical of eighteenth-century linguistics.

[7] See Seyhan 1992, 69.

[8] See also Barthes 1994, 2:1368–76.

[9] See especially Plato 1963, 383a. On the technical employment of 'motivation' here, see Saussure 1966, 131.

and strategies from apophatic theology). One result of this tendency has been a relative neglect of alternative, cratylian traditions. There are cogent reasons why Cratylism has fallen out of favour. It is ineradicably intertwined with ideology: it 'naturalizes' certain states of affairs at the expense of others. Moreover, it is often a product of nostalgia for impossible origins (in this case, Adamic language). In Chapter 10, I return to questions surrounding Cratylism to argue that Schelling's philosophy of language is *acratylian*. In this chapter, however, my focus is on cratylian remnants in eighteenth-century philosophy of language.

The natural sign is a motivated sign—a cratylian leftover from a pre-Lockean linguistic worldview. Its persistence in eighteenth-century philosophy of language was due to the problems that subscription to an unmotivated conception of language gave rise to. Mendelssohn describes these problems as follows:

> Everything in the language of philosophers remains arbitrary. The words and the connections among them contain nothing that would essentially agree with the nature of thoughts and the connections among them ... The soul finds nothing in the designation by means of which it could be guided to the designated subject matter ... For this reason, the slightest inattentiveness makes it possible for thought to lose sight of the subject matter, leaving behind merely the empty signs. (1997, 272–3)[10]

The arbitrariness of the sign hinders scientific progress, for, since the sign does not resemble the thing, the thing cannot be truly perceived from the sign alone. When the sign is given undue prominence, error ensues.

There is one overwhelming response to this state of affairs during the eighteenth century—to try and do away with language altogether. To progress to error-free knowledge, the arbitrary sign should negate itself. As Wellbery writes from the eighteenth-century viewpoint:

> Our ideal medium must be language. Not just any language, though, but a transparent one that sheds its semiotic character and yields without resistance to an intuitive-ideational process in the soul. It must be a language in which the signified idea is rendered present and is not held in absence by the arbitrariness of its signs. (1984, 68)

What is needed is a non-linguistic language! It is this attack on language (which I label 'anti-discursiveness') which I consider in various forms throughout the rest of the chapter. One way in which anti-discursiveness manifests itself is in the ideal of the natural sign, which reincorporates a pre-Lockean nostalgia for Adamic language into a Lockean framework.

---

[10] Locke himself acknowledges these problems (1993, 3.2.7).

Arbitrary signs have a merely conventional relationship instituted by the free choice of the subject; with natural signs, however, there is an actual objective reason for the choice of sign—the sign is naturally grounded in the thing itself.[11] The problem, however, is that there are very few examples of genuine natural signs (at least, on typical eighteenth-century philosophical assumptions). One example is onomatopoeia (Mendelssohn 1997, 181): onomatopoeic sounds are natural signs because there is a natural connection between their own being and that of the referent; this is not a connection dreamed up and imposed by the subject, but one objectively already there pre-existing the subject. Cries of emotion, metaphor, and mathematics are other examples. Natural signs are therefore those in which the sign is either contained within or is a natural consequence of the signified. In this way, the natural sign avoids the pitfalls of its arbitrary counterpart—it does not obscure the referent, rather it sheds light on it. Through the immediate relation the natural sign has to its referent, the mind manages to have a quasi-immediate relation to the referent as well. Through natural signs, Mendelssohn claims, 'one enjoys the advantage of providing an essential and non-arbitrary designation for discovering and grasping the truth' (1997, 265). There is little room for error.

It is because of these advantages enjoyed by the natural sign that Enlightenment semiotics often adhered to the imperative: transform arbitrary signs into natural ones! This was especially true within eighteenth-century aesthetics. Lessing contends, for example, 'Poetry must endeavour absolutely to elevate its arbitrary signs into natural ones' (1985, 134). Indeed, Lessing's ultimate solution to this problem is drama, for in drama linguistic signs are performed; here, 'the speech itself is an action . . . Sign and object are not only similar, but coincide' (Wellbery 1984, 225). Meaning is objectively connected to the sign in the drama, for here the meaning is performed in and by the sign.

Thus, within a generally Lockean framework, cratylian remnants remained entrenched. However, such cratylian traces occupied merely the fringes of theory and of language itself—drama, onomatopoeia, and metaphor are some of the rare instances of the natural sign. They are very much an exception.

Logosmystik

Another cratylian tendency within eighteenth-century linguistics which remained firmly on the fringes is the mystical interpretation of language called *Logosmystik* (Apel 1963, 20). *Logosmystik* refers to a disparate selection of thinkers who all placed language at the heart of theology. 'The Word become flesh' is made the model through which everything (including nature and

---

[11] See Mendelssohn 1997, 177–8.

human language) is to be interpreted. In Germany, *Logosmystik* has its roots in Eckhardt, Nicholas of Cusa, and Luther, then flourished among Böhme and the Swabian pietists (like Oetinger) after the Reformation. In late eighteenth-century Germany, it found its champion in J. G. Hamann.[12]

Logosmystiker therefore theologize on the experience of language. Language is so important to them because it disrupts 'sound, practical human reason' (Hamann 2007, 154). Hamann's treatise, *Neue Apologie des Buchstaben H*, is exemplary: he discovers in 'h' a scandal with which reason is unable to cope. Hamann pokes fun at contemporary calls to modernize German spelling (and in particular to drop the silent 'h' which appeared in the middle of many late eighteenth-century German words),[13] for such calls presuppose that language can be brought under the control of the principle of sufficient reason (2007, 150). Hamann counters that 'h' serves no rational purpose but still it survives—and this is because language has a religious and not a rational basis. 'H' indicates the divinity which underlies all linguistic use. Sheehan writes of Hamann's position,

> The *h* immoderately overflowed the parameters set by ... orthography insofar as its use was irregular, unpredictable and thoroughly unrestricted by the confines of proper pronunciation ... [It] was the very sign of superabundance and overflow in human language that harkened to God's hidden hand. (1998, 36–8)

As the alphabetic representative of breath or aspiration, 'h' most closely resembles the divine spirit which animates all things. Hamann's remarks here, idiosyncratic as they seem, draw on a whole tradition of theological thought and most particularly on Böhme, who had already written in 1623:

> The ancient wise men, judicious in this tongue inserted a [silent] H in the name JEOVA ... This was done with great understanding, for the H reveals the holy name, with its five vowels, in the outward nature. It shows how the holy name of God breathes itself out and reveals itself in the creature ... [It is an] instrument of the divine.[14]

At the centre of *Logosmystik* stands the principle: God's self-revelation is language. This has two corollaries: first, God's creation must be seen as a form of language and, second, human language is a form of God's revelation. In other words, creation expresses the Word;[15] nature is therefore divine language in corporeal form—*Natursprache*. Nature must be understood on a

---

[12] Such a list may suggest that Hamann emerged out of nowhere, and in the German context there is some truth to this. However, Hamann's understanding of language is certainly influenced by other eighteenth-century figures such as Warburton and Louth.

[13] See Sheehan 1998, 33–41.

[14] Quoted in Sheehan 1998, 37. See further Böhme 2001, 215.

[15] There are, of course, thorny theological issues at play here, and different thinkers liken creation to the Incarnation to very different degrees. All thinkers in this tradition, though, posit some analogy between them.

linguistic model: its products must be interpreted like words, behind which lie meanings, and ultimately all such meanings must be traced back to the author of the text.[16] Natural science, on this model, becomes a form of hermeneutics. This model applies to humanity as well: anthropology also becomes a branch of hermeneutics—the *imago Dei* resembles the *sermo Dei*. Böhme writes, in man 'the word of God speaketh, ruleth, liveth and willeth' (2001, 195), and thus man 'is the book of the Being of all beings' (198). However, humanity is also able to perpetuate and repeat God's revelation: God speaks in man and man's speaking is but the continuation of this originary word. As Baader wrote, 'To speak is to use the language of God.'[17] Divine revelation is redistributed in human language. A seventeenth-century follower of Böhme sums up this line of thought:

> Therefore *God* has determined all nature through the art of speech, indeed His words are shown through all the secrets of nature; therefore whoever speaks rightly...speaks as God.[18]

Since language is the proper model for divine revelation, human language takes precedence over nature as the most significant site of God's presence in the world. Language is the aspect of creation which most resembles God's original revelation; it is the closest finite approximation to the divine, and so it is the point in the created world in which God is most revealed. For *Logosmystiker*, human words reveal the divine nature; they are natural signs of God.

There is a further consequence of the *Logosmystik* conception of language which is perhaps not as immediately obvious—this is the identification of language and reason. Since humanity itself is part of God's self-expression, man's act of thinking forms part of God's act of speaking. In other words, human reason is an expression of divine Logos. Hamann writes, 'Language [is] the only, first and last organon and criterion of reason' (2007, 208).[19] Language is the paradigmatic model through which thought is to be understood. Of course, the very fact that the Greek term *Logos* means both reason and language is made much of in this regard, for it exhibits the original identity of language and reason. Moreover, its famous use at the beginning of John's Gospel further adds to its prestige: reason, language and God's Incarnation in the world are all bound together in '*Logos*'. '*Logos*' is therefore the proof par excellence for the *Logosmystiker*: human language and human reason are forms of God's Word.

---

[16] See Bayer 1983, 59; Griffith Dickson 1995, 139–43.

[17] Quoted in Susini 1942, 2:241.

[18] Quoted in Ingen 2001, 127.

[19] Baader held very similar views. See Susini 1942, 2:236–43. *Logosmystik* was not the only tradition in which the identification of reason and language was maintained (Wolff and Rousseau, for example, say very similar things); it is, however, a particularly crucial one.

Logosmystik entered a renaissance in Germany during the late eighteenth century. Not only did Hamann popularize this way of thinking, the first generation of Romantics enthusiastically championed many of the sources on which Hamann was drawing. Tieck, for example, proclaimed the virtues of Böhme in Jena in the late 1790s and seems to have introduced Schelling to his writings in 1799.[20] Simultaneously, in Munich Baader discovered Böhme and other mystics, devoting much of his life to reissuing their works.[21] Schelling's friendship with Baader on moving to Bavaria in 1803 strengthened his acquaintance with the *Logosmystiker* (although he had been aware of the Swabian pietists since his days in the Tübingen Stift[22]). *Logosmystik* was alive and well at the end of the eighteenth century, and so was an important vessel for the transmission of cratylian interpretations of language.

TAUTEGORY

Natural signs and the *Logosmystik* interpretation of language are two forms therefore in which Cratylism was preserved in the late eighteenth century. However, for our purposes, the most significant 'cratylian remnant' of German linguistic theory during the 1790s was the burgeoning discourse of symbolic language.

Yet, symbolic language did not merely assert a motivated relation between signifier and signified in opposition to the arbitrary sign; it flew in the face of arbitrariness by subscribing to tautegory—the union of signifier and signified. The relation between being and meaning in language, according to theorists of the symbol, is neither one of motivation nor of non-motivation, but one of ontological equivalence. Being is meaning; the signifier is the signified. On this basis, theories of the symbol not only diverge from the Lockean arbitrary sign, but also from the natural sign and the sign of the *Logosmystik* tradition.

Yet, of course, with such a radical view of language come problems— foremost among them the simple question: *can* tautegory be legitimately applied to language? One of the major issues for theorists of the symbol was the very possibility of symbolic *language*. If language is defined as sounds or images which refer to an external, intellectual meaning, then the idea of symbolic language begins to look self-contradictory. Gadamer, for example, describes the typical Western view of language as follows:

---

[20] On Tieck, see Mayer 1999, 55–60; on Schelling, see Gutmann 1936, xlv; Mayer 1999, 181–6.
[21] He published a new edition of Böhme's works in 1813 'so as to reawaken the mystic tradition' (quoted in Benz 1968, 7).
[22] See Benz 1968, 20–1, 56.

> *Pure indication* . . . is the essence of the sign . . . It should not attract attention to
> itself in such a way that one lingers over it, for it is there only to make present
> something that is absent and to do so in such a way that the absent thing, and that
> alone, comes to mind. (2004, 145)

In other words, the process of signification stands at the centre of our experience of language; it is the means by which a signifier refers to a signified
outside itself. The sounds of language (according to a standard picture) only
convey meaning by extrinsically indicating first a concept in the mind and
second the object in the world to which the concept refers. It is only by
transcending itself first into the mind and then into the world that language
operates successfully. Hence, the sign is not self-sufficient; it is not heautonomous: it requires something external to give it meaning. The sign's function is
to point away from itself—in this it is completely opposed to heautonomy.
This self-effacing 'essence' of language also problematizes any claim to tautegory. In the sign, meaning remains separate from and external to the being of
language. Such has always been the fundamental tenet of linguistics: meaning
exists outside of being—they cannot be unified. The whole point of the sign is
to be non-self-identical, to efface itself so as to point to some meaning external
to it. Signifier and signified remain separate and cannot be fused into one
another.

Hence, the task for theorists of symbolic language becomes to conceive
another, alternative model for language, a model on which language can
operate without giving rise to properties antithetical to the symbol. Only
thus can the idea of symbolic language be coherent. The requirement is for a
language in which meaning and being are unified. It is this aim I dub 'tautegory'. Tautegory is a first-order property which particularly applies to symbolic language (rather than symbols in general), for standard linguistic
theories are particularly virulent (as we have seen) in separating meaning
and being, so that tautegory is far more contentious in the realm of language
than it is elsewhere. Only a language which exhibits tautegory counts as a
symbolic language.

'Tautegory' is not a term Schelling or any theorist employs to refer specifically to the symbol; rather, my choice of this term is motivated by the writings
of the late Schelling who in his *Philosophie der Mythologie* employs 'tautegory'
in an almost identical way to how 'symbol' was employed in the *Philosophie
der Kunst*.[23] Myths are tautegorical because they are symbolic. While Schelling
uses 'tautegory' to refer to mythology alone, in this book I will extend its range
to cover the whole linguistic realm. 'Tautegory' is an appropriate term because

---

[23] See Tilliette 1970, 1:466 for a comparison. The term was coined, however, by Coleridge
prior to being appropriated by Schelling. In a footnote to the passage below (*SW* 11:196),
Schelling acknowledges this. For Coleridge's usage of 'tautegory', see Coleridge 1839, 296,
1993, 206.

even its etymology ('expressing the same thing as itself') suggests the identity of signifier and signified. Thus in the *Philosophie der Mythologie* Schelling writes:

> Mythology...has no meaning other than the one it expresses...Mythology is entirely proper, that is, it must be understood just as it expresses itself, and not as if it thought one thing and said another. Mythology is not *allegorical*; it is *tautegorical*. For mythology, the gods are the beings that really exist; instead of *being* one thing and *signifying another*, they signify only what they are. (*SW* 11:195–6)

This ideal of tautegory is that which forty years earlier also motivates Schelling's construction of symbolic language; hence, I use it in what follows to refer to the union of meaning and being in the symbol.

It needs to be stressed just how radical Schelling and other theorists of the symbol's pursuit of tautegorical language is within Western linguistics. The symbol does not refer to a referent outside itself; it participates in and so shares its being with this referent. The symbol presents *itself* and does not refer to anything outside of itself. It does not efface itself—because it is its own meaning. Such a conception of language is not even cratylian.[24] This is because, while the motivated sign possesses a 'natural' link to its referent in the manner of a faithful mimetic copy, the symbol goes one step further to become part of (or, in some cases, identical to) its referent. The symbol is not just a copy of its referent; it is its referent. This novel reinterpretation of the signifier–signified relation plunged theorists of the symbol during the *Goethezeit* into new waters.

Theorizing symbolic language hence became a special challenge. Theorists at the time were adamant that (in Frenzel's words), 'The poetic symbol is not merely referential, but possesses intrinsic value. It cannot be exchanged, nor can it be substituted like "x" in an equation...It is simultaneously what it stands for' (1963, 35–6). Yet, having made such negative assertions, it becomes more difficult to envisage the actual positive model for symbolic language— that is, if it is neither a conventional sign nor a motivated one, what form does it take? What other forms of language are there in which meaning is intrinsic? In this vein, Todorov writes (referring specifically to Moritz' work):

> Now is it not a generic character of every sign...to refer to something other than itself? Moritz thus needs to conceive of a new class of signs, characterized by their intransitivity. (1982, 161)

---

[24] Even Cratylus—characterized as holding an extreme position on language—admits 'the name is not the same with the thing named' (Plato 1963, 430a). Indeed, Socrates himself suggests that such an admission is the bare minimum required for there to be any common ground in discussing language. He later exclaims, 'How ridiculous would be the effect of names on things, if they were exactly the same with them!' (432b).

The task is to theorize a new class of intransitive signs—signs which do not refer to anything outside of themselves, but contain their own meaning. The task, then, is to conceive tautegorical signs—symbols. Each word must be an end in itself which enacts its own meaning and so requires nothing beyond itself.

THE POSSIBILITY OF SYMBOLIC LANGUAGE I: RESPONSES FROM CRITICAL THEORY

The next three sections of the present chapter are dedicated to unravelling the mysterious idea of a tautegorical language. Or, more specifically, they examine various criticisms of this ideal and admissions of its impossibility. First, in this section, I will consider some recent criticisms within critical theory of the *Goethezeit* quest for tautegorical language. Then I turn to the fate of symbolic language first in Kant and second in Goethe—both, as we shall see, implicitly admit that symbolic language is impossible and so linguistics is a domain into which the properties of the symbol can never be transposed. My purpose in considering these obstacles to symbolic language is to show how in fact they do not rule out symbolic language *tout court*, but *only one interpretation* of it. In short, it is only (I argue) when the 'romantic' interpretation of the symbol is transposed into linguistics that these criticisms or admissions of failure are valid. They are invalid for other interpretations of symbolic language. Ultimately, of course, my aim is to clear the way for both the possibility and the plausibility of Schelling's construction of symbolic language, since Schelling does not interpret it 'romantically' but in a very different manner.

The Naturalization of the Semiotic

De Man's 'The Rhetoric of Temporality' has provided—as we saw in the previous chapter—perhaps the most influential attempt to 'put into question . . . the assured predominance of the symbol as the outstanding characteristic of romantic diction' (1983, 198). He contends that theories of symbolic language were achieved by means of a violent 'suppression' (207) of the essence of language. De Man concentrates his criticisms on tautegory: a symbolic language committed to tautegory is one that ignores, and even suppresses, the fundamental abyss that actually separates signifier from signified.[25] This gap exists at the very heart of linguistics, so to conceive of a language without it is to

---

[25] Benjamin provides an important precedent (1998, 159–63).

no longer conceive of language at all. For this reason, symbolic language 'will never be able to gain an entirely good poetic conscience', but is rather a form of 'tenacious self-mystification' (208). In contrast, de Man vaunts allegory's superiority, its 'demystification of an organic world postulated in a symbolic mode' (222).

Indeed, the organicism of the symbol—its assertion of 'the priority of natural substances' (196)—is fundamental to de Man's denunciation of tautegorical language, as another of his essays, 'The Intentional Structure of the Romantic Image', makes clear. Here, de Man begins with Hölderlin's image in *Brot und Wein*:

> *...Nun aber nennt er sein Liebstes,*
> *Nun, nun müssen dafür Worte, wie Blumen, entstehn.* (1985, 2:90–5, ll. 89–90)
> [... But now he names his most loved,
> Now, for this reason, words, like flowers, must arise.]

According to de Man, this comparison of words to flowers sums up the underlying goal of symbolic language: language aspires to be a natural object. De Man writes, 'This type of imagery is grounded in the intrinsic ontological primacy of the natural object. Poetic language seems to originate in the desire to draw closer and closer to the ontological status of the object' (1984, 7). Symbolic language aspires to the objective presence of nature; indeed, 'Romantic thought and Romantic poetry seem to come so close to giving in completely to the nostalgia for the object that it becomes difficult to distinguish between object and image' (9). This, at first glance at least, seems to be the very point of tautegory: signs become ontologically indiscernible from the objects to which they refer; thus words become natural objects.

Moreover, de Man again criticizes such objectification for overriding the 'essence of language'. He writes, 'Words do *not* originate like flowers... It is in the essence of language to be capable of origination, but of never achieving the absolute identity with itself that exists in the natural object' (6). Natural objects are constituted by self-presence; language by irredeemable difference (by a permanent gap separating meaning from being). Tautegory therefore properly belongs to the natural object, and any aspiration to this condition by language is utterly futile. Symbolic language's 'nostalgia for the natural object' is doomed to 'ontological bad faith' (1983, 211). Language cannot be given 'material substantiality' (1984, 2).

Titzmann also criticizes this aspiration, which he dubs, 'the naturalization of the semiotic':

> The artwork approaches nature and nature the artwork...By means of the concept of the symbol, the difference between a semiotic field whose objects signify something and a natural field whose objects signify nothing is annulled. (1979, 660)

The symbol is conceived as a 'non-sign' (660–1). It is modelled on the silence and concealment of the opaque natural world. For example, Carlyle writes in *Sartor Resartus* (his affectionate pastiche of German Idealism), 'In a Symbol there is concealment and yet revelation; here, therefore, by Silence and by Speech acting together, comes a double significance' (1908, 164–5). Symbolic language, as well as speaking, conceals; it is inexpressive and non-disclosive. As Adams remarks of Carlyle's description, 'Like others in the symbolist tradition, Carlyle tends to treat symbols as opposed to language rather than as a kind of language or even fundamental to the nature of language' (1983, 82)—which is of course problematic when trying to account for the phenomenon of symbolic language!

In sum, symbolic language is naturalized and this leads to an abandonment of its linguistic character. Language turns against itself in order to become nature. The consequence of this is simple: symbolic language is not to be read or interpreted, but *perceived*—the mere sensory perception of the symbol is enough; no hermeneutic work is required on the part of the subject. As de Man puts it, language 'is defined as "symbolic" by the priority conferred on the initial moment of sensory perception' (1983, 193).

Interpretations of Heautonomy

Both de Man and Titzmann consider this naturalization of the symbol, and the resultant priority of perception, to be a consequence of tautegory. To unify meaning and being is, in their view, necessarily an imitation of the natural object—negating symbolic language's status as language. This, of course, is only compounded by the tendency to conceive this tautegory in organicist terms. In the very rhetoric used to articulate symbolic language, the naturalization and de-semiotization of language is already noticeable.

I agree entirely with the conclusions of this critique; however, the range within which they are valid is far more circumscribed than either de Man or Titzmann realize. It is not 'first-order' properties, like tautegory, in themselves which lead to these conclusions, but rather the second-order interpretation they are given by the 'romantic' interpretation of the symbol. The basis for distancing myself from de Man and Titzmann is, of course, the Schellingian symbol: Schelling's symbol shares first-order properties with 'the romantic symbol', but still manages to be discursive. Schelling's symbol is non-perceptual, whilst remaining tautegorical.

In Chapter 1, I argued that first-order properties radically underdetermine the symbol, and that a property such as tautegory (the union of signifier and signified) could be interpreted in at least three different, equally legitimate ways: the subject could take the signifier and signified as if they were one (the Kantian answer); the signifier could be absorbed into the signified, while the signified itself transcends it (partial tautegory); or finally the signified and signifier could be utterly identical (absolute tautegory). I am making a similar argument in this chapter. 'The romantic symbol' is understood along the lines of a natural object—that is, the signified inheres in the signifier in much the same self-evident way that, for example, green inheres in grass: one need only perceive the latter to know the former. Schelling, however, understands symbolic language in a very different manner: it does not display its meaning like a natural object, but produces or constructs it, like a Euclidean problem. Schelling provides an opposing second-order interpretation of the symbol, and in consequence his invocation of a symbolic language remains coherent. Neither tautegory nor any other first-order property of the symbol is itself responsible for the anti-discursive nature of some theories of the symbol.

What is it about how 'the romantic symbol' interprets symbolic language that brings about this process of naturalization? The answer, I contend, is the way in which it interprets the first-order property of heautonomy. Heautonomy, as we saw in the previous chapter, is the self-sufficiency of the symbolic image. It needs nothing external. Now, there are obviously many ways in which entities can be a self-contained whole, and for the purpose of this book I distinguish between two: first, the way in which a logical argument or mathematical equation is heautonomous and second the way in which a perceived natural object (like a blade of grass) is heautonomous. The former I label a 'rationalist' interpretation of heautonomy and the latter an 'empiricist' interpretation of heautonomy. I explore them in turn by considering an important proponent of each interpretation—Spinoza and Schiller, respectively.

1. Spinoza's epistemology hinges on a critique of ideas as 'impressions' received passively by the mind as it goes about 'seeing' what is outside it. In contrast, Spinoza emphasizes, ideas are actions; they are not passively received from without, but formed through the mind's own process of thinking.[26] This is also a critique of signs, but, in opposition to the more empirically minded thinkers I am otherwise discussing in this chapter, Spinoza does not think signs are problematic because they are not representational enough (i.e. because attention sometimes focuses on them, rather than the thing itself), Spinoza thinks signs are too representational. To the extent that they point away from themselves, they are inadequate. As Jacobi has Spinoza say from the vantage point of 1785, 'Truth cannot come from outside' (1994, 205). Spinoza gives the example of a conclusion without premises to illustrate an inadequate idea (1994, IIP28D): the idea does not show its own 'working'—it states its truth without explaining how this truth was reached. The adequate idea or syllogism, on the other hand, exhibits its own premises, and so requires

---

[26] See Spinoza 1994, IID3, IIP43S.

nothing external to justify its truth. Spinoza's theory of adequate ideas therefore shares the very same criterion of heautonomy as all symbols during the *Goethezeit*. Only that entity which is self-sufficient, which contains its own meaning within itself, is to be esteemed, for it is absolute (IIP34). Adequate ideas are active and rationally self-sufficient, but far from being modelled on a perceived natural object, such Spinozist heautonomy is modelled on a rational argument.

2. Schiller, as I indicated in the previous chapter, was one of the pioneers in importing heautonomy into aesthetics. He interprets heautonomy through an analysis of the subject's aesthetic experience: in encountering beauty, the subject perceives something which has already formed itself. The sense data the subject receives are structured without the mind's activity being required. It is, in Schaper's phrase, 'the appearance to the senses of intelligible perfection' (1979, 112). An intuition of a beautiful object is an intuition already imbued with form—the mind is merely passive in relation to it. In consequence, a beautiful object is one that merely needs to be perceived to be known. The subject is entirely passive faced with beauty: no hermeneutics or signifying inferences are required to recover its meaning; rather, it stands self-evident and 'ready-made' before the subject. Schillerian heautonomy is therefore a product of an 'initial moment of sensory perception'.

Each of these versions of heautonomy fed into different interpretations of the symbol. The rationalist variant informed the Schellingian symbol (as we shall see in later chapters) and the empiricist variant indelibly marked 'the romantic symbol'—and it is this latter influence I explore further in the rest of this chapter.

'The Romantic Symbol' and Anti-Discursiveness

My earlier claim concerning the regional validity of de Man and Titzmann's conclusions is dependent upon this contention that heautonomy is interpreted in different ways during the *Goethezeit*. The naturalization of the semiotic which de Man and Titzmann both see as a consequence of the idea of symbolic language is in fact only a consequence of a symbolic language interpreted through an *empiricist* form of heautonomy. Their arguments apply solely to 'the romantic symbol', because only 'the romantic symbol' employs an empiricist version of heautonomy.

What is more—and again this cuts against the grain of de Man and Titzmann's arguments—the symbol did not somehow create this anti-discursive empiricism in the first place. On the contrary, 'the romantic symbol' was embedded within a prevalent and long-standing trend within eighteenth-century Germany of understanding language in an empiricist and so anti-discursive manner. Rather than the structure of the symbol giving rise to anti-discursive sentiment, anti-linguistic tendencies are prior: it is the tradition of anti-linguistic thought in the Enlightenment as well as the *Goethezeit* which was the motor behind the naturalization of the semiotic and the priority of the perceptual. That is, it is anti-discursive sentiment which determines the way in which 'the romantic symbol' is interpreted, rather than vice versa.

One critic who has recently drawn attention to the development of an anti-discursive empiricism in the eighteenth century and its subsequent impact on the interpretation of the symbol is Halmi.[27] In *The Genealogy of the Romantic Symbol*, Halmi poses the following question, 'What cultural questions or needs motivated the formulation of symbolist theory, and what cultural conditions (philosophical, scientific, political) affected the forms that that theory assumed?' (2007, 26). In answer, one of the main narratives the book traces is a reaction against the alienation of science from everyday sense-experience. The *Goethezeit* inherited this 'anxiety about discursive representation' (152): in the climate bequeathed by the Enlightenment, abstract thought and language were to be distrusted. 'I'll believe it when I see it' became the underlying ethos of the age; the sophistries of language were veils hiding the self-evidence of the phenomena. It was within such a worldview that 'the romantic symbol' began to be interpreted on the model of a natural object—a model that does away with the corrupt mediation of the semiotic function.

Attacks on language were the order of the day. We have seen this already in my discussion of the natural sign; however, I now turn to a discussion of symbolic language in Kant and Goethe where we will see again (and this time in much more detail) that, while they took the eighteenth-century distrust of language to a new extreme, this remained a tradition they bought into, rather than an attitude they engendered themselves.

THE POSSIBILITY OF SYMBOLIC
LANGUAGE II: KANT

In Kant's critical philosophy, the symbol undergoes a revolution. While for all philosophers earlier in the eighteenth century symbols were a form of discursive knowledge, Kant transforms them into a perceptual *Darstellung*—completely opposed to any discursiveness. He states categorically, 'The intuitive in cognition must be contrasted with the discursive (not the symbolic). The former

---

[27] Halmi—in line with de Man and Titzmann (who are both cited approvingly (2007, 4, 13))—asserts the influence of this tradition on the fundamental constitution of the symbol itself: 'The privileging of sensible intuition demanded that the relation of signifier and signified be defined, paradoxically, in unitary rather than binary terms' (61). He explicitly places Schelling in this anti-discursive tradition (93, 153).

is ... *symbolic*' (1987, 5:352). The consequences for symbolic language are immense, especially considering the influence Kant's theory of the symbol was to have on later generations. Kant here erects the symbol on an empiricist interpretation of heautonomy—it is to be perceived, rather than constructed. In so doing, he inaugurates the specific 'romantic' interpretation of the symbol, a particularly anti-discursive interpretation. In this section, I describe how and why Kant made symbols perceptual at the expense of their discursiveness.

Pre-Kantian Symbolic Cognition

> Between Leibniz's *Meditations on Knowledge, Truth and Ideas* (1684) and Kant's *Critique of Judgment* (1790), the meaning of the *symbol* was radically transformed. From a mere arbitrary sign which is conventionally substituted for an idea, the symbol became intuitive presentation ... Kant consciously (and in a historically decisive manner) announces a rupture from the meaning attributed to the symbol by the Leibniz–Wolffian school.

> (Galland-Szymkowiak 2006, 73)

As Galland-Szymkowiak here implies, to understand the significance of Kant's transformation of the symbol and the 180° revolution in its meaning from discursive to perceptual, it is necessary to consider in more detail the position against which he was reacting.[28] In Chapter 1, I introduced the distinction between symbolic and intuitive cognition within eighteenth-century German epistemology. The two basic properties of intuition are immediacy and particularity, whereas symbolic cognition is defined by its mediacy (that is, its dependence on signs) and its universality (its conceptual content). Moreover, it is the arbitrariness of the signs it employs which makes symbolic knowledge fallible, for (since the sign does not resemble the thing) the thing cannot be truly perceived from the sign alone. The sign obscures what it marks.

This problem with the sign, and so with symbolic cognition, began to be increasingly flagged up as the eighteenth century progressed. I have already noted this growing distrust of language. Much of the impetus for this growing suspicion of the mediated nature of signs was the influence of British empiricism on the German intellectual scene. If knowledge is rooted in an act of perception, the philosophical merits of signs (and especially knowledge through signs) become harder to justify. Empiricism gradually defamed symbolic cognition. Humans are at present (the story goes) limited to two kinds of knowledge: the intuitive but clear knowledge they receive through sense-perception, and the

---

[28] A further analysis of symbolic cognition in pre-Kantian and Kantian German philosophy is to be found in Whistler 2012b.

distinct but symbolic knowledge achieved by the understanding.[29] The former is limited to the subject's immediate environment; the latter prone to error. The ideal for Enlightenment philosophy therefore is knowledge that is both distinct and intuitive. This would give man possession of an infallible and universal science; knowledge would be immediately of the things themselves, unmediated by the sign, and yet not limited to the finitely perceptible. Man would gain God's infinite and indubitable power of perception.

How though—the question was repeatedly asked—is this ideal possible when science is intrinsically dependent on symbolic cognition? The answer was located in language, for it is the sign that separates symbolic from intuitive cognition. As I have already indicated in my discussion of natural signs above, the imperative for the *Aufklärung* therefore becomes *to dissolve the sign without destroying science*. To quote Yuri Lotman, 'The striving for de-semiotisation, the battle against the sign, is the basis of the culture of the Enlightenment.'[30] Berkeley expresses this motivation most clearly:

> It were, therefore, to be wished that everyone would use his utmost endeavours to obtain a clear view of the ideas he would consider, separating from them all that dress and encumbrance of words which so much contribute to blind the judgment and divide the attention...We need only draw the curtain of words, to behold the fairest tree of knowledge. (1975, 88)

Such was the empiricist critique of language which became ever more popular in eighteenth-century Germany.

Kant's Expulsion of Language

Kant's philosophical roots lie in these developments. His early philosophical trajectory mirrors others of his era—an ever increasing awareness of the empiricist challenge to rationalism. What, however, is surprising considering this context is Kant's neglect of the sign. Semiotics makes no appearance in the critical philosophy. In spite of his predecessors' obsession with the issue of symbolic cognition, Kant is totally silent on the problem of signs. There is no such thing as symbolic cognition for Kant. As Surber puts it, 'Kant maintained a fairly consistent "silence" on language as a philosophical question' (2000, 316); each time a question of language occurs Kant pushes it back 'below the threshold of genuine philosophical interest' (315). It was, indeed, such absences which left his work open to metacritical attacks by Hamann and Herder.[31]

---

[29] This distinction draws on the technical meanings of 'clear' and 'distinct' current in the Leibniz–Wolffian tradition. See Leibniz 1998, 76–7.

[30] Quoted in Wellbery 1984, 35.

[31] Already in his 1784 *Metakritik über den Purismum der Vernunft*, Hamann (2007, 205–18) uses the absence of a treatment of language in Kant's work to criticize the very basis of the critical philosophy.

I want to argue that Kant's total silence in this regard is due to the fact that he solved the problem of the sign, and he does this by taking the negative, empiricist attitude of the *Aufklärung* towards language to its logical conclusion. He expels language from philosophy. Perhaps the best indication of this is his dictum, concepts without intuitions are 'empty' (2007, A51/B75), which sweeps away the very problem of symbolic cognition. Kant completely rejects its epistemological significance: symbolic cognition is premised on the possibility of knowing things without intuiting them; however, Kant counters, only what can be intuited can be known in any way; therefore, there is only intuitive cognition. Symbolic cognition is not cognition; it can provide no sort of experience.[32] Rather than man's finitude being marked by his dependence on the sign as the Leibniz–Wolffian tradition contended, for Kant man's finitude is due to his dependence on sensible intuition.

There is one paragraph in §59 of the *Kritik der Urteilskraft* which confirms this impression. Here, Kant does at least mention language, if negatively. This is the point at which Kant makes explicit the shift of the term 'symbol' from discourse to intuition by turning on its head the Leibniz–Wolffian distinction between symbolic and intuitive cognition. As we have just seen, philosophers of the eighteenth century conceived symbolic cognition in opposition to intuition due to its dependence on signs; Kant, however, completely disagrees with this usage: 'The intuitive in cognition must be contrasted with the discursive (not the symbolic)' (1987, 5:351). The major epistemological principle resides now not in the 'contrast [of] symbolic with intuitive *Darstellung*', but rather in the fact that symbols are a form of intuitive knowledge, and so 'must be contrasted with the discursive'. Kant writes:

> The more recent logicians have come to use the word *symbolic* in another sense that is wrong and runs counter to the meaning of the word. They use it to contrast symbolic with *intuitive Darstellung*. For the latter (the intuitive) can be divided into *schematic* and *symbolic Darstellung*: both are hypotyposes, i.e. *Darstellungen*, not mere *characterizations*, i.e. designations of concepts by accompanying sensible signs. (5:351–2)

'The more recent logicians' are Kant's forebears in the Leibniz–Wolffian tradition who employed the term 'symbol' for symbolic cognition. Both symbol and schema, as intuitive *Darstellungen*, are to be distinguished from 'mere characterizations'—that is, signs. This is because, while Kant finds symbols and schemata philosophically significant and gives them crucial roles in his critical project, signs remain extrinsic to philosophy. Here is how Kant defines the sign:

---

[32] Although he still holds open the possibility of employing 'empty signs' for thinking, rather than knowing.

Signs contain nothing whatever that belongs to the intuition of the object; their point is the subjective one of serving as a means for reproducing concepts ... They are either words, or visible (algebraic or even mimetic) signs, and they merely *express* concepts. (5:352)

Signs are merely subjective, arbitrary aids for communicating concepts. Kant relegates the problem of the sign to one of no philosophical importance: their only function is to 'reproduce' concepts already formed. The sign has nothing to do with epistemology whatsoever, but is solely a device for communicating already processed philosophical thought. Therefore, there is no such thing as knowledge gained through discourse alone for Kant. In this passage from the third *Kritik*, symbolic cognition disappears from philosophy. It is for this reason that Kant has almost nothing to say about language in his works.

Symbols are therefore to be opposed to language and to signs in general. To speak of symbolic language is a pure nonsense; instead, one must speak of symbolic intuitions. Kant takes the prevalent anti-discursive attitude of his era even further than it had been taken before: language (and especially any idea of symbolic language) is entirely banished from philosophy.

The Perceptual Symbol

The question naturally arises then as to what Kant means by symbolic intuition, and here one further development in the history of the symbol needs to be noted. As I discussed above, intuition in late eighteenth-century Germany had two defining characteristics: immediacy and particularity.[33] Notable by its absence from this list, however, is perception or sensation. As Hintikka has argued, 'There was no inseparable connection between the notion of intuition and sensibility in the writings of most seventeenth and eighteenth-century philosophers' (1969, 40–1). Indeed, Hintikka contends that to read our modern prejudices concerning *Anschauung* as perceptual vision back onto late eighteenth-century German thought would be a grave mistake (38–9). Perception was not (at least directly) associated with intuition. An obvious example here are the various forms of 'intellectual intuition' popular among seventeenth- and eighteenth-century rationalists; the very fact they could use the Latin *intuitus* to describe this form of knowledge demonstrates the term's non-perceptual connotations. Hintikka concludes, there was no 'direct conceptual connection' between intuition and perception (51).

Yet, with Kant this changed. One of the main tasks of the Transcendental Aesthetic in the first *Kritik* is to prove that all intuitions are perceptions, that intuition is solely grounded (for humans at least) in sensibility. In Hintikka's

---

[33] Kant's notion of intuition definitely partook of both these properties; see 2007, A320/B376–7.

words, 'Kant tries to show that all intuitions are sensible' (49–50). In light of this argument, Kant's designation of the symbol as a form of intuition can be further determined. Not only does the symbol become a form of immediate and particular presentation, but, owing to the argument of the Transcendental Aesthetic, it is now tied ineluctably to perception. Symbols are, Kant claims, to be perceived. Again, the radical shift from earlier uses of the term needs to be emphasized. For earlier eighteenth-century philosophers, symbolic cognition meant knowledge through discourse, interpretation, and concepts. Kant rejects this apparatus (at least when it is employed independently of perception). Symbols are particular images that are immediately perceived.

This shift had enormous consequence for the history of 'symbol' in the 1790s and into the nineteenth century. The symbol is now opposed to linguistic activity and linked, instead, to sensation.

THE POSSIBILITY OF SYMBOLIC LANGUAGE III: GOETHE

Goethe's work forms the culmination of this 'empiricist' tradition which naturalizes the semiotic into an object of perception. What is more, as I pointed out in Chapter 1, it is in Goethe's writings that the symbol is first explicitly worked out in the form that will come to be known as 'the romantic symbol'. Thus, this section comprises an examination of the way anti-discursiveness and the specifically 'romantic' interpretation of the symbol come together in his writings. As we shall discover, for Goethe the symbol is a natural object in the world in which meaning is 'ready-made' and available for perception. What de Man labels 'nostalgia for the natural object' here reaches fulfilment.

Seeing Symbols

One of Goethe's most famous statements on the symbol arises from a perceived disagreement with Schiller:

> On a slight disagreement between us ... I made the following reflections: There is a great difference whether a poet is looking for the particular that goes with the universal, or sees the universal in the particular. The first gives rise to allegory where the particular only counts as an example, an illustration of the universal; but the latter in fact constitutes the nature of poetry, expressing something particular without any thought of the universal, and without indicating it. Now whoever has this living grasp of the particular is at the same time in possession of the universal, without realising it, or else only realising it later on. (*M* §261)

Goethe polemicizes against signification and for perception.[34] While the allegorical poet 'looks for the particular that goes with the universal' (that is, has to exercise judgement concerning the appropriateness of a particular image to depict a general concept), the true, symbolic poet '*sees* the universal in the particular'. While the former requires intellectual effort in order to link particular to universal, for the latter the link is a matter of self-evident perception. Sørensen writes, 'According to Goethe, the "true" poet does not *search*, but he *sees*, i.e. his will and consciousness play in the moment of perception no active role; he comports himself intuitively' (1979, 633). The subject remains passive and receptive when confronted with a symbol.

The immediate self-evidence of all meaning to perception is one of the most persistent themes in Goethe's scientific work. Maxim §575 reads:

> Everything factual is already theory: to understand this would be the greatest possible achievement. The blueness of the sky reveals the basic laws of chromatics. Don't go looking for anything beyond the phenomena: they are themselves what they teach, the doctrine.

Perception already carries universal meaning within itself—no work is necessary on behalf of the subject to provide 'the doctrine'; it is ready-made. Theory exists self-evidently in the perception of fact. It is for this reason Goethe wrote, 'Thinking is more interesting than knowing; but more interesting than both is seeing' (*M* §1150). Goethe repeats again and again, perception is the major component in scientific method, while hypothesis-forming and reasoning are secondary. He conflates the conceptual and the perceptual to the extent that the idea is the perception and the perception the idea (*M* §39).

This is Goethe's interpretation of heautonomy. The universal is embedded objectively in the particular, independent of the subject, and the subject discovers it already pre-formed through perception. It is a presupposition of Goethean symbolism that 'meaning [already] necessarily inheres in all of the world's apparently accidental and meaningless phenomena' (Hayes 1969, 277). Or to put it another way, 'Reality must already have its own meaning... Reality must have meaning, so that art need have none' (Titzmann 1979, 658). The symbol is a 'ready-made'.

Goethe's Attack on Language

One of the most notable features of the Goethean symbol is that it is never applied to literature; indeed, Goethe never speaks (positively) of symbolic language at all. Goethe's references to the symbol are almost exclusively made in the context of the figurative arts—and especially sculpture. This

---

[34] See further Cassirer 1963, 81; Stephenson 1995, 63–73.

point has been forcefully made by Krueger (1990, 53): in her extensive survey of Goethe's allusions to symbol and allegory, Krueger discovers only one exceptional 'indication...that literary allegory might be suspect' (55).[35] As critics have pointed out (de Man 1983, 189–90; Krueger 1990, 59–60), much of Goethe's own literary output (especially the second part of *Faust*) uses allegory extensively, and so ignores his own apparent depreciation of the trope.

'The artistic symbol is plastic', states Benjamin (1998, 164), and it is definitely true that the development of the symbol in the *Goethezeit* was bound up with the pre-eminence of sculpture in Classicist aesthetics. Niklewski (1979, 95) claims that this preference for sculpture is due to its non-signifying *modus operandi*: sculptures do not (according to the tenets of Weimar Classicism) represent an external meaning; rather, their meaning inheres immanently. Sculpture was thus seen as paradigmatic of tautegorical representation. To become symbolic, art should imitate sculpture, put its meaning on display, and make it available for immediate perception. On this view, however, literature (dependent on signs for the production of meaning) becomes inferior (Niklewski 1979, 99).[36] It is for these kinds of reason that Goethe ends up criticizing the reading process itself as allegorical:

> There also exist works of art that scintillate through intellect, wit, gallantry, among which we also include all allegory: of these one can expect the least good, because they too destroy the interest in representation itself and drive the spirit back into itself, so to speak, and remove from its eyes what is actually represented. The allegorical distinguishes itself from the symbolic in that the former signifies directly, the latter indirectly. (*WA* I/47, 94–5; 1983, 397)

Interpretation and so reading are allegorical; they appeal to the intellect, whereas the symbolic sculpture appeals to the senses.

This depreciation of reading is confirmed when one takes into account Goethe's more general scepticism concerning language's capabilities—rarely has there been a poet who took such a dim view of poetic material! In the *Urfaust*, for example, language gets in the way of feeling; it obscures and veils emotional truth, leading to rationalistic falsehoods.[37] Instead of interpretation and signification, Goethe once more recommends the immediate self-presence of what is incommensurable with discourse. Similar attitudes surface throughout Goethe's corpus. His 1805 essay, *Symbolik*, begins with the statement that, 'Neither things nor ourselves find full expression in our words', and ends with the statement that the highest type of symbol 'based on intuitive perceptions alone, cannot occur in language' (*WA* II/11, 167–9; 1988, 26–7).[38] Goethe, it must be concluded, remained staunchly anti-discursive throughout his life.

---

[35] See also Todorov 1982, 204.   [36] See further Todorov 1982, 204.
[37] See *WA* I/39, 292, ll. 1143–50; 1987, ll. 3451–7.   [38] See further *M* §610, §720.

It is no surprise, therefore, that critics have noted Goethe's unease with the idea of symbolic language. Nygaard writes for example,

> [Goethe worries that words] tend to be more and more fully elaborated until they displace what they were meant to represent as the real centre of attention . . . All this evolves naturally from a consideration of the function of the sign in [his work], but is difficult to reconcile with some of the more fulsome platitudes commonly uttered about the Goethean symbol. (1988, 64)

While Nygaard is here right to draw attention to Goethe's problems with the word, she goes awry in claiming this critique of language is in tension with his theory of the symbol. The Goethean attack on language is a part of the 'romantic' interpretation of the symbol to which he subscribes. Dismissal of language is the very basis of Goethe's own affirmation of the symbol. Rather than being a critique of the symbol, Goethe criticizes language *in the name of the symbol*. Symbolism is established at the expense of symbolic language.

What is perhaps most striking about Goethe's position is how much it actually resembles de Man's criticisms of the symbol. Goethe, too, realizes that 'the romantic symbol' is inassimilable to the essence of language. Where they differ of course is that de Man holds on to language rather than the symbol, while Goethe values the symbol over language. However, they both agree that language and 'the romantic symbol' are polar opposites and the abyss separating them can in no way be bridged.

The story of the advent of 'the romantic symbol' is the story of the separation of symbols from discourse. When symbols are interpreted through an empiricist version of heautonomy, they become irreconcilable with language. Hence, theorists of 'the romantic symbol' opt for the symbol over language. Kant, for example, banishes language from philosophy, yet does not banish the symbol—instead, it is given a crucial place in the critical project. And this is because symbols are no longer seen as signs, but rather are opposed to signs—as intuitive images. Goethe brings this process to its culmination: language and signification are to be rejected in all their forms; only the self-evident object waiting to be perceived is a symbol. All that manifests a trace of semiosis is non-symbolic. Symbolic language is rejected in the name of 'the romantic symbol'. De Man and Titzmann are therefore right to contend that 'romantic' symbolic language is a contradiction in terms; however, where they go wrong is, first, in not seeing the extent to which theorists of 'the romantic symbol' agree with them and, second, in not realizing that there are *other* symbols which are more compatible with language.

Part II
System

.

3

The Symbol and the *Identitätssystem*

Schelling treated the theory of the symbol only in his *Philosophie der Kunst*... But, in fact, everything is a symbol... Philosophy is the symbolic science *par excellence*.

(Tilliette 1970, 1:404)

The symbol is the paradigm for the *Identitätssystem*.

(Niklewski 1979, 86)

As the above quotations suggest, Schellingian symbolic language is intimately bound up with Schelling's philosophical project as a whole. Not only is it a rigorous working-out of his metaphysical and epistemological principles in the linguistic domain, it is also a motif which expresses most intensely many of the patterns of his thought. Part II is therefore devoted to a sustained reading of Schelling's *Identitätssystem*. I argue that to understand what is going on in Schelling's construction of symbolic language, one must embed it in his more general thought of the period.

THE *IDENTITÄTSSYSTEM*

To begin, it is necessary to provide a preliminary sketch of the *Identitätssystem* and its place in Schelling's oeuvre.[1] One of the secondary aims of this book is to give an account of this *Identitätssystem*, since there is so little engagement with this period of Schelling's work even among Schelling scholars.[2] Beiser depicts traditional attitudes towards Schelling as follows:

[1] The name '*Identitätssystem*' was only used once by Schelling in the Preface to the 1801 *Darstellung* (SW 4:113; 2001a, 348). He later came to regret that this particular name stuck (SW 10:107; 1994d, 120). (For the abbreviations used in my citation of Schelling's writings, see the Note to the Reader at the beginning of the book.)

[2] In English, only Vater's essays (1976, 1984, 2000), the last 100 pages of Beiser 2002, and Toscano's piece on construction (2004) are worth reading on the *Identitätssystem* in particular. The situation is hardly any better in Germany: one has to return to Zeltner's work (for example, 1975) for the last high-profile consideration of the *Identitätssystem* as such. Only in France (the

For all too long [Schelling] has been treated as a predecessor to others, 'an intermediate figure' between Kant and Hegel...[Historians] value Schelling essentially as a stepping-stone for later developments. Schelling is rarely taken as a figure in his own right, deserving close examination for his own sake. (2002, 465)

Yet, if this is true of Schelling's work as a whole, then the *Identitätssystem* in particular is merely a transitional phase in a transitional philosopher's oeuvre. In what follows, I argue, on the contrary, that the *Identitätssystem* should not be valued merely because of what came before or what came after it, but on its own terms.

The *Identitätssystem* begins at 'the moment', Schelling describes retrospectively, 'when the light burst upon me in philosophy, in 1801' (*SB* 3:222). It is this moment—the moment marked, as Schelling continues, by the publication of his *Darstellung meines Systems* in May 1801—which is the decisive one of his philosophical career. The 'light' of 1801 marks the beginning of the *Identitätssystem*, the philosophical project which he pursued for five years from 1801 to 1805. Although it would be too much to claim that Schelling's position during this period remains identical, it is clear that he considered his work of this period as a unified whole and I shall treat it as such in this book.[3]

Schelling was 26 years old in May 1801 and had already been publishing philosophy for seven years. This early work prior to 1801 should be seen as a creative apprenticeship to Fichte. It begins in 1794 with his first publication, *Über die Möglichkeit einer Form der Philosophie überhaupt*, and culminates in his famous *System des transzendentalen Idealismus* of 1800. Despite the fact that today the *System des transzendentalen Idealismus* is still taken as most representative of Schellingian philosophy, Schelling himself always maintained that it was written 'under the exterior [*Hülle*] of Fichtean thinking' (*SW* 10:96; 1994d, 111). It was his next major work—the 1801 *Darstellung meines Systems*—that Schelling considered the inaugural piece of his philosophical maturity. Beiser writes:

With the *Darstellung meines Systems* Schelling finally comes into his own. True to its title, this work represents *his* philosophy in contrast to Fichte's... [He] made it plain that he was no longer toeing a master's line. If the possessive adjective in the title was not a formal act of repudiation, it was still a declaration of independence. (2002, 551)

spiritual home of Schelling scholarship since 1970) is there a plethora of sustained engagements with the *Identitätssystem*.

[3] The periodization of Schelling's philosophy is a particularly contentious issue. For a very different assessment to mine, see Grant 2006, 4. As the above suggests, the idea of an '*Identitätssystem*' is premised on the coherence of Schelling's philosophical project between 1801 and 1805. There have been various attempts in the literature to separate out different sub-periods or strains within the *Identitätssystem* (Tilliette 1970, 1:371, Fischbach 1999, 248); however, none radically put into question the overriding similarities of the works from this period: they all 'point in one direction', in Courtine's words (1990, 114).

The end of the *Identitätssystem* is less clear-cut. The years 1805 to 1808 mark Schelling's slow retreat into philosophical silence. When he did emerge from that silence in 1809 with the publication of the *Freiheitsschrift*, it was with a very different philosophical voice and very different concerns. The *Freiheitsschrift* marks the beginning of a different philosophical trajectory (Schelling's 'middle period'). Where exactly to draw the line marking the end of the *Identitätssystem* is therefore debatable; in this book, I have assumed that, since after 1805 Schelling did not reaffirm the metaphysical principles on which the *Identitätssystem* is based, then (even if he did not conversely explicitly reject them) this serves as a convenient moment to mark the end of the *Identitätssystem*.[4]

The major works of the *Identitätssystem* can be listed as follows:

1801 *Darstellung meines Systems der Philosophie*
1802 *Bruno*
      Fernere Darstellungen aus dem System der Philosophie
      Über das Verhältnis der Naturphilosophie zur Philosophie überhaupt
      Ideen zu einer Philosophie der Natur (second edition)
1803 *Vorlesungen über die Methode des akademischen Studiums*[5]
      Über die Construktion in der Philosophie
1804 *System* (published posthumously)
      Philosophie und Religion
1805 *Aphorismen zur Einleitung in die Naturphilosophie*

All these works will figure prominently in what follows.[6]

However, at the centre of my argument stand Schelling's lectures on the *Philosophie der Kunst*, for in §73 of this work Schelling gives his construction of symbolic language.[7] Schelling gave these lectures first at the University of Jena in the winter semester 1802/3 and subsequently at the University of Würzburg in the winter semester 1804/5. They were only published posthumously by Schelling's son from the surviving lecture notes in 1859. It will be important to bear in mind in what follows that Schelling did not prepare them for publication, and, in fact, later in life requested that the manuscript be intentionally lost.[8] Nevertheless, portions of the Jena lecture course were published by Schelling at the time of

---

[4] During 1805, on the other hand, Schelling is at pains to 'affirm afresh' the metaphysics of the 1801 *Darstellung* (SW 7:114; 1984b, 246).

[5] In what follows, I refer to this work as *Über die Methode*.

[6] Another work to which I refer is I. P. V. Troxler's notes (1988) on a lecture course on metaphysics Schelling gave in Jena in late 1801. For the English titles of the works cited above, see the translations listed in the Bibliography.

[7] My emphasis on the importance of the *Philosophie der Kunst* brings my position close to that of Shaw, who also stresses that 'the philosophy of art maintains a privileged place in Schelling's thought' throughout the *Identitätssystem* (2010, 90–1).

[8] See Tilliette 1999, 152. The SW version of the *Philosophie der Kunst* is certainly based on the Würzburg set of lectures (SW 5:xvi); the difference between the Würzburg *Philosophie der Kunst*

the lectures: the last lecture of his 1803 *Über die Methode* is a reproduction of the introduction to the *Philosophie der Kunst* and a short essay which appeared in the *Kritische Journal*, *Über Dante in philosophischer Beziehung*, replicates sections on Dante from the lecture notes.

Such then is the systematic context to Schelling's construction of symbolic language; in the rest of the chapter, I wish to draw attention to the intimate connection that holds between this theory of symbolic language and the *Identitätssystem*.

SPECULATIVE TRANSFORMATION

The idea which informs this book that the Schellingian symbol can only be understood in relation to Schelling's philosophy as a whole may not seem controversial; however, in the context of scholarship on the symbol, it is. Traditionally, it has been assumed that the baroque intricacies of Schelling's philosophy are irrelevant to an understanding of the meaning and role of his theory of the symbol.[9] And this, it is claimed, is because he plagiarized the symbol from his predecessors. Schelling copies Kant, Goethe, and Schlegel, and so his own thought is irrelevant; what matters are the sources on which he drew.

In Chapter 1, I discussed these sources (Kant, Goethe, A. W. Schlegel), and argued that Schelling was considerably influenced by them. Indeed, Schelling's lectures on the *Philosophie der Kunst* as a whole are not, on the face of it, his most original contribution to philosophy. In Fackenheim's words, 'None of Schelling's works is so dependent on the ideas and research of others as his *Philosophie der Kunst*' (1954, 310).[10] We should remember, for example, as I related in Chapter 1, that Schelling wrote the *Philosophie der Kunst* with a copy of A. W. Schlegel's Berlin lectures in front of him, and he readily admits that access to this manuscript 'spare[s] me much inquiry' (*SB* 2:436). There has seldom been such a clear-cut admission of plagiarism.

On the basis of this evidence, the overriding critical 'temptation' (Fackenheim 1954, 310) has been to write off Schelling's symbol as slavishly reproducing the work of his more innovative predecessors. And from this follows the conclusion that Schelling's own thought can be safely ignored by historians of the symbol. Sørensen, for example, claims, 'It is scarcely worthwhile noting the

and the Jena *Philosophie der Kunst* can easily be perceived from comparing this version to the notes made by Henry Crabb Robinson (1976) in Jena.

[9] Sørensen (1963), Titzmann (1979), Todorov (1982), and Halmi (2007) all make claims about the Schellingian symbol without analysis of the *Identitätssystem*.

[10] Influences on the *Philosophie der Kunst* include Moritz, Winckelmann, Vitruvius, Diderot, Rousseau, A. W. Schlegel, Goethe, Schiller, Jean Paul, Fiorello, Sulzer, Tieck, Wackenroder, Hemsterhuis, and Geneli. See Tilliette 1970, 1:439, 1:455, 1999, 153.

many idiosyncrasies of this theory as laid out in the *Philosophie der Kunst* for two reasons: first, as an aesthetician Schelling was extremely dependent on his predecessors and second, [his presentation] loses much in clarity [from those of his predecessors]' (1963, 260–1).[11] The Schellingian symbol is merely a replica: it may bring together disparate elements from Kant, Goethe, and the Schlegel brothers, but its only merit is to thereby synthesize pre-existing material. There is nothing, it is claimed, truly innovative about Schelling's theory of the symbol.

Yet, the evidence laid out above in no way proves (as critics have assumed) that Schelling thereby appropriates his sources unthinkingly. To claim this would be to misunderstand the nature of the scientific enterprise as Schelling conceived it. He is not concerned with plagiarizing these pre-existent theories of art, but with *performing a speculative operation* on them—that is, with transforming them. Sørensen, for example, fails to recognize the properly philosophical work to which other theorists' ideas are subjected in Schelling's writings.

The letters Schelling penned to A. W. Schlegel (when requesting a copy of his lecture notes) not only make this perfectly clear, they can be read as a sort of manifesto for such creative assimilation:

> In the future, I will fully avoid establishing a *theory* of art…which must neces-sarily be empirical. Just as there are real or empirical things, there is real and empirical art, and to this *theory* refers. However, just as there are intellectual things, things *in themselves*, so too is there *art in itself*, of which empirical [art] is only the appearance. It is by means of this that there is a connection to philosophy of/on art [*Philosophie auf Kunst*]. You can easily discern how—in this way—my philosophy of art is able to be more a universal philosophy than a theory of art. In the former one can in no way speak of empirical art, but only the root of art, as it is in the absolute. (*SB* 2:435–6)

Schelling contends that, while his philosophy of art may have the same subject matter (art) as previous aesthetic theories, it differs from them fundamentally in how it considers it. He is concerned with the essence (not appearance) of art, and because of this his work can never be treated as one more 'theory of art'. Schelling's phrase '*Philosophie auf Kunst*' is particularly revealing: he is not concerned with discoursing about art or providing rules for artistic practice, but with performing a philosophical operation *on* art. Art and aesthetics form the material on which Schelling's speculation works.

It is for this reason that when Schelling goes on to draw attention to 'my power of assimilation' (2:437), this is no admission of plagiarism, but a statement of his creative assimilation of Schlegel's ideas. Such ideas will be transformed from a mere empirical theory into genuinely philosophical

---

[11] See also 249.

speculation. The context of Schelling's comment that Schlegel's lectures will 'spare me much inquiry' makes this transformation particularly clear:

> Your manuscript would be of excellent service to me, so as to keep me orientated and to bring me back to the intellectual from the empirical in art (which, according to your outline, you have sufficiently dealt with)—and so spare me much inquiry which would perhaps not have led me to the goal and would certainly have hindered the formation of the speculative. (2:436)

Schelling's focus is on developing the proper speculative account of art. For this task he needs material on which the 'speculative attitude' can labour, and A. W. Schlegel's Berlin lectures (as well as, by extension, all the other aesthetic theories on which the *Philosophie der Kunst* is dependent) are a convenient, ready-to-hand source for this work.[12]

What is more, this is precisely the viewpoint Schelling takes up within the *Philosophie der Kunst* itself. Schelling eschews history of art or a technical theory of art in favour of 'the completely speculative science...one not directed toward the cultivation of the empirical intuition of art, but rather of its intellectual intuition' (*SW* 5:344–5; 1989, 3). Philosophy of art 'is the presentation of the absolute world in the form of art' (350; 7). *Philosophy* of art is inherently philosophical: it works on aesthetics until the latter manifests the genuine subject matter of philosophy—the absolute.[13] Schelling continues:

> Only to the extent that the science of nature or of art presents the absolute within it is this science genuine philosophy, *philosophy* of nature, *philosophy* of art ... [Otherwise] the science under question cannot be called philosophy, but rather only a *theory* of a particular subject, such as a theory of nature or a theory of art. Such a theory could, of course, *borrow* its principles from philosophy, as for example the theory of nature does from the philosophy of nature. For just this reason, however – because it only *borrows* them – it is not philosophy. In the philosophy of art I accordingly intend to construe first of all not art *as* art, as this **particular**, but rather *the universe in the form of art*, and the philosophy of art is *the science of the All in the form or potency of art*. Not until we have taken this step do we elevate ourselves regarding this science to the level of an absolute science of art. (368–9; 16)

Philosophy of art raises its subject matter into the absolute. It is this, Schelling maintains, that distinguishes his discussion of art from all previous aesthetics.

We must not therefore write off the Schellingian symbol as derivative. While Schelling did draw on Goethe, A. W. Schlegel, and Kant, he transformed (or, at the very least, he claims to transform) their work in the very process of appropriating it. The Schellingian symbol is a symbol constructed from the viewpoint of speculative metaphysics rather than empirical theory.

---

[12] See further Fackenheim 1954, 310–11; Mayer 1999, 16–17.

[13] Hegel will express very similar sentiments; for a brief comparison of Hegel and Schelling's practices of speculative transformation, see Chapter 11.

There are two issues at stake here: one concerning the speculative grounding of the Schellingian symbol, another concerning the specific form this grounding takes. Indeed, this is implicit in the phrase 'speculative transformation' which I am using to designate the operation Schelling performs on the symbol: it is not just that what is empirical becomes 'speculatively grounded'; in the process it is also materially altered. First, Schelling claims his is the first properly speculative grounded theory of the symbol. This is not to say—as Schelling points out—that previous theories did not 'borrow' their principles from philosophy. In fact, we have seen how 'the romantic symbol' presupposes certain metaphysical and epistemological models (like analogy). Schelling's point is, rather, they merely 'borrow' such models from philosophy—where 'borrow' has a twofold significance: first, it implies that previous theories of the symbol hid their presuppositions to give themselves the air of being purely empirical (hence, 'the romantic symbol' does rely on metaphysical and epistemological presuppositions, but for the most part attempts to hide them behind a veil of empiricism); second, 'borrow' implies that previous theories of the symbol rely on such principles in a non-rigorous manner. They are not philosophically constructed from these principles by a direct, cogent process, but are erected unconsciously and (consequently) shakily on their unacknowledged metaphysical ground. Since the process of construction is unconscious, it is not rigorous.

Thus, Schelling claims to have produced the first theory of the symbol whose foundations are not merely 'borrowed' but are premised rigorously. However, more than that (and this is the second point), Schelling also claims that his theory of the symbol is materially different from previous theories, because it is premised on different (and, in Schelling's view, better) philosophical foundations. Schelling's *Identitätssystem* in general diverges considerably from other philosophies of its time, and—because it is constructed from the *Identitätssystem* in a rigorous manner—his theory of the symbol also departs considerably from previous theories of the symbol.

The conclusion to be drawn is that Schelling's theory of symbolic language depends heavily on his general philosophical assumptions. The symbol is bound up in his metaphysical and epistemological innovations of that period and cannot be dissociated from them. The critical prejudice is therefore false: acquaintance with Schelling's philosophy is a necessary prerequisite for understanding his construction of symbolic language. It is for this reason Part II is devoted to this end.

SCHELLING'S PECULIARITY

However, this is to anticipate. So far we have merely considered Schelling's programmatic statements which imply the peculiarity of his theory of the symbol; we have yet to record any evidence that this is in fact the case. Thus, it is worth pausing to see if there is any preliminary evidence for taking Schelling's claims seriously. The purpose of this task is twofold. First, exhibiting (even if only provisionally) the peculiarity of the Schellingian symbol shows that Schelling did not plagiarize his predecessors, and so the context of his construction of symbolic language (the *Identitätssystem*) is worth taking seriously. Second, such a procedure also 'cashes out' much of what I claimed in Part I of the book: Schelling's symbol is unlike any other; he interprets the three first-order properties (heautonomy, syntheticism, tautegory) in a unique manner. Thus, the following example will hopefully hint at the accuracy of my argument in Part I.[14]

In Chapter 5, I will argue that at the centre of the *Identitätssystem* stands the doctrine of quantitative differentiation—that is, the metaphysical rejection of all forms of qualitative negation in favour of a conception of differentiation through differing degrees of intensity. Schelling repeats this doctrine within his construction of the symbol; thus, he rejects the qualitative distinction erected by Goethe between symbol and allegory as well as the qualitative distinction established by Kant between symbol and schema. In their place Schelling proposes relations of quantitative intensity between symbol, allegory and schema.[15]

Schelling's description of Dante's *Divine Comedy* as a 'partial mythology' (*SW* 5:156; 1988b, 242) makes this position clear. Dante occupies an intermediary position between symbol and allegory—a position that would be impossible if the two were dichotomously opposed. Schelling writes,

> To present the ideas of philosophy and theology in symbols was impossible [for Dante] because there was no symbolic mythology in existence. No more could he make his poem completely allegorical, because it would then no longer be historical. Therefore it had to be a completely unique mixture of the allegorical and the historical. (155; 241)

That is, 'a completely unique mixture' of the allegorical and the symbolical, as Schelling makes clear in the following paragraph:

> Dante's poem is not allegorical in the sense that the figures simply stand for something else, without being independent of this meaning and thus something in themselves. On the other hand, none of them is independent of the meaning in such a way that it becomes one with the idea itself, and more than allegorical of it. There is thus in Dante's poem a quite unique middle point between allegory and symbolic-objective forms. (156; 242)

The *Divine Comedy* stands between the two modes of presentation; in Sørensen's words, it 'mediates between the extreme possibilities of pure allegory and pure symbol' (1963, 257).

---

[14] Of course, this is not to say that what follows is the only difference between the Schellingian and 'romantic' theory of the symbol, nor even the most significant one. However, it is a useful introduction to what makes the Schellingian symbol so 'peculiar'.

[15] Nevertheless, the only commentators to have recognized the significance of quantitative difference for Schelling's theory of the symbol are Wanning (1988, 87–8) and Szondi (1974, 2:236).

Why is this significant? In short, because such a 'middle point' is inconceivable for any other theorist of the symbol. Goethe is the relevant point of contrast, since he insisted on the symbol/allegory dichotomy most forcefully. For Goethe, symbol and allegory are strictly opposed: 'The allegorical distinguishes itself from the symbolic in that the former signifies directly, the latter indirectly' (*WA* I/47, 95; 1983, 397). Symbol and allegory form a binary between which no mediation is possible: a middle term between direct and indirect signification is not available (the same is, of course, true for Kant in the *Kritik der Urteilskraft* in relation to schematism and symbolism). There is only symbol or allegory. In consequence, Schelling's reading of Dante makes no sense from a Goethean standpoint. Yet, it does make sense from the standpoint of Schelling's own *Identitätssystem*. That is, only by considering the 'metaphysical' differences between Schelling and Goethe's philosophies can this anomaly be explained. In short, the relation between allegory and symbol for Schelling is quantitative rather than qualitative. Allegory is not the flip-side of the symbol; it is instead a lower intensity of symbolism. Schelling's universe is not one of binaries (universal or particular, direct or indirect), and on this basis Schelling's seemingly incongruent claim about Dante makes perfect sense.

Schelling therefore establishes a three-term series of schema/allegory/symbol in which the terms are not qualitatively, but quantitatively distinguished. This difference illuminates Schelling's substantive departures from the Kantian-Goethean orthodoxies. Schelling writes:

> That *Darstellung* in which the universal means the particular or in which the particular is intuited through the universal is *schematism*. That *Darstellung*, however, in which the particular means the universal or in which the universal is intuited through the particular is *allegory*. The synthesis of these two, where neither the universal means the particular nor the particular the universal, but rather where both are absolutely one, is the *symbolic*. (*SW* 5:407; 1989, 46)

Schelling's three-term series grafts Goethe's symbol/allegory dichotomy onto Kant's symbol/schematism dichotomy. This is often used as evidence of the Schellingian symbol's derivative status. Schelling's only claim to originality is to have brought together Kant and Goethe's theories of the symbol. Yet, in deploying Goethean allegory and Kantian schematism in this passage, Schelling is not endorsing or synthesizing them, but implicitly criticizing them. The Goethean symbol is criticized for being too schematic and the Kantian symbol for being too allegorical. Neither of them, Schelling implies, attains the true indifference point between universal and particular.

In Chapter 1, I quoted Sørensen's telling assessment of the universal/particular relation in Goethe's theory of the symbol: 'The universal outweighs the particular' (1963, 111). This is precisely Schelling's criticism of Goethe. By utilizing Kant's conception of schematism, he suggests that the opposition Goethe establishes between symbol and allegory is really only the opp-osition between schematism and allegory. For Goethe, either the particular is prior (in which case the exhibition is allegorical) or the universal is prior, and while Goethe designates this latter case 'symbolism', Schelling argues that it cannot in fact be symbolic, because it does not manifest the requisite identity of meaning and being, of universal and particular required by the properties of tautegory and syntheticism. Therefore, Goethe's symbol is merely schematic. Thus, when Schelling writes, 'The dominating element in the schema is the universal, although the universal in it is intuited as a particular' (*SW* 5:407; 1989, 46), he could easily be describing the Goethean symbol under the guise of schematism. The Goethean symbol does not exhibit the identity of universal and particular; it is therefore not symbolic enough. Goethe forecloses on the possibility of a third point of indifference and Schelling criticizes him for it.

In a similar vein, Schelling uses Goethe's category of allegory to criticize the Kantian symbol. In Kant's theory of the symbol, a particular *Darstellung* is forced to represent an idea of reason by means of a process of analogy. In the *Philosophie der Kunst*, Schelling describes this kind of process as follows, 'In allegory the particular merely *means* or *signifies* the universal' (409; 47). There is again no identity between meaning and being, universal and particular: Kant's symbol is in no way tautegorical. Meaning and being remain separated, and in conse-quence the former is only won from the latter by means of an artificial process of analogous reasoning. Symbolism in Kant is constituted by the very process by which Goethe defines allegory—'looking for the particular that goes with the universal' (*M* §261). The Kantian symbol is in fact allegorical.

Schelling uses Kant and Goethe to attack each other: the Goethean symbol is shown up by Kant as merely schematic, while the Kantian symbol is shown up by Goethe as merely allegorical. In this manner, Schelling criticizes (rather than plagiarizes) the two major theories of the symbol on which he was drawing. His theory of the symbol does not copy these previous theories, but it is instead constituted through a critique of them. Schelling—as we saw earlier in the chapter—does not appropriate his sources unthinkingly; he transforms them. The Schellingian symbol cannot therefore be aligned with 'the romantic symbol'; it is in fact premised on a critique of it. Such is the preliminary evidence for its peculiarity.

READING AND MISREADING
THE *IDENTITÄTSSYSTEM*

The next three chapters embark on a reading of Schelling's *Identitätssystem*, a reading that will bear fruit in Chapter 7 when I show how it necessitates the 'peculiarity' of the Schellingian symbol. As a preliminary to this, in what follows I provide three maxims which orientate my reading of the *Identitätssystem*.

First, the *Identitätssystem* is not a precursor to the Hegelian system. Often, Schelling's *Identitätssystem* is read as a deficient version of the dialectical absolute idealism which Hegel later perfected, an abortive first sketch of Hegelianism. One strain of this 'pro-Hegelian prejudice' (Tilliette 1987, 112) portrays Schelling as a 'poetic' or 'unconscious' philosopher whose initial explorations were later systematized by the mature Hegel.[16] Even Schelling scholars have sometimes understood their relation in these terms. Vater is a prime example: 'The *Phenomenology*,' he states, 'represents an advance beyond Schelling's philosophy of identity, or at least a liberation for Hegel from the obvious drawbacks of Schelling's concepts' (1984, 91). He goes on to conceive the *Identitätssystem* as a 'blurred image' of Hegelianism (85).[17] There are of course undeniable connections between Schelling and Hegel's philosophies; however, the idea that Schellingianism is a 'blurred' form of Hegelianism is one I combat in this book. In short, Schelling's *Identitätssystem* is irreducible to and incomparable with Hegel's system; it pursues very different ends and employs very different means to achieve its ends. The relation between Schelling and Hegel's system of philosophy is a *differend*, not an *Aufhebung*.[18]

Second, the *Identitätssystem* does not merely repeat earlier German Idealist insights in an extreme form. In order to maintain a narrative of philosophical development, critics have tended to see Fichte as radicalizing his Kantian heritage and Schelling, in turn, radicalizing what he inherits from Fichte. Thus, the *Identitätssystem* is merely Kantianism drawn to its most extreme conclusions. There is of course some continuity between Schelling's early more Fichtean, works and his *Identitätssystem*; in fact, Schelling's Preface to his 1801 *Darstellung* makes precisely this point:

> No one should think that I have altered my system of philosophy. For the system that appears here for the first time in its fully characteristic shape is the same one that I always had in view in the different earlier presentations, which I constantly used as my personal guiding star in both transcendental and natural philosophy. (*SW* 4:107–8; 2001a, 344)

Yet, the very same Preface also makes the opposite point. Schelling criticizes his earlier work and claims to only now have attained the true system:

---

[16] See Harris 1995, 191–8; Lukács 1975, 249, 1980, 134–5. Hegel is of course partly responsible for this view (1896, 3:512–44).

[17] For an antidote, see Uslar 1968, 503; Esposito 1977, 9.

[18] See Toscano 2004, 126. In consequence, I will not be concerned with defending Schelling's position against Hegel's criticisms in the *Phänomenologie*.

> I regard each of them [that is, the earlier presentations which were limited to either transcendental philosophy or *Naturphilosophie*] as nothing more than a one-sided presentation of that system...With the present exposition I situate myself at the indifference point between them. (108; 344)

It is only with the 1801 *Darstellung* that Schelling is at last able to present the fundamental system and its 'first principles... *for the first time*' (113; 348; my emphasis).

Vater is therefore right to point out that 'the Preface has a double, if not contradictory, burden: to convince the reader that Identity Philosophy is not new...and that it is new'.[19] In this book, I emphasize the latter point. My description of Schelling's philosophy will begin with the 1801 *Darstellung* and make no sustained reference to what preceded it or even how the post-1801 views emerged out of Schelling's earlier writings. There are a number of reasons for this emphasis: first, the break that the *Identitätssystem* constituted in relation to Schelling's earlier work has not been sufficiently emphasized in the critical literature; second, outside of the Preface to the 1801 *Darstellung*, Schelling is at pains to emphasize the rupture in his thinking in 1801; third, while the earlier works may be helpful in understanding Schelling's *Identitätssystem*, they are *not necessary* for such comprehension (i.e. almost all the works written between 1801 and 1805 attempt to be self-sufficient presentations of the entirety of the Schellingian philosophy); finally (and more pragmatically), space does not permit me from being diverted into discussions surrounding the origins and development of Schelling's *Identitätssystem*—the purpose of this book, to repeat, is a full grasp of §73 of the *Philosophie der Kunst*, not of the *Identitätssystem* as a whole.[20]

The third and final maxim which will orient my reading runs as follows: the *Identitätssystem* is not significant merely in relation to Schelling's later philosophy. On this reading, the *Identitätssystem* is some sort of botched attempt at system-building which—in the very process of failing—provides the negative stimulus for Schelling's much more interesting (or so it is claimed) later work. Schelling's metaphysics of the period is a *reductio ad absurdum* of speculative philosophy, giving rise to the 'positive philosophy' of the 1820s and beyond.[21] This interpretation is a product of the renaissance of Schelling's

[19] Michael G. Vater, 'Translator's Introduction' to Schelling 2001a, 339.

[20] One concrete consequence of this restriction is that the *System des transzendentalen Idealismus* is not given as much attention as is customary. Indeed, Marquet's warning should be borne in mind, 'The *System des transzendentalen Idealismus* is paradoxically the work most known by Schelling, the only one which has succeeded in being installed amidst the classics of philosophy, and yet far from marking a summit or even a resting point in the development of a still juvenile thought, it represents, on the contrary, a moment of transition which only in the following years will find its denouement' (1973, 174).

[21] Schelling himself was the first person to read his *Identitätssystem* in this light (*SW* 10:123–5; 1994d, 133).

later philosophy: whereas traditionally the *Identitätssystem* was seen as the apogee of Schelling's development and the later philosophy an afterthought, current opinion is exactly the reverse. This has made reading the *Identitätssystem* in light of the later philosophy extremely popular, leading critics to concentrate exclusively on the apparent failures and aporia of the *Identitätssystem*. White, for example, states categorically,

> That Schelling never published the system of identity in its entirety suggests that the system is fatally flawed; examination of the system confirms the truth of what the publication record suggests... Schelling's strict science ultimately fails in that there are fundamental problems that it can neither avoid nor solve, the major goal of the following analysis is to reveal those problems, for they determine the further course of Schelling's development. (White 1983, 74)

Bowie is similarly explicit about his interest solely in 'the still viable aspects of the identity philosophy' in which are found 'the beginnings of arguments that re-emerge in the later critiques of Hegel and form the basis of his significance for subsequent philosophy' (1993, 56–7). Symptomatic of this type of reading is the topic which dominates most accounts of the *Identitätssystem*: the justification of finite existence. It is compulsory, it seems, for examinations of the *Identitätssystem* to devote considerable energies to Schelling's (supposed) repeated, failed attempts to account for the origins of finitude.[22]

Schelling's *Identitätssystem* need not, however, be read for the benefit of his later philosophy; it need not be seen as a failure. If Schelling's *Identitätssystem* is understood on its own terms, a very different picture emerges. Indeed, as we shall see, the whole problem of the finite that so obsesses contemporary critics is a pseudo-problem which dissipates under the harsh light of Schellingian monism. One should follow Challiol-Gillet's advice here (even if she fails to herself) and 'not make the system of identity into a caricature which refuses all finitude' (1996, 26).

All three hermeneutical maxims are therefore concerned with the integrity, distinctness, and even singularity of Schelling's thinking at this period. And it is only through such a reading strategy that what is distinctive about Schellingian symbolic language will gradually be revealed.

---

[22] See Beierwaltes 1983, 95; White 1983, 93–101; Vater 1984, 40; Bowie 1993, 87–90; Challiol-Gillet 1996, 33–7; Brito 2000, 51–8; Shaw 2010, 90–1. The undue prominence of *Philosophie und Religion* in these accounts is also symptomatic.

4

Schelling's Metaphysics

'Philosophy is entirely within the domain of the absolute and never goes outside it' (*SW* 5:278; 1966, 73). The *Identitätssystem* is a philosophy of the absolute, and in consequence is characterized by nothing more than its metaphysical ambition. This chapter is concerned with outlining this metaphysics by means of answering the question, 'in what does reality consist?' I begin by stating four names Schelling gives reality, before treating at length the immanence and monism of that reality. In the second half of the chapter, I then examine how this reality is constituted, contrasting Schelling's conception with Platonic emanation and transcendental representation.

NAMES FOR REALITY

Schelling gives four preliminary answers to the metaphysical question, 'in what does reality consist?' To begin, I merely state them and only in later sections will their significance become clear. Schelling employs all four terms practically interchangeably: while different works favour different terms, they are all at bottom synonymous. Moreover, none of the names is privileged as *the* proper name for reality; each of them is equally improper (I return to this issue in Chapter 11).[1]

1. *The absolute.* Schelling inherits the first, most common name for reality in the *Identitätssystem* from his German Idealist forebears. The absolute is reality—the two terms are synonymous (*SW* 4:129; 2001a, 359).

2. *Identity.* As one might expect from a 'philosophy of identity', a defining name for reality is identity. The proposition 'A = A' stands at the heart of Schelling's philosophy of this period, and reality is defined both by and as

---

[1] It is worth making clear from the start that, just because these names are 'improper', it does not mean they are inadequate (that reality somehow exists above and beyond them). This is not apophaticism. There are in fact five such improper names, because of course 'reality' should itself be included in this list. On the above, see further Whistler 2012a.

this law of identity: 'The ultimate law...for all being is the law of identity, which with respect to all being is expressed by A = A' (*SW* 4:116; 2001a, 350).

3. *Indifference.* Reality also bears the name of 'indifference'. The term emerged from Schelling's *Naturphilosophie*, specifically the study of magnetism; it designates the neutral point on the magnet where neither of the poles dominates. A number of critics have attempted to distinguish between Schelling's use of identity and indifference (Wanning 1988; Courtine 1990; Fischbach 1999) and there are perhaps some slight differences: for example, indifference is often employed with respect to form (so more in epistemological contexts) and identity with respect to essence (so more in metaphysical contexts).[2] However, basically the two are used synonymously: reality is defined as identity *and* as indifference.

4. *God.* Before mid-1802 and after 1806, God does not name reality; instead, God is a determinate entity within reality. This is still true as late as the *Fernere Darstellungen* (*SW* 4:417). However, between late 1802 and 1805, God does become synonymous with reality. Reality is given a theological name at this juncture—even if Schelling's 'God' of this period bears little relation to any other religious or even philosophical formulation of the divine.

THE IMMANENCE OF THE ABSOLUTE

'In what does reality consist?' As we shall see, Schelling's contemporaries usually interpreted this as a question about the fundamental principle on which reality rests. Schelling, however, interrogates the very presuppositions of such foundationalism. His question after 1801 is no longer 'what grounds reality?', but 'does reality have grounds?'

Before and After 1801

Schelling's very early work, especially the 1795 treatise *Vom Ich*, is derivative of much early German Idealism in its search for one, sole ground of reality. Schelling employs the term 'absolute' to designate this ground and, in consequence, the main thrust of his work before 1796 is geared towards determining precisely in what the absolute consists. In *Vom Ich*, for example, the absolute ground is characterized as infinite (§8), one (§9), indivisible (§11), substantial (§12),

---

[2] What is more, outside of the *Identitätssystem* the two terms are often employed distinctively. See, for example, *SW* 3:258–9; 2004, 185.

omnipotent (§14), and eternal (§15). As such a list indicates, Schelling transfers the properties of the traditional deity onto his post-critical 'absolute I': the absolute is for Schelling (at this stage) a supersensuous principle residing above and beyond reality.

Ineffability is one consequence of this transposition. In *Vom Ich* in particular, Schelling insists repeatedly on the ineffability of the absolute ground of reality. Concepts, discursive thinking, and even consciousness in general are unable to grasp it.[3] As critics have pointed out,[4] Schelling here approximates to a crude form of negative theology, and his epistemological advocacy of a mystical act of intuition as the only means to discern this absolute (*SW* 1:181–2; 1980b, 85) certainly owes much to such traditions. The result is that Schelling establishes an utterly equivocal relation between reality and the absolute. Nothing from the world of ordinary experience can in any way compare to what is experienced in intellectual intuition. Schelling's early philosophy situates the supersensible beyond and above the sensible. This is an extreme formulation of a 'two-world' metaphysics in which reality and the ground of reality exist as qualitatively opposed realms.

Unsurprisingly, Schelling's first forays into philosophy came under heavy criticism. In October 1796, J. B. Erhard published a caustic review which attacked both the ineffability of Schelling's absolute and also the very search for an absolute which his early project presupposes.[5] Hölderlin expressed similar concerns to Schelling at this time.[6] Schelling took such criticism to heart. Two months later he published an *Antikritik* in which he disingenuously claims that he knew all along foundationalism was to be avoided, but was merely presenting his work in foundationalist language to aid an uncomprehending public (*SW* 1:242–3; 1980b, 127–8). Moreover, he did thereafter move away from the position of *Vom Ich*: he never again wrote of the absolute as a transcendent, ineffable principle, nor did he ever again pursue the German Idealist search for grounds so naïvely. The next few years are full of attempts (which do not concern me here) to begin philosophy without foundations. It was only in 1801, however, that Schelling came upon a satisfactory position that overcame Erhard and Hölderlin's objections.

In 1801, Schelling abandoned all search for grounds; he abandoned 'the absolute' as the name for something which conditions reality; he abandoned, in fact, all distinction between the absolute and reality. From 1801 onwards, there was no more 'two-world' metaphysics. The ground of reality is not beyond reality but is itself reality. The *Identitätssystem* effectively commences with Schelling's claim, 'Absolute identity is not the cause of the universe, but

---

[3] See especially *SW* 1:178; 1980b, 78—191; 85—216; 110.
[4] Tilliette 1987, 66–70; Beierwaltes 2002, 395–8.
[5] See further Frank 2004, 48–9.   [6] See Frank 1992, 108–15, 2004, 107–8.

the universe itself' (*SW* 4:129; 2001a, 359). Combating philosophy's 'long and profound ignorance about this principle', Schelling rediscovers the 'true' relation the ground of reality holds to reality itself—one of absolute immanence. 'Absolute identity is the universe itself' (129; 359); 'outside [of it] is nothing, and in it is everything' (115; 350). The absolute is identical with reality and reality is identical with the absolute. In short, '*Everything* is absolute' (*SW* 4:387).

Of course, as the above quotations make clear, Schelling remained committed to the term 'the absolute', but it plays a very different role in his post-1801 philosophy. For the early Schelling, 'the absolute' names the ground of reality as something distinct from reality itself; it implies some form of distinction between them. After 1801, 'the absolute' does not in any way name something distinct from reality; it is reality itself under a different name. The two names ('the absolute' and 'reality') designate 'merely different views of one and the same thing' (*SW* 5:366; 1989, 14–15). Schelling thus subverts the vocabulary of German Idealism for his own purposes: he appropriates it for the sake of a philosophy of immanence, and in so doing changes its meaning.

Immanence and Monism

Schelling rejects the view basic to his early work (and the majority of the tradition which preceded him) that the foundation of reality is transcendent of the reality it grounds. On the contrary, he insists that the absolute 'cannot be considered as separated from everything that is' (*SW* 4:125; 2001a, 357). It is for such reasons he calls 'the sole true method of philosophy . . . the one under which everything is absolute and nothing is the absolute' (*SW* 4:406; 2001b, 393). There is no one, single foundation above or beyond reality ('nothing is *the* absolute'); instead, reality itself is its own ground ('everything is absolute'). The ground of reality is reality.[7]

The absolute immanence of the ground of reality to reality itself is a constant defining principle of Schelling's philosophy between 1801 and 1805. One consequence is that being is univocal. There are no separate realms or worlds; there is no qualitative hierarchy in the cosmos. 'I absolutely do not,' Schelling insists, 'acknowledge two different worlds, but rather insist on only one and the same, in which everything . . . is comprehended' (*SW* 4:101–2). There is but one world and this is the absolute. From the 'two-world' metaphysics of *Vom Ich* and the equivocal relation it maintained between the

[7] See Plessner 1954, 71; Seidel 1976, 94. It is also worth comparing Schelling here with Fichte who claims, 'Philosophy has to exhibit the ground of experience, and the ground lies necessarily outside of what it grounds' (1982, 27). The heautonomy of the organism provides Schelling with a model for self-grounding.

sensible and supersensible, Schelling has therefore reversed his position: everything is encompassed univocally in one immanent realm.

The basis for Schelling's commitment to absolute immanence is his monism. Everything is the absolute and the absolute is everything—and (between 1801 and 1805 at least) this 'is' should be taken in the strongest possible sense. Reality is therefore characterized by its unity and ultimate oneness: 'All that is is, to the extent that it is, One ... *There is everywhere only One Being, only One true Essence*' (*SW* 6:156; 1994c, 153). All is one, for all is absolute. One obvious problem with this monism is that 'the absolute' is singular whereas 'all' is plural. Only in the next chapter will this tension ultimately be reconciled; however, a preliminary answer can now be given: it is a presupposition of much classical metaphysics that the One and the All are convertible. This is the very meaning of the slogan so important to Schelling and his generation—*hen kai pan* (the one and the all). Schelling interprets it to mean, the One is the All and the All is the One: 'Absolute identity is absolute totality' (*SW* 4:125; 2001a, 357).[8]

As will become clear over the forthcoming chapters, one consequence of this monism is that in Schelling's universe there are no discrete individual substances. According to Schelling, finite individuals are illusions (which is not to say that the finite, or even individuals, per se are illusions). They conceal the essential oneness of reality. Our everyday belief in a plurality of finite beings is misguided. Hence, he states categorically, 'Considered in and of itself, nothing is finite ... No finitude exists anywhere' (*SW* 6:161; 1994c, 156). In short, there is only the absolute. Therefore, to say that 'the absolute is equivalent to reality' requires qualification. This is not 'reality' as one ordinarily understands it, the reality of commonsense. 'In its relationship to common sense the world of philosophy is in and for itself an inverted world' (*SW* 5:13; Hegel and Schelling 1985, 283).[9] Schelling maintains that commonsensical views of the world fundamentally distort and misrepresent reality. In consequence, reality is ultimately different from what it phenomenally appears to be.

The Here-and-Now

It is worth giving further examples of Schelling's resolute rejection of transcendence, since many critics still attribute to him some sliver of transcendence or remnant of a 'two-world' metaphysics. Vater, for example, labels Schelling's *Identitätssystem* 'otherworldly in its direction' (1984, 91). Schelling's absolute, Vater claims, exists '*behind* appearances' (44), invisible and ineffable (76). However, Vater's criticisms entirely miss the point: of course,

---

[8] See Uslar 1968.   [9] See further *SW* 4:362; 2001b, 377.

for 'finite cognition' (91) Schelling's absolute is otherworldly and ineffable, but Schelling repeatedly argues that finite cognition erroneously conceives all absolutes as otherworldly. Schelling attacks those (like Kant and Fichte) who separate the absolute out from reality and think of it as beyond consciousness, beyond appearances and beyond nature. He calls 'the unconditional require-ment that *the absolute be kept outside oneself*... the fundamental error that has lurked unchallenged at the base of almost all recent philosophical efforts' (*SW* 5:109; 1985, 368). Similarly, he attacks those previous philosophers who have assumed that 'the absolute remains an idea, a Beyond' (5:12; Hegel and Schelling 1985, 281).[10] When one adopts the proper philosophical viewpoint, one realizes that reality and the absolute are identical.

Another helpful example is found in Schelling's polemics against Eschen-mayer in *Philosophie und Religion*. Eschenmayer contends that the *Identitäts-system* (and indeed all philosophy) remains incomplete without a theological supplement. He asserts the radical transcendence of God against Schelling's immanentist conception of the absolute:

> It is as little possible to overcome the main antithesis between the *here-and-now* and the *Beyond* as it is true that all antitheses in the sphere of knowledge are revoked in absolute identity... The *here-and-now* is [that in] which knowledge is chained to the finite... The *Beyond*, on the contrary, implies the freedom of all directions and the immortal life of genius.[11]

The absolute is not enough; the *Identitätssystem* is incomplete, Eschenmayer argues. A transcendent deity remains a necessary addition to all philosophy.

Schelling's response is simple: Eschenmayer is wrong. To conceive of God transcending the absolute is to misconceive the nature of the absolute: 'The person who posits another *God* above the absolute of reason has not genuinely understood [the absolute] as absolute' (*SW* 6:21). There is nothing beyond the absolute, because to posit something beyond in this manner would limit the absolute's unconditional absoluteness. To posit a transcendent God would be to negate the absolute: 'The inquiry into what is above and beyond the absolute implies, in my view, an immediate contradiction' (51). Hence, all there is is the immanence of the absolute—and Schellingian reality is free from transcendent entities.

The foundation of Schelling's *Identitätssystem* is therefore to be sought in its rejection of all foundations. The very idea of an *archē* on which reality depends is vehemently rejected by Schelling after 1801; reality is instead self-grounding and so immanent.

---

[10] See Beiser 2002, 559–60.   [11] Eschenmayer, quoted in Lukács 1980, 156–7.

Early Modern Metaphysics of Immanence

The historical resonance of Schelling's commitment to immanence may already be clear to some readers; however, in the present section, I want to make Schelling's appropriation of early modern metaphysical sources more explicit. Schelling found in Spinoza and Bruno (to name the two crucial figures) allies and precursors in his pursuit of a philosophy of immanence. Spinoza and Bruno began the modern epoch by dismantling the hierarchy of being which pervades Renaissance metaphysics; they erected a plane of immanence on which to think reality. Transcendence was eliminated in favour of monism.

Schelling's engagement with Spinoza was long and eventful; however, relevant here is solely Schelling's adulatory attitude between 1801 and 1805.[12] Time and again, we must look to Spinoza to understand Schelling's thought, for he is present in the very detail of the *Identitätssystem*.[13] Similarly, there is no doubting the influence Bruno had on Schelling's thought of this period. It is unlikely that Schelling had access to Bruno's thought first-hand, but Jacobi's extended summaries of *De causa* in the second edition of the *Spinoza-Briefe* had a marked impact.[14] The main piece of evidence is Schelling's *Bruno*: not only is the title a direct homage to the Italian philosopher, but also within the dialogue itself the character who espouses Schelling's own views is named 'Bruno'. As Lukács observes, Schelling 'made Giordano Bruno the patron saint of his philosophy' (1980, 137).

The crucial question becomes: what was so important to Schelling in Spinoza and Bruno's writings? There are, I contend, three elements to an answer.

1. Renaissance thought is structured by an ontological hierarchy that is Neoplatonic in origin. Beginning from God, reality is constituted by a series of descending realms of being. Modernity commences, crudely speaking, with the abolition of this hierarchy, and it is in the work of Bruno that we first witness this.[15] Bruno extends Copernican cosmology into ontology: no rigid hierarchy constrains being any longer. Thus, one of Bruno's central refrains (borrowed from Cusa, but transformed in the process) is 'the centre is the circumference' (1988, 89). There is no centre—no foundation of meaning which orients all other points: centre and circumference are indiscernible. No overarching ontological schema

---

[12] For example, the *Fernere Darstellungen* form, in Tilliette's words, an 'unconditional elegy to Spinoza' (1970, 1:410).

[13] For Schelling's most explicit acknowledgements of Spinoza's significance, see *SW* 4:113; 2001a, 348—*SW* 2:71; 1988a, 53–4. At the end of the 1804 *System*, the *Ethics* is appropriated almost verbatim. Reality is temporarily named substance (*SW* 6:551) and the good is identified with increase in activity through the cultivation of adequate ideas (555).

[14] See further Vieillard-Baron 1971, 416–19; Boenke 2003; Otto 2003.

[15] I here follow Michel 1973; Ingegno 1988.

of value differentiates them. Bruno 'discards all idea of hierarchy' (Michel 1973, 87). Therefore, when Schelling attacks transcendence, he is closely following in the footsteps of early modern metaphysicians who were also intent on a philosophy of immanence.

2. At the heart of this critique of Renaissance thought lies what Zourabich-vili has labelled the 'strategy of the chimera' (2002, 112). According to Zourabichvili, Spinoza (and also, I would contend, Bruno) 'uses old terms in new ways such that a new subversive notion is created' (Gangle 2010, 26).[16] Spinoza and Bruno employ traditional philosophical vo-cabularies 'in ways that shift or distort their traditional senses, imposing unfamiliar meanings' (26). Bruno's use of the Cusan maxim, 'the centre is the circumference', is a case in point: a key concept is taken from the philosophical tradition to be utilized against this tradition. Originally formulated by Cusa to safeguard divine transcendence it is now mutated in Bruno's work to subvert divine transcendence. Myriad examples could also be cited from Spinoza's *Ethics*—foremost among them, Spinoza's use of 'God'. In being equated with nature, for example, God cannot remain a transcendent entity, but rather becomes an immanent principle. Spinoza and Bruno subvert the philosophical tradition by mutating its vocabulary and concepts for the sake of immanence. We have already seen something similar at work in Schelling's *Identitätssystem* with the notion of 'the absolute'. While retaining the vocabulary of his and Fichte's earlier thought, Schelling now subverts its meaning: no longer is the absolute the ground of reality, it is instead reality itself. This is the same process of mutation at work in Spinoza and Bruno. Another name for this process is 'speculative transformation', which I considered in the previous chapter in relation to aesthetics. There we saw how Schelling transforms the aesthetic tradition in the name of an absolute account of art. Schelling, Spinoza, and Bruno all speculatively transform the philosophical tradition they inherit.

3. Being becomes univocal in Bruno, Spinoza, and Schelling. In Spinoza's *Ethics*, this univocity becomes immanence. Substance (or God) is neither an occult force standing behind its phenomenal manifestations nor a thing-in-itself external to appearances. Substance is its phenomena; it exists only in the phenomena themselves. As Bruno puts it:

God is no exterior intelligence making the universe turn in circles; it has to be worthier for him to be an internal principle of movement, that is, the very nature, the very space, the very soul which possesses all animated beings.[17]

---

[16] Gangle is here paraphrasing Zourabichvili 2002, 112.   [17] Quoted in Védrine 1967, 328.

Bruno himself is never quite sure of the consequences of this move: no sooner does he make seemingly sincere appeals to the existence of a transcendent Deity than he brackets him off as irrelevant to the study of reality.[18] Nevertheless there emerges in Bruno's wake a fundamental law of early modern metaphysics which reads: what is exists only in being manifested—there is nothing more than such manifestations.[19] Concerning Spinoza, for example, one critic has written:

> It is important to note that, if Spinoza's God is a reality which underwrites the possibility of the material world, it is not because there is something essential to his nature which does not find total expression in that world... There is in this God no reality which fails to find expression under each of his attributes. (Lloyd 1996, 41)

Such is the model of reality with which Bruno and then Spinoza replace the Neoplatonic hierarchy of being. In it, the ground of reality is reality. The similarities to Schelling should be evident: Schelling too conceives the ground of reality as immanent to reality itself. Just as Bruno and Spinoza conceive God as the immanent principle of all things, so too does Schelling.

THE FORM/ESSENCE DISTINCTION

Schellingian reality is not static: 'The absolute is by nature an eternal act of producing. This producing is its essence' (*SW* 5:482; 1989, 99–100). The task of the rest of this chapter is to comprehend how the absolute produces itself. In the previous section, I discussed the immanence of the Schellingian absolute; what is now at issue is how the absolute is immanent, the process of self-constitution it undergoes so as to exist immanently. I argue that a description of this process ultimately leads to a discussion of the complete rejection of the categories of *representation* and *emanation* by Schelling during the *Identitätssystem*.

The Dynamic Law of Identity

One of the defining characteristics of the absolute is identity. The absolute exemplifies the law of identity ($A = A$), but also produces this law in the first place. To understand this, the distinction between form and essence needs to be introduced. Schelling sees the absolute as comprised of two elements—an essence and a form. While these two elements are utterly identical (as we shall

---

[18] See Védrine 1967, 324–5; Michel 1973, 78–9.   [19] See Deleuze 1990, 27.

see at length in what follows), the philosopher is able to isolate them individually, distinguishing between the quintessential identity which constitutes the essence of the absolute and the form of identity in which this essence subsists.[20] That is, reality consists in two types of identity: essential identity and formal identity.

(a) Essential Identity

Reality is in essence indeterminate identity. If one formulates the law of identity notationally as 'A = A', then essence corresponds to the symbol, '=' (the two 'A's are inessential).[21] This is why Schelling is insistent that 'A = A' does not best articulate the absolute, if too much focus is placed on the 'A's and not the '='. The law must not, in other words, be understood in a synthetic manner, as the bringing together and making equal of two distinct elements ('A' and 'A'), nor even as a tautology (or repetition) of 'A' (*SW* 4:142; 1984a, 142). Only the equal sign ('=') refers to the essence of the absolute:

> The proposition A = A, conceived universally, says neither that A on its own *is*, nor that it is as subject or predicate. Instead, *the unique being posited through this proposition is that of identity itself, which accordingly is posited in complete independence from A as subject and from A as predicate.* Since abstraction is made from the being of A in its own right, and also from its status as subject and predicate, the sole thing remaining from which abstraction cannot be made, which is therefore really posited in this proposition, is absolute identity itself. (*SW* 4:117; 2001a, 351)[22]

(b) Formal Identity

It is a fundamental presupposition of the whole *Identitätssystem* that essence cannot exist without form nor form without essence. Existence involves both. Thus, while the philosopher is able to isolate one or the other, this is an artificial operation which bears no resemblance to what actually is. The two are in fact indissociable. Essence always exists formed—there are no exceptions.

---

[20] More technically, form and essence are distinguished ideally, not really. A detailed discussion of the meaning of form and content is seemingly unforthcoming in the *Identitätssystem*; for criticisms, see Harris 1995, 192; Vater 2008, 85–6; for a cogent defence, see Marquet 1973, 210. It is particularly unfortunate for me that Schelling fails to analyse sufficiently the concept of form considering the significance I ascribe to it in later chapters.

[21] Terminologically, I here follow Tilliette 1970, 1:328. There are questions concerning the status of this mathematical symbolism: is it metaphorical or literal? Can the absolute really be adequately expressed in this way or is it merely an illustration? I provide an answer to such questions in Chapter 11.

[22] The editor adds, '[The] A in the subject position and the other in the predicate position is not what is really posited; what is posited is only the identity between the two' (117).

Thus, the absolute does not exist as pure essence (not merely as '=') but as formed, and this form is the law of identity.[23] In short, '=' exists as 'A = A'. A further mathematical analogy is helpful here: '=' on its own is not a well-formed mathematical proposition, and to that extent the pure utterance of equality ('=') is meaningless. Only a well-formed proposition is a meaningful proposition, and so '=' must take on determinate, articulated forms, such as 'A = A'.[24] The same is true of reality: it must exist as well-formed, as determinate.

What is absolutely crucial here is that 'A = A' expresses the very same truth as '='—identity. Both the essence and form of the absolute are expressions of identity; it is just that essence expresses such identity quintessentially, whereas form does so in a determinate manner. Form and essence express the same truth and so they are identical (*SW* 4:120; 2001a, 353). In the absolute, there is no distinction between essence and form; they are both expressions (one essentially, one formally) of identity.

The Ineluctable Formation of the Absolute

The absolute exists as formed. Marquet glosses Schelling most clearly on this point. 'Identity must itself take on form', he writes (1973, 228), continuing, 'All manifestation always takes place *in* something, in a *form*' (284). The absolute 'is irredeemably engaged in its form' (258). There is therefore no such thing as the unformed absolute; there is no such thing as essential identity free from formal identity. The absolute (or reality or identity or God) always and necessarily exists as formed:

> The proposition A = A expresses a being, that of absolute identity; this being, however, is inseparable from its form. So there is here a unity of being and form, and this unity is the supreme existence. (*SW* 4:126; 2001a, 357)

This is another way of affirming immanence: just as Spinozist substance does not exist apart from its modes, so too the Schellingian absolute always exists in form and never as a formless abyss. Reality is always already determinate.[25]

In other words, form and essence are identical. The essence of the absolute does not exhibit anything which is not in turn exhibited by form. Both articulate identity in equally adequate (if divergent) ways. Mathematical symbolism is helpful once again here: '=' (essential identity) is very literally reproduced fully and adequately in 'A = A' (formal identity) without anything

---

[23] A = A 'belongs not to its essence but only to the form or mode of its being' (*SW* 4:120; 2001a, 353).

[24] See *SW* 4:120; 2001a, 353.

[25] This shows the falsity of Lacoue-Labarthe and Nancy's claim that 'the properly idealistic direction of Schelling's philosophy ... leads beyond all *Bildung* and indeed beyond all *Darstellung* towards a pure revelation of the absolute absent from all form' (1988, 111).

being lost or distorted. Between form and essence, there is no alienation, no diminution, no distortion, and no loss; there is merely a relation of strict identity between them.[26] It is for this reason Schelling speaks in the 1801 *Darstellung* of 'the identity of identity' (4:121; 2001a, 354).

Form is essence. Nothing indeterminate exceeds the determinate. There is no essence hiding behind reality; rather, identity is fully and adequately expressed in what is. As such, everything is manifest in reality; nothing remains hidden behind the manifestations. 'A = A' is a full and complete translation of the essence of the absolute into an adequate form. There is no ineffable 'behind' or 'beyond' to what is expressed that never manifests itself; there is no hidden transcendence.

SCHELLING'S CRITIQUE OF
REPRESENTATION AND EMANATION

What then of the relation between essence and form? So far I have spoken in terms of an 'adequate translation' or a 'complete expression' of essence in form; yet, however natural such a way of speaking may seem, we will discover that it is precisely such terminology that Schelling puts into question. In other words, Schelling departs from conventional ways of understanding the relationship between elements of being. There are schematically two conventional ways of understanding such a relationship—representation and emanation. Schelling rejects them both, and this rejection stands at the heart of his whole *Identitätssystem*.

On a representational paradigm, form mirrors or copies essence; it is a qualitatively different repetition of the essence that still attempts to be as faithful as possible to it. The logic is that of original and copy. A corollary of representation is therefore correspondence: the extent of the correspondence between form and essence is the criterion by which the success of the representation is to be judged. What is at issue is therefore how 'adequately', 'fully', or 'completely' form mimics essence. The key presuppositions of the representational paradigm are the pre-existence of essence to form (since form must try to capture what already exists), the superiority of essence to form (since form depends on essence but not vice versa), and the ideal of *mimesis* (form must become as similar to the pre-existing essence as possible). In consequence, representation is built on failure—the likely failure of form to

---

[26] As Courtine puts it, 'Essence takes form and assumes a figure proper to it. By this, one must understand that essence is not sheltered behind form nor reserved within it, but it passes completely into form' (1990, 125).

adequately imitate essence. Form is typically inferior to or a diminution of essence; it certainly never improves upon it.

Although emanation is a very different model, it has very similar presuppositions.[27] On this paradigm, form emanates from essence—essence's very act of existing necessarily leads it to produce form from itself. This outflow of form is an inferior repetition of essence, and so form is a derivative product of essence's existence. Again, therefore, emanation presupposes the pre-existence of essence to form and the superiority of essence to form. On the other hand, unlike representation, emanation rejects the model of *mimesis* in favour of production (since form is essence repeated on an inferior scale). Yet, even here there are similarities to representation: emanation too is built on failure—form can only ever be inferior to essence, never adequate. Form necessarily exists on a lower, more derivative level of being.

Schelling rejects both these models. He rejects the metaphysical assumption common to both paradigms that some elements of being are necessarily inferior versions of others, that there is a hierarchy of being. Both models contravene his commitment to the univocity of being: there is no hierarchy in reality, no necessary superiority of originals over copies.

In the following section, I treat Schelling's rejection of representation and in the next Schelling's rejection of emanation. In order to do so thoroughly, however, I also consider these two paradigms in the guise of their most celebrated practitioners—Kant and Plato. The rejection of representation is the rejection of Kant and the rejection of emanation a rejection of (at least some forms of) Platonism. Only through understanding these wider critiques does the extent of Schelling's elimination of these two forms of thinking from his philosophy become clear.

The Rejection of Representation

Schelling breaks with transcendental philosophy in his *Identitätssystem*. Of course, put in such a bald form, this thesis is insufficient: there is much in Schelling's work between 1801 and 1805 that is thoroughly indebted to Kant. However, this does not gainsay the fact that Schelling consciously attempts in the *Identitätssystem* to discard the paraphernalia of critical idealism in favour of a metaphysics of production. We must take seriously, I am arguing, Schelling's contention of 1799 that 'philosophically [Kant] is dead' (*SB* 2:189). Indeed, when Fichte read the 1801 *Darstellung*, he did not consider it a new version of transcendental idealism; instead, he wrote, 'What must one say of this new— transfigured!—Spinozism?'[28] While Fichte's tone is disputable, his contention

---

[27] Hence, Deleuze's postulation (1994, 333–4) of the origins of representation in emanation.
[28] Quoted in *SB* 2:384.

that Schelling's *Identitätssystem* is a 'new Spinozism', rather than a post-critical system, is not. Attacks on critical philosophy can be found throughout Schelling's work of the period,[29] and one of the philosophical motivations behind such attacks is his rejection of the post-Kantian search for grounds.

A transcendental argument is one which discovers the universal and necessary conditions of experience. Its premise is that there are conditions of experience graspable in isolation from experience itself. Kant therefore begins the first *Critique* with the following claim, 'I entitle *transcendental* all knowledge which is occupied not so much with objects as with the mode of our knowledge of objects' (2007, A11/B25)—a claim which presupposes that 'the mode of our knowledge' can be distinguished from its content. Transcendental cognition is of the conditions of our experience, and not of our experience itself. Moreover, the search for metaphysical grounds has the same transcendental justification as that for conditions of experience—both refocus philosophy away from reality to what makes it possible. However, as we have already seen at length, Schelling breaks with this very search for grounds. He rejects the idea of a condition of reality in order to focus on reality itself. Reality has no ground outside of itself. In consequence, transcendental philosophy's obsession with the conditions of reality becomes redundant.[30] This is the key claim of the *Identitätssystem*.

This is one reason why Schelling rejects transcendental thinking; moreover, it is also the basis from which Schelling launches his attack on representation. Representation is a fictional ground which Kant (and then Reinhold) falsely privilege.

According to Kant, experience always proceeds through representations. Representation is a necessary condition for the possibility of experience. Dickerson, for example, has labelled Kant a 'representationalist': all conscious states are representations and nothing present to the mind escapes being represented. Representation is thus 'a primitive property of the mental', the ground on which Kantian epistemology is built (Dickerson 2004, 4–5).[31] Reinhold promulgated this view in 1790s Jena, making representation 'the ultimate and proper foundation of philosophy' (1985, 67). That is, he locates the ground of reality in the structure of representing: 'The science of the *entire faculty of representation as such* ... [is] the common foundation to both *theoretical* and *practical* philosophy' (67). Reinhold's argument for this is simple: 'I can never reach out to a rose which would be different from my impression of it, which would not occur in my representation.' There is therefore no experience that is not structured by representation. Representation, Reinhold concludes, is 'the source of all

---

[29] For Kant, see *SW* 4:350–3; for Fichte, 353–6.

[30] I do not mean to imply here that Schelling never makes a transcendental argument for the existence of the absolute; my point is rather that the absolute does not have transcendental status. In fact, in Schelling's universe, there is no such thing as the transcendental. There is nothing that is merely a condition of reality without in fact being that reality.

[31] See also Rockmore 2002, 345–6.

knowledge'; it is 'the ultimate thing that we cognise and for that reason cannot be derived from anything more primitive'. Representation is a primitive 'fact of consciousness' (56–7).

While Fichte and Schelling may have temporarily succumbed to Reinhold's search for grounds, they always disagreed vehemently with the ground Reinhold himself suggested. From 1794 onwards, both Fichte and Schelling are adamant: representation does not ground reality. Instead of remaining satisfied with the brute fact of representation, Fichte and Schelling both attempt to find the conditions of representation itself. They attempt to surpass Reinhold in discovering 'the principle for explaining the origins of our representation' (*SW* 1:412; 1994b, 110). The most pressing question for Fichte's early philosophy, for example, is, 'Whence arises the system of representations?' (1982, 31).[32] What are the conditions for the 'fact' of consciousness? Fichte's answer is the self-positing of the I, the activity by which the self first constitutes itself. 'The self is originally a doing' (1982, 66) and this doing is the 'act by means of which representations are produced' (1992, 98). Hence, beneath Reinhold's *fact* of consciousness (*Tatsache*), Fichte discovers a more primordial *act* of consciousness (*Tathandlung*). Representation is therefore a derivative structure of the mind dependent for its possibility on an original act, a positing of the self as itself.

Fichte and Schelling's philosophical trajectory begins with a critique of the category of representation. They critique Reinhold's fact of consciousness for reasons similar to those which motivate theorists of the symbol to criticize signs. This early attempt to ground philosophical thought in a category other than representation could be one philosophical motivation for Schelling's later adherence to the symbol. Moreover, an argument could be made in favour of Schelling proceeding further in this regard than Fichte (Esterhammer 2000, 83–4). Schelling, unlike Fichte, realizes that a critique of representation necessarily implies a critique of all signs. When Fichte attempts to deduce the transcendental necessity of the arbitrary sign in *Von dem Sprachfähigkeit und dem Ursprung der Sprache*,[33] he fails to pursue the consequences of the critique of representation he and Schelling both wage against Reinhold. Schelling, however, does move from this critique of representation to an attack on the arbitrary sign, and so to a theory of the symbol.

It is worth pursuing Schelling's attitude towards representation further into the *Identitätssystem*, for here we find exactly the same dismissal of the representational relation as philosophically insignificant, and a similar attempt to discover a different model for reality. Like Heidegger,[34] Schelling objects to the implicit premise of representation (expressed in the German, *Vor-stellung*) that the subject is to be set over and against the object. The general name

---

[32] See Rockmore 2002, 350–4.   [33] See Chapter 2.
[34] See Bowie 1993, 60–1, for a comparison.

Schelling gives this kind of assumption is 'reflection'. Reflection designates all that is wrong with our habitual mode of thinking, and ultimately this wrong-ness boils down to the creation of oppositions, including the subject–object opposition.

It is in the opening salvoes of the 1804 *System* that this critique is most evident. Schelling begins, '[The] very distinction between a subject and an object in knowledge constitutes the fundamental error in all knowledge' (*SW* 6:137; 1994c, 141) Such a distinction gives rise to both representation and correspondence. Schelling, on the contrary, asserts, 'Our own proposition states the *opposite* of this; namely, that there exists neither a subject *as subject* nor an object *as object*' (138; 140).[35] Hence, representation is rejected—that is, 'We now abandon forever that sphere of reflection that discriminates between the subject and the object' (140; 143).

Such is one more example of Schelling's continual rejection of representa-tion, and it is for this reason Toscano dubs Schellingian thought 'the first philosophy in the wake of Kant to undo, in great part through his appropri-ation of Spinozism, the strictures of representational dualism' (1999, 69). Representation is no longer a plausible candidate for how reality operates; it is no longer the defining ground of what is. Representation is rejected in all its variants and consigned to reflection as an inadequate way of understanding how the world works.

The Critique of Emanation

Another model for reality is emanation. Such a model is rooted in the Platonic tradition; therefore, Schelling's dismissal of emanation is bound up in his partial rejection of Platonism. The *Identitätssystem* has frequently been read as a revival of Platonic thought. Schelling's contemporaries called it 'the Neoplatonism of our times',[36] and this sentiment has been repeated in recent scholarship.[37] While there is of course some truth to this assessment, it is not the whole story. On the one hand, Schelling does welcome the influence of one type of Platonism on his ideas, but, on the other hand, he also rejects another strand of Platonic philosophy. That is, Schelling (following Spinoza and other early modern philosophers) rejects otherworldly, apophatic Platonism in favour of the 'one-world', immanentist Platonism found in the *Timaeus*.[38]

---

[35] For further analysis of this argument, see Frank 1985, 119–21; Beiser 2002, 590–2.

[36] J. F. Winzer, quoted in Beierwaltes 1972, 107.

[37] See (for example) Beiser 2003, 71.

[38] See Grant 2006, 26–58. The implication that Platonism has been transmitted into modern-ity in two forms—a 'two-world' metaphysics and a 'one-world' physics—has its origins in Lovejoy's *The Great Chain of Being*: 'There are two conflicting major strands in Plato and the Platonic tradition ... otherworldliness and this-worldliness' (1936, 24).

Schelling makes it very clear to his readers that he rejects 'two-world' Platonism and he does so by parodying it. The dialogue *Bruno* opens with a presentation of a classic 'two-world' outlook. The arguments made in the opening pages by the character Anselm (in itself a significant name—suggesting perhaps that it is not merely Platonism, but a whole theological tradition that is here under scrutiny) result in a dualistic worldview of the sort usually associated with Plato. Yet, this is a position immediately undermined by Schelling. As soon as the eponymous hero of the dialogue, Bruno, begins to speak, he distances himself from this metaphysical position. Indeed, Bruno's subsequent presentation of the one, true philosophy is a critique of the inadequate Platonism Anselm exemplifies.

Anselm's worldview is dualistic: he establishes a stark opposition between archetype and copy. The task for the philosopher is 'to show men the archetypes of all that they are accustomed to seeing in images' (*SW* 4:233; 1984a, 134). Anselm sounds in fact a lot like Schelling's early self in *Vom Ich*. Yet, now Schelling parodies this otherworldly strain of Platonism. From the moment Bruno begins to speak, his reluctance to endorse Anselm's viewpoint is clear. '[I] beg your forgiveness,' Bruno apologizes, 'if I expound the one true philosophy I know, rather than [what you requested]' (234–5; 135). Bruno is insistent on the need to tone down Anselm's rhapsodic invocation of the supersensible. Of course Bruno still espouses a form of Platonism, but the difference remains crucial: there is no more dualism; archetypes and copies are one and the same thing. As Schelling writes elsewhere, 'The innermost mystery of creation' consists in the 'the divine identification of original and copy which is the true root of every being' (*SW* 4:394; 2001b, 386).[39]

Vater has argued at length for the significance of this internal critique within the dialogue:

> [Bruno] disassociat[es] himself from the simple Platonic dualism Anselm espoused. Whereas Anselm thinks in terms of simple oppositions such as time and eternity, soul and body, archetype and individual thing, Bruno will put forth an analysis of things in terms of three elements [the potencies] ... The difference is most clearly seen in the case of the relationship between concept and thing. Anselm presents them as simply opposed, while Bruno sees them as ... distinct aspects of the individual thing ... As the discussion unfolds it will become apparent that Bruno (Schelling's *persona*) is no dualist.[40]

Vater is even blunter elsewhere:

> [When] Bruno assumes direction of the discussion, [he] immediately disassociates himself from the peculiarities of Anselm's way of thinking ... He thus distances himself from Anselm's Platonism, and from the simple dichotomy of the eternal and the finite that the latter's argument presumed. (1984, 23)

---

[39] See further Lacoue-Labarthe and Nancy 1988, 108; Wanning 1988, 70; Courtine 1990, 128–9.
[40] Translator's Note to Schelling 1984a, 231.

In short, within *Bruno*, 'two-world' Platonism deconstructs itself into Schellingianism.

This dramatization of the differences between Anselm and Bruno is Schelling's clearest statement of his relation to Platonism. Indeed, it is also a dramatization of the difference between Schelling's extremely dualistic early work and his anti-dualistic position in the *Identitätssystem*. Schelling here confronts his earlier self in the guise of Anselm, and refutes him successfully. His Platonism is not to be mistaken for the classic 'two-world' Platonism for which Anselm is the mouthpiece.

The model of emanation is grounded in the very 'two-world' metaphysics Schelling rejects. The distinction between copy and archetype is brought about by the process of emanation. Pre-existing archetypes produce inferior copies of themselves, and these subordinate and dependent entities constitute the material world. Schelling's rejection of the archetype/copy distinction, as well as his attack on 'two-world' Platonism in general, implies the elimination of a model of emanation from his system. However, one need not rest content with such implicit attacks, for Schelling is very explicitly disdainful of emanation as well. In *Philosophie und Religion*, for example, he denounces the 'illegitimacy' of emanation, especially as it appears in 'the works of the Neoplatonists' (*SW* 6:35–7).[41] Emanation is designated an inadequate, reflective model for reality.

Indeed, not only is emanation rejected in this manner, but all conceptions of the self-externalization of reality are vehemently and continually scorned. As we saw earlier in the chapter, the absolute is in no way the cause of reality, but is reality itself. One significant result of this principle is Schelling's commitment to the following: the absolute is not involved in a process of generating 'entities' outside of it, neither by emanation, creation nor self-externalization. God 'does not bring about anything, for he *is* everything' (*SW* 7:157; 1984b, 256). The absolute never steps forth from itself—such a principle holds unconditionally, no matter how such externalization is conceived. The One does not become the All; it already is the All from all eternity:

> The most basic mistake of all philosophy is to assume that absolute identity has stepped beyond itself and to attempt to make intelligible how this emergence occurs. Absolute identity has surely never ceased being identity... True philosophy consists in the demonstration that absolute identity has not stepped beyond itself and everything that is, insofar as it is, is [the absolute] itself—a proposition that Spinoza alone of all previous philosophers acknowledged... There is here no transition, no before and after. (4:119–20; 2001a, 353)

---

[41] Of course, the extent to which Schelling's description of emanation resembles any Neoplatonic version of the doctrine is open to doubt. See further Beierwaltes 1983, 95–9.

All there is is the absolute and the absolute does not produce anything else. It is 'the most basic mistake of all philosophy' not to have realized this, and to have repeatedly tried to deduce or derive reality from some pre-existing, fundamental ground. Schelling explicitly aligns himself with Spinoza's dictum (as interpreted by Jacobi): there is no transition between the infinite and the finite.[42]

Yet, despite Schelling's insistence on this point, this 'most basic mistake' has been endlessly repeated in Schelling scholarship, as I pointed out in Chapter 3. Again and again, commentators have failed to take seriously Schelling's claim that there is no transition, no deduction of reality and, instead, made the 'problem of the emergence of the finite' central to the *Identitätssystem*. To take two examples: first, 'Schelling certainly never ignored the necessity of explaining, from the absolute, the finite . . . It is this without doubt which led him to abandon the system of absolute philosophy bit by bit' (Challiol-Gillet 1996, 33); second, 'Schelling's central difficulty [is] to demonstrate how the transition from the infinite to the finite is possible, to show how the finite world arises within the absolute' (Shaw 2010, 90). As we shall see repeatedly in what follows, such widespread sentiments miss the entire point of Schelling's metaphysics of this period: Schelling refuses the idea of a finite world derived from the absolute (as if it were a ground); indeed, he denies the very idea of pure finitude entirely.

SCHELLING'S ALTERNATIVE

Representation and emanation are found wanting; what is the alternative? The task of the present section is to elucidate a third, alternative model for the form/essence relation. The foundation on which Schelling's alternative is built is the principle (discussed earlier) that formation is inescapable. In consequence, essence is not prior to form—neither temporally nor logically. Instead, the opposite is true: essence is completely dependent on form. Schelling, that is, reverses the traditional binary of Western thought in which form is seen as derivative of essence, to posit form as prior. Essence depends on form; essence is produced through form. It is here we return to Schelling's statement, 'The absolute is by nature an eternal act of producing' (*SW* 5:482; 1989, 99–100). Essential identity is the product of this act and formal identity is that through which it is produced. The absolute exists by producing its own essence through a process of formation.[43] Schelling, as will become clearer as the book proceeds, is *a philosopher of form*.

---

[42] See Troxler 1988, 38–9, where this connection is made explicit.

[43] The importance of 'production' is a constant throughout Schelling's career. It gives rise to the imagery of procreation which Schelling uses to describe the constitution of reality. See *SW* 5:405; 1989, 44—*SW* 2:189; 1988a, 151.

The major consequence of this model is that there is no pre-existent essence against which all subsequent productions can be measured. Correspondence no longer applies: there is nothing archetypical to which productions can refer back. All there are are various forms which produce essence. To talk of a form 'adequately', 'fully', or 'completely' expressing essence is therefore nonsense, for there is no benchmark such forms can adequately, fully, or completely express. There is no more adequacy on Schelling's metaphysical presuppositions. All that remains are different intensities with which essence is produced, where 'intensity' does not refer back to the perfect intensity of the original essence. All this will become clearer in the next chapter when I discuss Schelling's doctrine of quantitative differentiation; suffice it say that the process of potentiation (or the intensification of form) is not a means of returning to a pre-given perfection but is rather an infinitely increasing production of essence.

The point can be illustrated by means of a disagreement between Schelling and Fichte. After reading the 1801 *Darstellung* in which the above argument is proposed, Fichte countered: the absolute as absolute cannot be formed, for such formation would diminish its absoluteness. He therefore warns Schelling, 'The absolute would not be absolute if it existed in any specific form' (*SB* 2:381; Fichte and Schelling 1997, 89). However, this comment betrays a complete misunderstanding of the thrust of the *Identitätssystem*, for it tries to force Schelling's logic of production back into a logic of emanation or representation. Fichte argues that to form the absolute would be to lose something of its essence, that formation is always necessarily a process of alienation. This is precisely what Schelling rejects. Formation does not distort a pre-existing essence; it is what produces essence in the first place. Determinate forms therefore not only can express the essence of the absolute, essence can only be (and so must be) expressed in a determinate form. It is on this principle that the *Identitätssystem* stands or falls. Formation constitutes (rather than loses) essence. Schelling thus writes in a later work (implicitly responding to Fichte's comment), 'The true [absolute] is not formlessness, but is delimited in itself, is finished *by* itself and is thus perfect' (*SW* 7:143; 1984b, 246).

In short, whereas representation and emanation presuppose the failure and inadequacy of their forms, Schellingian philosophy conceives form as always *excessive*. The produced essence is always more than it was prior to production (for, prior to production, it did not exist). Determination is not a prison which stops us reaching what matters most; what matters most is in fact first produced in the very act of determination. Formation can never be a diminution, alienation, distortion or loss of essence, for there is no essence prior to form. Schelling here agrees entirely with Goethe's criticism of Plotinus:

> A spiritual form is by no means diminished by emerging into appearance, provided that its emergence is a true procreation, true propagation. What is

begotten is not inferior to the begetter, and indeed, the advantage of live begetting
is that what is begotten can be superior to that which begets it. (*WA* I/48 196;
1989, 420)

Such then is the relation of essence to form: each form produces essence to a
greater or lesser degree of intensity. Every form is a means of producing
essential identity. Moreover, these forms do not succeed or fail at producing
identity in comparison to some pre-existing standard; instead, there is a
perpetually excessive surplus of essence. At the heart of the *Identitätssystem*
therefore stands the process of formation. Everything depends on it: reality is
constituted by this process, essence is produced by it. The whole of Schelling's
philosophy between 1801 and 1805 revolves around the question of form.

THREE MODELS FOR PRODUCTION

Reality produces itself—such is the basic claim of Schelling's *Identitätssystem*.
So far I have considered this act of self-production in relation to the form/
essence distinction; however, there are other, complementary ways in which
Schelling describes this process. There are three I consider further in this
section: the model of self-affirmation, the dialectic of *Ineinsbildung*, and the
self-knowledge of the absolute. Schelling seemingly sees no contradiction
between all the different models, and they do broadly articulate a very similar
idea—the immanent self-constitution of reality; however, each has its own
emphasis and consequences which do not always sit well with the other
models. Foremost here is the question of difference (what is difference and
how does it relate to the identity of the absolute?); the various answers
Schelling gives to this question engender the different strands of the
Identitätssystem.[44]

Self-Affirmation

The first model is the simplest: the absolute affirms itself and in so doing
reality is constituted. While Schelling does use this kind of language in the
1801 *Darstellung*, it is the 1804 *System* which insists most forcefully on it.
'God,' Schelling writes, 'is His own absolute affirmation' (*SW* 6:148; 1994c,
148), continuing, 'He is only to the extent that He *affirms Himself*' (151; 150).
The act of production we were considering in the last section is here described
as the self-affirmation of the absolute: the absolute affirms itself *as identity*,

---

[44] On these different strands, see Tilliette 1970, 1:371.

and this affirmation is simultaneously the formation of reality and the production of essence. To affirm identity is to articulate it and so to give it a form
in which it exists. Identity exists as formed through this eternal act of self-
affirmation.

This model is quite different from a dialectic process of achieving identity
through mediation. No mediation or negation is necessary here, merely the
immediate affirmation of identity as identity.[45] By structuring this model
around the image of affirmation, Schelling banishes negation. This has significant consequences for the status of difference in the *Identitätssystem*. In short,
since reality affirms itself immediately as identity, difference is excluded.
Schelling thus claims, 'The absolute is absolute only through the absolute
exclusion of difference from its essence' (*SW* 4:375). Self-affirmation excludes
difference.

Yet, this is in need of qualification, for it is only qualitative difference which
is excluded in this manner; quantitative difference, on the other hand, can be
reconciled with the absolute's self-affirmation. The next chapter is devoted to
the whole issue of quantitative differentiation; what is at issue now is how
quantitative difference is reconcilable with the model of self-affirmation, and
the answer to this question is to be found in the concept of *refraction*. Schelling
proposes a version of the ancient idea of 'the great chain of being',
the manifestation of being across a spectrum of different entities: 'The absolute
manifests and actualises itself across degrees of being...The absolute
shines...like a diamond with a thousand faces' (Maesschalck 1989, 83).
Schelling conceives this 'spreading out' of the absolute over reality along the
lines of the refraction of light.[46] The result is a 'refraction of identity' (Tilliette
1970, 1:404). The self-affirmation of identity is refracted throughout reality,
giving rise to quantitative (not qualitative) differences. Reality can affirm itself
as identity while still leaving room for some form of difference.

The Dialectic of *Ineinsbildung*

While the beginning and end of the *Identitätssystem* are marked by the stark
simplicity of the model of self-affirmation, the years 1802 and 1803 are
characterized by the intricacies of dialectic. This dialectical process revolves
around the concept of *Ineinsbildung*, introduced in the *Philosophie der Kunst*
as follows,

> The splendid German word 'imagination' [*Einbildungskraft*] actually means the
> power of *mutual informing into unity* [*Ineinsbildung*] upon which all creation is
> really based. It is the power whereby something ideal is something real, the soul

[45] See Groves 1999, 34.   [46] See *SW* 6:441, 7:172.

simultaneously the body, the power of individuation that is the real creative power. (*SW* 5:386; 1989, 32)

'All creation' rests on a process of 'mutual informing into one' or *Ineinsbildung*. Imagination is thus no longer a faculty, it no longer resides in the subject; rather, the power of forming into one, *Einbildungskraft*, is an ontological process.

On this model, the absolute's act of self-production is a process of forming itself into one. The presence of *Bild* (form) in *Einbildungskraft* is key, for here Schelling provides concrete detail on how the process of formation takes place. A philosophy of *Einbildungskraft* charts the *Bildung* of the absolute—the production of its essence through formation, and this formation is thereby conceived as a kind of unification:

> The absolute . . . converts itself . . . as sheer identity into the real, into the form, and conversely, in equally eternal fashion, resolves itself as form, and to that extent as object, into the essence or subject. (*SW* 2:62; 1988a, 47)

Reality is formed in two stages: first a multiplicity of forms are created and second they are identified. The two moments are thus the differentiation of all reality and its subsequent[47] re-identification. Schelling also dubs this process subject-objectivization: reality is first made subject and then made object (and so the indifference of subject and object).[48]

Ineinsbildung is a two-stage process in which what occurs in the first stage is negated in the second. Difference is first posited and then negated. On the first model of self-affirmation, difference was excluded from the absolute since identity was immediately affirmed as identity; on this second model, however, a moment of difference is part of the process by which the absolute is self-constituted. Identity is affirmed '*across* or *thanks to* difference' (Courtine 1990, 116). Schelling here approaches (and was perhaps influenced by) Hegel's definition of the absolute as 'the identity of identity and non-identity' (1977a, 156). Mediation is also central: the absolute is not immediately affirmed as identity (*per* the first model), rather it only achieves identity by means of an intermediary stage of differentiation. In Vater's words, '*Ineinsbildung* is an intermediation of strict identity' (1976, 288). Identity expands into difference, and then reverts back into identity—and together these two movements comprise the process of *Ineinsbildung*.

Schelling frequently uses the image of 'reflection' to designate such mediation. Reality must be reflected into difference to regain identity, and so the reflected world of appearances is a necessary stage in this becoming identical.[49] Only once

---

[47] This is logical, not temporal (*SW* 4:417).
[48] *SW* 5:317–18; 1966, 115—*SW* 2:62–4; 1988a, 47—*SW* 4:391; 2001b, 384.
[49] See Courtine 1990, 128.

reason is able to recognize (as if in a mirror) essential identity dispersed amidst this multiplicity of forms is the dialectical process complete.

The Self-knowing of the Absolute

There is also a third model Schelling employs—absolute knowing. 'The self-affirmation of God may also be characterized as a process of self-knowledge', he writes in the 1804 *System* (*SW* 6:168; 1994c, 162). This is of course the most idealist of Schelling's ways of describing reality: reality is constituted through an epistemological process of knowing. The absolute becomes an idea of itself, and (in so doing) it determines and forms itself.

This epistemological model immediately raises the question: *who knows?* Schelling answer is concise, if polemical: 'The fundamental error in all knowledge is ever since Descartes the "*I* think, *I* am". Thinking is not my thinking, and being not my being, for everything is only God's or the All's' (*SW* 7:148; 1984b, 250). The absolute knows. In the 1804 *System*, Schelling stresses this need to abstract epistemology from the individual subject,

> In *reason* all subjectivity ceases ... In reason, eternal identity is at once the knower and the known—it is not *me* who recognizes this identity, but it recognizes itself, and I am merely its organ. Reason is *reason* precisely because its knowledge is not subjective; instead, an identity in it comes to recognise itself as the self-same. (*SW* 6:142–3; 1994c, 144)

Schellingian epistemology therefore treats the self-knowledge of the absolute alone; all individual knowledge is merely 'its organ'. The individual is not the subject of knowledge: 'Reason is not a faculty ... There is no reason at all which we could have, but only a reason which has us' (*SW* 7:148; 1984b, 250). All there is is God in his eternal act of self-knowing, and this self-knowing is one more way of elucidating the immanent self-constitution of reality.

Reality has many names (identity, indifference, God, the absolute), but no hierarchical structure, nor anything that transcends it. It is notionally distinguished into form and essence, but, unlike traditional metaphysics, form is not dependent on a pre-existing essence, but is what produces essence in the first place. This can be described variously as the self-affirmation of reality, the *Ineinsbildung* of essence and form, or the self-knowing of reason. Such is a summary of Schellingian metaphysics; it is the task of the next chapters to show the ways in which these abstract principles impact concretely on Schellingian symbolic language.

5

Quantitative Differentiation

Schellingian symbolic language is derived rigorously from the principles of the *Identitätssystem*, so only by reconstructing these principles can it be properly understood. I continue this reconstruction in the present chapter. In my account of Schelling's metaphysics in the previous chapter, I spoke of 'reality' in a rather abstract manner. Questions remain, therefore, concerning the type of individuals which populate Schellingian reality and how they are to be reconciled with his monism. It is to such questions I turn in this chapter. In the first section, I consider the nature of the entities which comprise Schellingian reality; they are to be understood, I argue, as *Darstellungen* or ideas. In the second section, I turn to the question of reconciling individual existence with monism, and contend it is precisely Schelling's theory of quantitative differentiation that allows him to do so. Finally, using the resources provided by my examination of quantitative differentiation, I give readings of, first, reflection and, second, the *Potenzlehre*.

IDEAS

At the beginning of the previous chapter, I posed the following metaphysical question: in what does reality consist? To this question, I gave the answer: it consists in a process of immanent self-constitution. Yet, a more concrete and straightforward answer has yet to be given, and it is this I give in the present section. In short, reality consists in ideas.

Beyond Epistemology

The claim that reality consists in ideas is Schelling's most idealist moment during the *Identitätssystem*. This assertion seems to suggest that metaphysics is reduced to epistemology, so all reality can be analysed in terms of mental entities. Yet, to read Schelling thus would be to misunderstand him, because, while Schelling certainly draws on idealism for his vocabulary, he transforms the notion of idea so that it no longer designates something merely ideal, but the identity of real and ideal. It is not the case that metaphysics is reduced to epistemology therefore, but rather the language of epistemology is a crucial resource on which Schelling draws to explicate reality metaphysically. Just as the model of the self-knowing of the absolute is a metaphysical description of reality (as we saw in the previous chapter), so too is 'idea' freed from subjectivity and from its usual reference to mental (purely ideal) entities.

This can best be seen in terms of the sources Schelling draws on for his *Ideenlehre*. 'Idea' obviously has a Platonic ring to it;[1] yet, unlike traditional interpretations of Plato, Schellingian ideas do not exist in an intellectual heaven distinct from the world of appearances; copy and archetype cannot be separated (again, as we saw in the previous chapter). They are not withdrawn entities only known in intellectual contemplation, but immanent entities within the world. In fact, the Platonic terminology hides a Spinozist meaning as well.[2] Spinozan ideas are acts by which substance affirms itself ideally; they are immanent affirmations of substance in thought. The same is true for Schelling: ideas are productions of essence in determinate forms. The major difference between Schelling and Spinoza here is that Spinozan ideas are purely ideal, whereas Schellingian ideas are defined as the identity or indifference of ideal and real. They are metaphysical entities, not purely epistemological ones.

The Proliferation of Identity

In the previous chapter, I began to consider the process of formation through which reality constitutes itself and essence is produced. Essential identity exists as formal identity, as the law of identity ($A = A$). An obvious question to which I then alluded is how formal *identity* can give rise to the irreducible multiplicity of everyday life. There are many answers to this. First, Schelling does not think that such multiplicity is ultimately irreducible: our common-sense assumptions about a plurality of finite substances are misguided. Second, he contends, in line with much of the metaphysical tradition, that the One and the All are convertible. Third and most significantly, Schelling insists that form (even formal identity) is not singular; there is a plurality of formal identities in existence. It is false to maintain that the law of identity can only be expressed in one form; rather, all forms express the law of identity. There are two different claims

---

[1] See *SW* 6:185–6; 1994c, 173–4. Leibnizian monads are also a crucial precedent, see *SW* 2:64; 1988a, 48. The term 'idea' is missing from the 1801 *Darstellung* and makes its first appearance in the 1802 Platonic dialogue, *Bruno*.

[2] See *SW* 4:373; Marquet 1973, 278; Vater 1984, 12.

implicit here: first, more than one form expresses the law of identity to exactly the same extent as 'A = A'; second, all forms express the law of identity to different extents. Schelling is committed to both these claims, as we shall see: his theory of ideas presupposes the first claim and his conception of *Darstellungen* the second. I deal with the first claim in this section.

In the previous chapter, I noted Schelling's appeal to the concept of refraction. Reality's self-constitution is refracted into multiple instances of identity. This is how plurality arises in the Schellingian cosmos. In Tilliette's words, 'Identity unfolds into an efflorescence of forms, a streaming forth and profusion' (1999, 147).[3] Reality is not merely formed as A = A, but also B = B or Z = Z etc.—a multiplicity of expressions of the law of identity are engendered when reality constitutes itself. In fact x = x (where 'x' stands for any value) is perhaps the most accurate formula for reality's self-constitution. This proliferation of identities was not available to Fichte and the early Schelling, since they conceived of the absolute on the model of the I, and in consequence the statement I = I held a privileged position—it possessed more truth than any other statement of identity. For Schelling after 1801, this is just not true: all identity-statements are equally valid. Schelling's *Identitätssystem* is indifferent to content; all that matters is the extent to which formal structures exhibit the law of identity, i.e. the extent to which they approximate to x = x.

Schelling designates these various manifestations of the law of identity 'ideas'.[4] Ideas are what constitute reality; they are the absolute as it is produced in the universe. They are therefore what compose reality when it is properly viewed. Schelling is committed to the view that everything individual that exists (when reality is viewed adequately) is an idea: 'Every particular object is in its absolute status idea' (*SW* 4:405; 2001b, 392) He writes elsewhere, 'True being is only in the ideas' (*SW* 4:389). All ideas express, in essence, the same thing—identity—and they all do so maximally. That is, all ideas are completely 'adequate' manifestations of the law of identity: they are 'perfect' manifestations of the indifference of the absolute in idiosyncratic—but parallel—forms.[5]

The Nature of Ideas

Formal identity is the identity of two terms, A = A. These two terms are generated by reality's act of self-constitution, and they are generated as equal to each other.

---

[3] See also Grant 2006, 172.   [4] See *SW* 6:191; 1994c, 177.

[5] The scare-quotes around 'adequate' and 'perfect' are reminders that in fact Schelling's metaphysics (I argued in the previous chapter) does away with adequacy and all other evaluative terms based on correspondence. Thus, in what follows, I resort to other terms like 'intense' and 'maximal' which do not imply a comparison with a pre-existing benchmark.

Ideas therefore exist as the identity of two terms—for example, the identity of real and ideal, finite and infinite, or universal and particular (*SW* 6:184; 1994c, 172). Moreover, because ideas are what are produced by the absolute under the form x = x, in them form and essence are identical. They exemplify formal identity (x = x), and so both their form and their subsequently produced essence are defined by the property of identity. 'Form and substance are one in the idea' (193; 179). Such is Schelling's point when he calls the ideas 'the absolute positing of infinite reality' (191; 177), or when he more explicitly (and rhapsodically) writes:

> [Ideas] furnish the unique possibility of comprehending absolute profusion within absolute unity, the particular in the universal, and precisely by that also the absolute in the particular—blessed beings, as some designate the first creatures who live in the immediate sight of God, which we shall more accurately say, are gods themselves, since each is for itself absolute, and yet each is included in the absolute form. (*SW* 4:405; 2001b, 392)[6]

There are a number of points which follow from this determination of the ideas. First, it implies that the correct view of reality equates the finite and infinite, the real and the ideal. Ideas (and therefore reality itself) consist in the identity of these binaries; they never exist in separation. There is, for example, nothing purely finite or purely infinite: 'The infinite in and for itself and the finite in and for itself... are really only one' (*SW* 4:385). All things are finite *and* infinite. Thus Schelling speaks in terms of 'infinite finitude' (*SW* 4:248; 1984a, 148): the finite can only be said to exist at all insofar as it is infinitely finite; there is no finitude *as such*. Here again those critics who look to the *Identitätssystem* for a derivation of the finite are shown to be mistaken: the finite at no point exists as merely finite.

The same is true of the relation between real and ideal. 'We could never assert that a purely ideal being existed, nor a purely real one either' (254; 155). Instead, as the 1804 *System* phrases it, 'The ideal is immediately also the real' (*SW* 6:149; 1994c, 148). Nothing is purely mental or purely physical, but all things include both domains of being. Indeed, Schelling goes so far as to write, 'The first step to philosophy and the condition without which it cannot even be entered is the insight that the absolute-ideal is also the absolute-real' (*SW* 2:60; 1988a, 44).[7] Schelling's position here is a form of panpsychism (and panphysicalism) modelled after Spinozan parallelism: all that exists in the physical world is a mental entity as well, and conversely there are no purely mental entities but only mental entities which simultaneously possess physical existence. All things are 'both real and ideal at every point' (*SW* 5:219; 1966, 13). Again, we see the identity of epistemology and metaphysics in Schelling's philosophy: 'idea' is not a purely epistemological term, but the identity of real and ideal.

---

[6] See further *SW* 2:64; 1988a, 48.   [7] See *SW* 5:216–17; 1966, 9–10.

Second, it follows that the correct way of looking at reality is that which perceives ideas and only ideas: 'What is genuinely real in all things is strictly their idea' (*SW* 6:183; 1994c, 172) Ideas are the only material out of which reality is (or even can be) formed. What is ordinarily seen as merely finite is, in fact, an idea in which the finite is simultaneously infinite. Vater writes, 'Neither the finite nor the infinite is intrinsically real . . . The eternal ideas alone are real, and they are the indifferent subsistence of the finite and the infinite.' When common sense claims to discern purely finite, phenomenal individuals, it perceives 'but images of ideas, ideas perceived from the limited standpoint of reflection' (1984, 31). It is reflection (a distorted form of thinking) which inhibits us from recognizing the ideational nature of reality. 'Ordinary reflection,' Schelling insists, 'which is the opposite of philosophy, remains necessarily in an antithetical relation to the universal and the particular' (*SW* 6:185; 1994c, 173)[8] From the standpoint of reason as opposed to reflection, the logic of reality is the logic of ideas. This is a 'both . . . and . . .' logic—infinite and finite, real and ideal, whereas reflection attempts to separate and oppose this original identity. It stops us realizing 'all is idea'.

All beings are ideas; therefore, all beings are both finite and infinite, both real and ideal; and philosophy 'is simply the capacity to see the universal in the particular, the infinite in the finite, the two combined into a living unity' (*SW* 4:362; 2001b, 377). Schelling thus concludes, 'Philosophy has but one sole object of study, the idea' (*SW* 4:243; 1984a, 143).

Darstellungen

Ideas are forms of reality, when that form is equivalent to x = x. However, they are not the only individuals to populate the Schellingian cosmos. There are in fact all kinds of individuals, even if ultimately they are all reducible to ideas. In short (and to summarize an argument I make later in the chapter), 'x = x' exists in different amounts, and this distinction in quantity is what differentiates entities. The ideas are those forms in which 'x = x' is manifest to the maximum possible extent; however, this implies that 'x = x' is not necessarily manifested maximally: other individuals manifest 'x = x' to lesser extents; they are dimmer versions of the ideas. This is the second claim I set out above: forms can exhibit identity to different extents and this is another way by means of which multiplicity arises. Therefore, for Schelling there are two ways multiplicity is engendered—extensively and intensively. Extensively, there are different forms of the law of identity and these different forms are designated

---

[8] Indeed, to oppose the finite to the infinite and thus to misconceive ideas is, for Schelling, the basic error exhibited by 'the empty philosophizing of the mass of men' (*SW* 4:384).

ideas; moreover, there are also different intensities of each idea, and such determinate intensities also subsist as individuals.

Significantly, Schelling labels all individuals—both ideas and their intensively dimmer variants—as *Darstellungen*. In so doing, he draws on Kantian terminology. Kant's epistemology could crudely be summarized as a description of the mechanisms by which a human subject produces *Vorstellungen* (representations of an object). Yet, alongside *Vorstellung*, there is another form of 'presentation': this is *Darstellung*. Gasché distinguishes the two thus,

> As opposed to *Vorstellung* or representation which Kant uses very broadly to designate the mode in which something is given to a subject, *Darstellung* has a technically very concise and limited meaning... Presentation, or *Darstellung*, is intuitive, sensible presentation of pure concepts. (1990, 91)

Darstellung designates a sensible presentation that *exhibits* a concept or idea; it is thought made sensible, given objective existence or reality. In short, each *Darstellung* realizes a concept. In *On the Progress of Metaphysics*, Kant writes under the heading, 'How to Confer Objective Reality on the Pure Concepts of Understanding and Reason':

> To represent a pure concept of the understanding as thinkable in an object of possible experience is to confer objective reality upon it and in general to present [*darstellen*] it. Where we are unable to achieve this, the concept is empty, i.e. it suffices for no knowledge. (2002, 20:279)

Thinking is not enough for Kant; it is a mere playing with concepts. To really matter and become objectively valid, concepts and ideas need to realize themselves in intuition. '*Darstellen*' designates this process of 'conferring objective reality on concepts' by 'exhibiting' them in intuition. *Darstellungen* are therefore ways in which concepts take on shape and figure. They are the original *Bildung* of concepts into intuitions, their temporal and spatial figuration.[9]

Schelling follows Kant closely. There are, however, crucial differences. First, Schelling completely eliminates the category of *Vorstellung* from his philosophy: we have already rehearsed this rejection of representation (especially Kantian representation) in the previous chapter. There are therefore only *Darstellungen*.[10] Second, Schelling does not merely consider *Darstellung* as an epistemological category; he extends its range to cover all entities whatsoever (not merely mental ones). All individuals are *Darstellungen*. This, as we have seen, is quite consonant with the *Identitätssystem* as a whole, which frequently transfers epistemological categories into metaphysical discourse. Third, *Darstellungen* for Schelling are not merely the immediate exhibition of

---

[9] See Beaufret 1973, 103–4; Flach 1982, 455; Lacoue-Labarthe and Nancy 1988, 31.
[10] See Helfer 1996, 9.

concepts as they are for Kant, but rather the immediate exhibition of identity. Essence is formed into *Darstellungen*; thus each *Darstellung* is a manifestation of absolute reality. Finally, of course, in line with Schelling's more general metaphysical polemics, Schelling disagrees with the 'revelatory model' on which Kantian *Darstellung* is based whereby a pre-existing concept emerges into time and space; instead, Schelling refigures *Darstellung* around his own metaphysical model in which form is prior: therefore, nothing pre-exists *Darstellungen*—identity, reality, the absolute are all produced out of them.

To the question, 'in what does reality consist?', the simplest Schellingian answer is thus, *Darstellungen*. They are the individuals that populate Schelling's universe; forms which exhibit essential identity to various extents.

QUANTITATIVE DIFFERENTIATION

All *Darstellungen* exhibit essential identity; therefore they all have exactly the same content. How then are they to be differentiated? This is a problem that all monisms face; Schelling, however, makes things more difficult by also adhering to the qualitative identity of all forms as well. All forms are ultimately the same, since they all—to various degrees—are formulations of the law of identity. In consequence, Schelling permits no qualitative differences whatsoever, neither in terms of essence nor in terms of form. The only possible mode of differentiation left is *quantitative*—it is 'to various degrees' which is the crucial differentiator in Schelling's cosmos.

Quantitative differentiation is often seen as an albatross around the neck of Schellingian philosophy—from Hegel's dismissals of the concept in the *Phänomenologie* and the *Logik*[11] to Beiser's recent failure to take it seriously (2002, 568). Plessner's reaction is typical: it is 'an unwisely chosen concept' (1954, 73). However, in what follows I will present what is usually seen as a weakness as a key strength; I will follow Zeltner in asserting that quantitative differentiation 'is a cornerstone of the *Identitätssystem*' (1975, 87).

Theories of Judgement

To begin to understand Schelling's theory of quantitative differentiation, it is first necessary to take a short detour through theories of judgement in German Idealism. For Schelling during the *Identitätssystem*, all judgement is thetic

---

[11] Vater (1984, 83–5) summarizes Hegel's criticisms.

judgement, and in consequence there is no such thing as synthetic or antithet-ical judgement.[12]

Post-Kantian German philosophy identified three forms of judgement: thetic, antithetic, and synthetic. Drawing out a distinction present *in germo* in Kant's works,[13] Fichte's account of judgement runs as follows:

> Just as there can be…no synthesis without antithesis, so there can be neither without a thesis—an absolute positing, whereby an A (the self) is neither equated nor opposed to any other but is just absolutely posited. (1982, 113)

When I = I is 'posited absolutely' (93), this is a thetic judgement, and such a judgement is the fundamental presupposition for all other judgements. It is the ground of thought. In a thetic judgement, 'the self posits itself absolutely as infinite and unbounded' (225). Thetic judgement is therefore characterized by its indeterminacy. Such judgements also give rise to 'the category of reality' (100): being is one of its consequences.[14]

For Fichte, equally necessary for consciousness is a second form of judge-ment—antithetical judgement (A $\neq$ $\sim$A). As soon as the I constitutes itself, it immediately distinguishes itself from the not-I: 'The essence of reason consists in my positing myself, but I cannot do this without positing a world in opposition to myself' (1992, 83). In other words, to know what something is it is necessary to separate it from what it is not. To be something determinate it is necessary not to be other things. *Omnis determinatio est negatio*, as Spinoza famously put it. Division is therefore a necessary precondition for synthetic judgement (A = B). Predication is possible only after an antithetical judgement has taken place. Fichte writes, 'Nothing is known regarding what something is without the thought of what it is not.'[15]

For Fichte and the early Schelling, this account of the threefold generation of judgements provides a definitive answer to Kant's guiding question, 'how are synthetic judgements possible?' Owing to their discovery that 'thesis precedes antithesis, and that both precede synthesis', they both claimed to have 'now answered [Kant's question] in the most universal and satisfactory manner' (*SW* 1:195; 1980b, 95). Schelling sums up this line of thought clearly in his *Philosophical Letters*, '*Synthesis* comes about only through the mani-fold's opposition to the original unity.' And he continues a page later,

---

[12] For the close relation between quantitative difference and the rejection of synthesis and antithesis, one need only remember that in the *Kritik der reinen Vernunft* Kant places negation (antithesis) and limitation (synthesis) under the category of quality (as opposed to quantity) (2007, A80/B106).

[13] Not only in his distinction in the table of judgements between affirmative, negative, and infinite judgements (2007, A70–3/B95–8), but also in his pre-critical discussion of being as a form of positing. For more on the origins of thetic judgement, see Frank 2004, 84–93.

[14] See *SW* 1:221; 1980b, 114.

[15] Quoted in Frank 2004, 87.

'Synthesis as such is thinkable only under [the] condition . . . that it be *preceded* by an *absolute* unity' (1:294–6; 1980c, 164–5). Both a primordial thesis and then an antithesis are needed for synthetic judgements to be possible.

One of the tasks of transcendental philosophy (as Fichte and the early Schelling understood it) was to recover the original, grounding thetic judgement underlying all antithesis and synthesis.[16] Philosophy aims at re-presenting the ground of thinking. Hence, in 1795 Schelling insists in line with this synthetic method, 'In theoretical as well as in practical respects, reason aims at nothing but absolutely thetic theorems, equal to the theorem I = I' (*SW* 1:229; 1980b, 118). He is even clearer a year later, 'All philosophy demands absolute thesis as the goal of all synthesis. Absolute thesis, however, is thinkable only through absolute identity. Hence, [philosophy] necessarily strive[s] for absolute identity' (1:327–8; 1980c, 187). Thesis is absolute identity; it takes the form of A = A; and philosophy's task is to regain this primordial state of indifference.

One of the most fundamental implications of Schelling's *Identitätssystem* is that: there are only thetic judgements.[17] This is, in many ways, a development from his earlier view. The goal of philosophy has now been reached, and so all it need do is repeat the original thetic judgement. While in 1795 Schelling wrote, 'Where there is thesis there is I, and where there is I there is thesis' (*SW* 1:225; 1980b, 116), in 1801 the I has become the absolute and all there is is the absolute; hence, his statement would now read, 'Everywhere there is the absolute, everywhere there is thesis.' 'We never emerge from A = A', is the guiding thread of the *Identitätssystem*.[18]

Perhaps the easiest manner in which to see Schelling's commitment to thesis and thesis alone is his rejection of synthetic and antithetic forms of judgement. For example, the absolute is not a synthesis of A and A, but the point of indifference which generates these very terms to begin with. The absolute is not a result, but the origin (*SW* 4:128; 2001a, 359). Throughout his *Identitätssystem*, Schelling remains true to the insight that what reflection perceives as the synthetic, third moment which unites two pre-existing contraries is, in fact, their 'common root', the original first moment: 'What appears in experience as third is in itself again the first' (*SW* 2:107; 1988a, 83–4).[19] Schelling vehemently attacks synthesis as 'an absurd putting-together

---

[16] This is another version of the quest for grounds I discussed in the previous chapter.

[17] It needs to be pointed out from the very beginning that the subject here doing the judging is reality. If one finds it hard to conceive of being itself judging, then one could speak of thetic positing.

[18] This statement is found in a footnote added by the editor of the *SW*. It continues, 'All difference consists just in this: A = A is posited in one direction or tendency' (*SW* 4:137; 2001a, 365). See also Troxler 1988, 34.

[19] See also *SW* 6:182; 1994c, 171. All of this holds for the model of self-affirmation discussed in the last chapter, rather than for the dialectic of *Ineinsbildung* which still retains a moment of antithesis and synthesis (as its designation 'dialectic' suggests).

of opposites' (*SW* 4:379). Indeed, he maintains that 'all objections that have been raised against the system of identity rest on this misconstrual'—seeing reality as 'a product of synthetic thought' (*SW* 6:163–4; 1994c, 158). Synthesis, that is, is the error which hinders universal recognition of the *Identitätssystem*'s cogency.

This also holds true of antithesis: it is not a distinct form of judgement to thesis, but merely an inadequate manner of conceiving such thesis. Since the absolute is the thetic positing of identity and identity alone, there is no room for negation (or, at least, antithetical, qualitative negation) in Schelling's universe.[20] Identity, Schelling makes clear, 'cannot be negated anywhere and in no manner' (*SW* 6:179; 1994c, 169). He writes elsewhere, 'Reason posits neither the negation of opposites nor even any opposites... Negation is not posited' (*SW* 7:154; 1984b, 253–4).[21]

Having excluded synthesis and antithesis, only the model of the thetic can be used to describe reality. This point is stressed in the 1801 *Darstellung*:

> Each A = B considered in itself or as referred to itself is an A = A, therefore something absolutely self-identical.—Were this not true, there would be nothing real, since everything that *is*, subsists only to the extent it expresses absolute identity under some determinate form of being. (*SW* 4:133; 2001a, 362)

As Schelling puts it succinctly a page later, 'An A = B is an A = A', and this is because '*what is in existence* is always and only indifference' (134; 363).[22] Synthesis (A = B) is reduced to a form of thesis.[23]

In short, Schelling's hope expressed in 1795 that all syntheses *should* become theses is now realized. There are no longer any synthetic propositions, only thetic ones. As Schelling puts it elsewhere in the work, 'Absolute identity can never be abolished as absolute identity' (119; 352).[24] There is nothing which is not part of the absolute positing of the absolute: 'The same identity is posited throughout... even [in] A = B' (137; 365). This line of thought is summed up in a passage from the 1804 *System*:

> The infinite substance produces, in an infinite fashion, only the absolute *thesis*, just as it itself is only absolute thesis... [In reflection] instead of the thesis, the synthesis is produced, and what is first in the absolute or in itself is third in the

---

[20] At least, when setting aside the dialectic of *Ineinsbildung*.

[21] The aphorism continues, 'Not the negation, therefore, for then the unity would be a merely negating and therefore conditioned unity.' See also *SW* 6:179; 1994c, 169.

[22] In 1804, Schelling similarly writes, 'B = A dissolves into A = A' (*SW* 6:209; 1994c, 190).

[23] Similarly, Schelling now has nothing but scorn for the synthetic method pursued by Fichte and in his earlier work. He rejects the employment of syntheses as a means of accessing primal thetic judgements. Synthetic method, Schelling still admits, is 'a true image of absolute method', but one 'pulled apart in reflection' (*SW* 4:399; 2001b, 390).

[24] See *SW* 6:156; 1994c, 153.

replica; this is the universal law of all reflex. (*SW* 6:228–9; translated in White
1983, 85)

This theory of judgement has one crucial consequence for Schelling's theory of
differentiation: individuals are not generated through a synthetic procedure of
determination. The Spinozist maxim, *omnis determinatio est negatio*, is firmly
rejected. Thetic judgements comprise all that there is, and therefore the only
thing that can distinguish one entity from another is the intensity with which
the thesis is posited in different cases. This is a classically monist point: there is
only one substance that comprises all there is; the only differentiating attribute, therefore, is the degree to which this substance is instantiated. This is
what Schelling means when he speaks in the second edition of the *Ideen* of
'degrees of the absolute' (*SW* 2:64; 1988a, 48), or when he writes in the *Fernere
Darstellungen* of 'different grades of identity' (*SW* 4:431) or of individuality
arising out of 'a partial positing of infinite reality' (387). It is also what Grant
means when he speaks of 'the quantity of identity' each entity possesses for
Schelling (2006, 174) or of the fact that 'there can be no differences in kind, but
only in degree' (147).[25]

Quantitative Difference

Two things have now hopefully become clear: first, differentiation is a matter
of form rather than of essence, and, second, it is a matter of the degree to
which the individual produces essential identity. Quantitative differentiation
follows quite simply from these two points.

The *locus classicus* for Schelling's actual formulation of the theory of
quantitative differentiation is the 1801 *Darstellung*. §23 reads, 'None other
than quantitative difference is at all possible between subject and predicate'
(*SW* 4:123; 2001a, 355). Such a thesis has two corollaries. First, 'Any qualitative difference between the two is unthinkable', because 'it is the same equal
absolute identity that is posited as subject and object' (123; 355). That is,
qualitative difference is impossible, because subject and predicate are the same
thing: A = A is universal and no qualitative distinction holds between 'A' and
'A'. Second, Schelling continues,

> Since there is no possible difference between the two in terms of being itself
> (because they are equally unconditioned as subject and object, thus the same in
> essence), there remains only a quantitative difference, i.e. one that obtains with

[25] See also §61 of the 1804 *System* for a remarkable passage in this vein (*SW* 6:212–14; 1994c,
192–4). It should already be clear—and it will become clearer in what follows—that I conflate
intensity and extensity in my discussion of Schelling's account of magnitude. Like form, this key
aspect of the *Identitätssystem* is never thematized. Nevertheless, my hunch is that by speaking of
'potency', Schelling attempts to borrow features of both intensive and extensive magnitude.

respect to the *amount* of being, such that the same identity is posited, but with a predominance of subjectivity or objectivity. (123; 355)

What is crucial in distinguishing entities is the 'amount of being' (or, in Grant's paraphrase, 'quantity of identity' (2006, 174)). Individual *Darstellungen* are not to be thought of as distinct subjects and objects but as various grades of the production of the absolute.

Schelling here spells out explicitly much of what we have already discerned in his thought: he is a monist, therefore in essence all things are one (that is, are absolute identity itself); moreover, this essential identity is always posited *as* identity (i.e. in formal identity). The only possible difference is the different 'amounts' with which such identity is posited. It is this difference in intensity which gives rise to distinctions between subject and object. Difference is quantitative. The same series of moves is made throughout Schelling's *Identitätssystem* often using different terminology, but always making the one basic point: for a rigorous monism, quantity is the only way to distinguish individuals. Hence, rather than the Spinozist 'all determination is negation', Schelling proposes the dictum, 'all determination is quantification'. There is no negation here, merely, in Groves' words, 'the reiterated [thetic] affirmation of [reality's] own existence' (1999, 34). That is, differentiation occurs through excess and surplus: all beings are excesses; it is just how much they are excesses which distinguish them. It is 'this idea so shocking and bizarre of a "surplus"' (Tilliette 1970, 1:260) which marks Schelling's *Identitätssystem* apart from so many other philosophies. Difference is a product of exuberance; there is no lack, no failure, just different amounts of excessive production.

Schelling often speaks of quantitative differentiation in terms of 'relative identities' (4:264) or 'relative points of indifference' (414). In other words, the various different intensities with which essential identity is produced can be roughly schematized into three groupings: a preponderance of the subjective intensity, a preponderance of the objective intensity, and 'a perfect quantitative balance of subjectivity and objectivity' (*SW* 4:127; 2001a, 358). This is the 'threefold mode of appearing' in which one and the same identity is made manifest in three different 'amounts' (*SW* 4:413). Schelling makes this clear in §54 of the 1804 *System*: 'The particularity of all finite things . . . can be grounded either in a reciprocal dominance of one factor [real or ideal] over the other or in the equilibrium of the two . . . These are the only possible differences' (*SW* 6:209–10; 1994c, 191). The *Potenzlehre* will be founded on this threefold grouping.

Schelling's famous magnetic line depicts these three quantities of being (Fig. 1). The middle point is that of relative indifference; on the right side, there is an excess of the subject position (hence the '+' over the 'A'); on the left side, there is a preponderance of the predicate position or of the object (hence the '+' over the B). As Schelling himself writes in respect to this diagram:

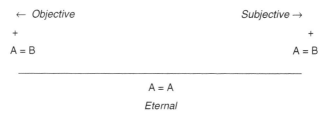

Fig. 1. *The magnetic line* (SW 4:137; 2001a, 365)

> Absolute identity's form of being can thus be universally conceived through the
> image of a *line* where the very same identity is posited in each direction, with A or
> B in the opposite directions, while A = A itself falls at the point of equilibrium.
> (We signify the predominance of one factor over the other by the + sign)... The
> same identity is posited throughout the line, and even at A = B $^+$... Thus we never
> leave the form of subject-objectivity, we never emerge from A = A. All differenti-
> ation consists just in this: A = A is posited in one direction or tendency. (137; 365)

Each point on the line is an affirmation of the self-same identity;[26] however,
each point posits different intensities of this identity, and these intensities can
be grouped into three 'directions or tendencies': the subjective, the objective,
and the indifferent. The direction to the right of the middle indicates an
increasingly positive intensity of indifference; the left of the middle designates
an increasingly negative intensity of indifference.[27] The middle point is that of
relative indifference.

One consequence Schelling draws from the above depiction of the magnetic
line is the overall indifference of the cosmos. While each point on the line
specifies a specific 'amount' of indifference, equilibrium reigns in the All, since
these quantitative differences balance each other out to form a total quantitative indifference. Schelling writes:

> Our assertion is this: if we could view everything that *is* in the totality, we would
> perceive in the whole a perfect quantitative balance of subjectivity and objectiv-
> ity... however much in the perspective of the individual a preponderance might
> occur on one side of the other. (SW 4:127; 2001a, 358)

Schelling's theory of quantitative differentiation is neither analogical nor
dialectical, and this is because there is no qualitative differentiation in Schelling's philosophy, or in other words there is no negation in Schelling's
philosophy. Analogy is founded on a conception of qualitatively distinct
realms of reality, and this alone is enough to see that Schelling cannot hold
to a theory of analogy. Things are not analogously related, for everything is the
same! Phenomena exhibit different degrees of what is identical, and as such

---

[26] 'Identity recurs at all possible stages, changing in form only' (SW 5:272; 1966, 66).

[27] See SW 4:124; 2001a, 356, where Schelling speaks in terms of 'a positive or negative power
of A'.

cannot participate in the complex and delicate balancing of sameness and difference on which theories of analogy, participation, and emanation are founded. As Grant has emphasized in his recent work on Schelling's *Natur-philosophie*, Schelling is not 'another analogizer' (2006, 155).[28] A similar story can be told in respect to Schelling's dismissal of dialectic: dialectic is motored by negation—by the repeated negation and so sublation of qualitatively distinct *Gestalten*. Again, Schelling cannot in any way subscribe to this: differentiation is not for him a product of reiterated negation, but rather of reiterated affirmation or production. Uslar writes, 'The inner movement of Schellingian absolute identity is fundamentally different from Hegel's dialect-ical movement... And the fundamental difference is that Schelling conceives the inner movement of the absolute *without negation*' (1968, 503). Uslar continues, the basis of Schellingian thought 'is not a negation of the negation, but the finite potentiation of an identity of identity' (507).[29] Quantitative differentiation sets the *Identitätssystem* apart.

REFLECTION REVISITED

At this point in the chapter, it is worth returning to the problem of reflection and the manner in which it distorts reality, for Schelling insists that ignorance of quantitative differentiation forms the precondition of all reflection. It should be pointed out from the beginning that there are holes in Schelling's theory of reflection. First, Schelling never decides whether reflection is a property of thinking or being—that is, does the philosopher distort reality or is reality already distorted? He often speaks as if the former is the case, but, as we know, he also rejects the idea that anything but the absolute knows. Ultimately, we should not be surprised at this ambiguity, since we have already seen at length the indissociability of metaphysics and epistemology (being and knowing) for Schelling. Second, there is a correlate problem concerning the origin of reflection: is it an avoidable error or a necessary feature of reality? I incline towards the latter, since Schelling also names the first potency (on which more later in the chapter) the potency of reflection (4:418), suggesting thereby that reflection is an ineluctable part of the distribution of being; however, this does not square with the genealogy of reflection I am about to describe. Once again, Schelling is not clear on this point.

---

[28] See also Grant 2006, 19, 54, 184.
[29] Schematically, one could assert that Schelling sides with Goethean *Steigerung* over Hegelian dialectic. To repeat, this is not so obviously true in respect of Schelling's own dialectic of *Ineinsbildung*.

Everything is in essence identical: 'Identity is universal, all-pervasive and all-encompassing' (*SW* 4:256; 1984a, 157). The entities which produce this identity maximally are named ideas; they express 'clear unclouded identity itself' (*SW* 4:128; 2001a, 358). All distinction is formal and so inessential: there are no distinct substances, nor any qualitatively distinct entities. There are just different quantities or degrees of this self-same identity. Schelling writes, 'We have a single fundamental pattern repeated with continual quantitative variations' (*SW* 5:341; 1966, 140).

In line with all other rigorous monisms, such a worldview leaves no room for falsity. In *Bruno*, for example, Schelling contends, 'No falsehood is possible in nature' (*SW* 4:222; 1984a, 124). Even false thoughts must be productions of absolute identity. The question, then, naturally arises: in what way are they false? And the answer is simple: they possess a low 'amount of being', a minimal degree of productivity. False thoughts are what least produce essential identity. So, again, there is no qualitative distinction between the true and the false, but only a quantitative one: true and false opinions differ in the intensity to which they affirm reality—they differ in degree.

What is important here is that there is no dualism or rupture between reason and reflection.[30] Qualitative thinking is not a different *Gestalt* from quantitative thinking; rather, qualitative difference is reinterpreted by Schelling as a small amount of quantitative difference. This is the reason reflection is designated the first potency: it is not excluded from Schelling's worldview as purely false, but is seen merely as less intense. As always there is a spectrum of positions, not a binary or hierarchy.

In order to see the working of reflection in detail, it is worth looking at two examples of error in Schelling's philosophy and how they need to be interpreted as expressing reality to a low degree.

Qualitative Opposition

The best place to start is the very error Schelling is combating with his theory of quantitative differentiation—a worldview that postulates a plurality of qualitatively distinct substances. It is quite easy to see why such a view only expresses the absolute to a minimal degree. Ideas are the most intense products of absolute identity, because they are structured around the identity of real and ideal, finite and infinite. They are based on identity. They therefore express the nature of the absolute to a maximal extent. Qualitative oppositions, however, are structured around the very opposite notion—the inequality of two things. They presuppose the pervasiveness of antithetical

---

[30] I am following Tilliette (1970, 1:371), *pace* Fischbach (1999, 228) and Lukács (1975, 441–3).

judgements: substance A ≠ substance B. This is, according to Schelling, 'an arbitrary separation of the individual from the whole effected by reflection' (*SW* 4:125; 2001a, 357).[31] Such oppositions express the disunity of all things. Qualitative opposition articulates itself therefore in direct opposition to identity, and so this view of the world produces almost none of the absolute's nature (essential identity). Productivity of qualitative opposition → 0. In Schelling's own words, distinction 'appears as opposition only to one who finds himself outside indifference, who fails to view absolute identity itself as primary and original' (128; 358–9).

Qualitative opposition is therefore a complete misrepresentation of the nature of reality. It is the very worst way of thinking about the world.

Causality

The second 'error' I examine—causality—is a corollary of qualitative opposition. Causality is a product of a world conceived oppositionally, and therefore shares with oppositional thinking a lack of productivity.[32] The notion of causation[33] is premised on a distinction between cause and effect: the two must first be thought of as self-sufficient in themselves and excluding each other for it to make sense to think of them as coming occasionally and accidentally into contact. Causation presupposes distinct substances, thus a worldview of qualitative oppositions. Causal thinking 'tears apart the infinite identity of the idea... and puts the separated factors into a relation of cause and effect' (*SW* 4:283; 1984a, 181).

Hence, in the *Fernere Darstellungen*, Schelling is quick to dismiss any form of cognition that assumes causal relations between things. Any 'type of knowledge which in general rests on the law of mechanism' is labelled 'an eternal and flowing source of error' (*SW* 4:343–4). Genuine philosophy is based on the rejection of causation: 'The main criterion [by which absolute cognition is discerned] is the complete avoidance of the causal law and that worldview in which it is valid' (345).[34]

---

[31] Schelling continues, 'But in itself this separation simply does not happen, since everything that *is* is one.'

[32] Schelling often designates temporality another correlate of oppositional thinking, and so another error of reflection (*SW* 4:115; 2001a, 349—*SW* 4:251; 1984a, 151). This is because what is organically and intrinsically connected in the absolute is separated out and connected merely causally in time. However, such claims are extremely problematic when it comes to the possibility of history. See Zeltner 1975, 103; Wanning 1988, 36.

[33] By 'causation' Schelling means efficient, mechanistic causation of the sort holding between two colliding billiard balls—'lifeless motion' as he pejoratively calls it (*SW* 4:315; 1984a, 209).

[34] See further Hegel 1977a, 116.

A Genealogy of Reflection

Reflection is a form of oppositional thinking. 'Reflection works only from oppositions and rests on oppositions', as Schelling himself puts it (*SW* 4:113; 2001a, 348). In the previous chapter, we saw this in regard to the category of representation—the fact that the subject is said to represent the object presupposes that subject and object are originally opposed and distinct. Such a presupposition, however, is precisely what Schelling questions and we can now understand why. The category of representation fails to acknowledge the quantitative differences which hold between individuals. Reflection (and so representation) is to be defined as minimally expressive thought (*SW* 4:298; 1984a, 195). Reflection is the very worst way of thinking about reality, for it fails to affirm the identity at the heart of all things. 'Reflection dismembers absolute unity' (251; 151). In the 1804 *System*, Schelling puts it as follows:

> The idea is the complete identity of the particular with its universal. Ordinary reflection, which is the opposite of philosophy, remains necessarily in an anti- thetical relation to the universal and particular. It knows the universal and the particular only as two relative negations, by conceiving of the universal as the relative negation of the particular [and] the particular the relative negation of the universal. (*SW* 6:185; 1994c, 173)

No identity or indifference is made manifest by reflection.

What is more, according to Schelling (and this will become increasingly important as I go on to consider the theological dimensions of the *Identitäts- system*), the pervasiveness of reflection has its roots in Christianity: 'The modern world is in general a world of antitheses... [and] dualism [is] an inherently necessary and necessarily recurrent expression of the modern era' (*SW* 5:272–3; 1966, 66–7). It is a particularly modern (or post-Classical) phenomenon. The binaries of sensible and supersensible, human and divine, matter and spirit, body and soul which so define modern thought are all products of reflection, of a way of thinking which qualitatively distinguishes and opposes pairs of phenomena.[35] This cultural inheritance must, Schelling presses, be rejected wholesale. This is the urgent task facing thought. In other words, reflection has 'only *negative* value' (*SW* 2:14; 1988a, 11),[36] and Schel- ling never stops working towards its elimination. His attitude to reflection is summed up in the following,

> As soon as man sets himself in opposition to the external world... reflection first begins; he separates from now on what Nature had always united, separates the object from the intuition, the concept from the image, finally himself from himself... *Mere* reflection, therefore, is a spiritual sickness in mankind, the

---

[35] See *SW* 4:314–15; 1984a, 209.

[36] This is a significant difference between Schelling and Hegel even before 1807.

more so when it imposes himself in dominion over the whole man, and kills at the root what in germ is his highest being... Identity. (*SW* 2:13–14; 1988a, 10–11)

THE POTENCIES

Let us return to the magnetic line. As we saw, Schelling conceives of three different types of 'relative identity'. These three groups are the three different manners in which the absolute is produced, and are designated more technically, 'the three potencies'. As Plessner puts it, 'The respective degree of identity of subject and object is signified by the word "potency"' (1954, 73) Or, in Zeltner's words:

> Potency designates determinate forms or modes of being of absolute identity, corresponding to their respective quantitative difference of subjective or objective. Absolute identity remains unchanged itself; what changes is only the mode, the way of being. (1975, 88)[37]

The three potencies therefore correspond to the three moments on the magnetic line: the third potency (named, 'the eternal') affirms the absolute indifferently (and so corresponds to the ideas); the first potency emphasizes the finite or the objective pole; while the second potency emphasizes the infinite or the subjective pole.

The Recursion of the Potencies

The magnetic line is so important to Schelling because it exhibits one of the most crucial properties of the potencies—their infinite recurrence. 'All potencies repeat themselves' (*SW* 4:419). If one takes any point on the line, the same structure which is present over the whole line will there recur in miniature: 'The same identity is posited throughout the line... What holds for the line as a whole, holds too for each individual section of it unto infinity... The constructed line is divisible unto infinity' (*SW* 4:137–8; 2001a, 365). For example, on the right hand side of the line (which in general is subsumed under the first potency), the same three potencies recur in miniature, and so the structure of the magnetic line as a whole is reproduced on this smaller scale. To quote Schelling once more:

> Each point of the line, depending on how it is viewed, is the indifference-point and pole or its opposite... Every point can also serve as indifference-point

---

[37] See *SW* 5:365–6; 1989, 14.

relative to some other, or become now one, now the other of the two opposed end-poles, depending on how I divide the line. (138; 366)

This process takes place *ad infinitum*, which is, of course, the case with magnets too: any part of a magnet recapitulates the same polar structure (i.e. with one end magnetized to the North, the other to the South, and a point of indifference in between); hence, no matter how small one breaks up a magnet, the parts will still take on the properties of the whole. It is for this reason the magnetic line 'is the symbol for a potency as such' (139; 367).

In terms of the theory of the potencies itself, it is quite evident why they must repeat themselves *ad infinitum*. The first potency, for example, in emphasizing the finite (or objective), does not exhibit just the finite element of the ideas, but rather it exhibits identity finitely. Hence, identity is still the one and only content and essence of reality, merely expressed in a different way: 'Absolute identity is in the individual under the same form under which it is in the whole... It is *entirely* in every individual' (132; 361). Each potency recapitulates the structure of identity: each potency thus re-presents all three potencies while still emphasizing one. In consequence, 'The original identity is maintained in each of these three identities' (*SW* 4:425). The threefold grouping of relative identities is implicit within each particular potency.

It is this property of infinite recursion which gives rise to the baroque Porphyrian trees which plague Schelling's works (as well as works on Schelling). For example, reality as a whole can be split into three potencies:[38] the finite which corresponds to the natural world, the infinite which corresponds to the ideal world, and the point of indifference between the two which corresponds to reason. Within the natural world, the three potencies recur as matter, light, and organism; within the ideal world they recur as thought, act, and art. To take just art as our example: within the realm of the artwork, the three potencies recur again: as 'formative art' (i.e. non-verbal art), verbal art, and a problematic third term (to which we will return in a later chapter). Both types of art are again split into three. To take the example of formative art alone, it is formed of the three potencies of music, painting, and sculpture; furthermore, music, for example, is in turn split into three: rhythm, modulation, and melody. And, of course, in principle this splitting could go on endlessly: 'Just as this three-in-oneness expresses itself in the whole of philosophy, so too it is, in turn, expressed in every single part of it' (424).

This portioning up of reality is one of the most problematic-seeming elements of Schelling's philosophy and critics from Hegel onwards have not stinted in mocking it.[39] However, it is crucial to see the necessity of infinite

---

[38] The following schema is a generalized one; different formulations have their own idiosyncrasies. See Tilliette 1970, 1:417–21.

[39] See Hegel 1977b, §§51–3.

recursion within the *Identitätssystem*. If identity is all there is and this identity always manifests itself in a threefold manner, then all productions of the absolute will have three elements to them. Everything that exists (as we have seen) is a quantity of identity, and, as such, possesses exactly the same properties as any other quantity of identity. Hence, musical rhythm is just as much subject to the law of the threefold appearance of identity as light or as action. 'Everything that is is reducible to three potencies' (340).

The *Potenzlehre* is not an inchoate dialectic. The *Potenzlehre* and dialectical thought are absolutely incommensurable, and this is because the former is grounded on a quantitative and the latter on a qualitative conception of reality. Dialectics, it is true, often has a threefold structure, but these three elements are successively produced by means of negating the previous elements in the series. There is a relation between them of opposition and sublation. No such structure applies to the theory of the potencies: each potency possesses a degree of productivity which is more or less than the others. The differences between them are strictly quantitative. Moreover, in consequence, while the dialectic is a process where each element succeeds the previous one, this is not necessarily true of the potencies. Everything, in Szondi's words, 'is always already given and developed' for Schelling (1974, 1:223). Or, in other words, potencies can co-exist. 'The potencies must be thought as contemporaneous', as Marquet rightly points out (1973, 225).[40] Schelling's theory of the potencies is not a preliminary version of anything, but a fully-fledged understanding of the way reality works, which is to be set in opposition to dialectical understandings.

The Three Potencies

All three potencies are present in all things, even if one potency dominates there. So, for example, the first potency is that of finitude; it corresponds to the natural world. However, there is also an element of the ideal world where the first potency predominates (thought), as well as aspects of the natural world in which the other potencies predominate. We return here to Schelling's insistence that nothing is purely finite or purely infinite, purely real or purely ideal. Everything is a compound of the two, or, more precisely: in everything all three potencies recur. To speak, then, of the natural world as real or even to speak (as Schelling himself often does[41]) of an 'ideal world' is to reduce what is complex to what is simple. The natural world does not precisely correspond to

---

[40] See further Tilliette 1970, 1:377, 422–4; Zeltner 1975, 88. Marquet also rightly points out that, as the *Identitätssystem* progresses, Schelling becomes increasingly fond of thinking of the potencies as a historical sequence. See Marquet 1973, 319–23; Fischbach 1999, 248.

[41] See *SW* 2:65; 1988a, 49, or *SW* 4:417.

the first potency; in the natural world, the finite is dominant, but is still only one aspect of the threefold mode in which the absolute expresses itself. There is no simple one-to-one correspondence between entities and potencies: all entities are a compound mixture of all three potencies. One potency may be more fully present in any one entity, but the other two will always be found somewhere in the mix.

Again, we see that there is no such thing as a finite entity or pure finitude for Schelling. Everything that exists is a mixture of finite, infinite and eternal: 'All potencies are once again contained in all things' (*SW* 4:418). In short, a crucial principle of the *Identitätssystem* is the necessarily compound nature of all things.

What differentiates the three potencies is the different extent to which they produce identity. 'These unities,' Schelling writes, 'each of which signifies a definite degree of embodiment of the infinite into the finite, are represented in three potencies' (*SW* 2:68; 1988a, 51).[42] That is, the potencies are grouped according to amounts of intensity, and each potency produces the absolute more intensely than the last.[43] 'Potency' is a mathematical term synonymous with power or indice: each potency expresses a determinate power of reality ('reality squared' and so forth). Yet, we must be clear that there is no such thing as reality prior to potentiation: 'Identity... is always potentiated' (Zeltner 1975, 88). As Schelling puts it, 'The absolute is beyond all powers or it is strictly devoid of power' (*SW* 6:212; 1994c, 192), by which he means that the absolute 'as such' is a fiction (and a pernicious one at that); it is nothing or 0.[44] In other words, nothing exists outside of form. Reality, beginning from nothing, gradually potentiates or affirms itself into more and more intense forms until finally the surplus reaches its maximum (in the idea or the eternal).

The third potency (the eternal) therefore produces essential identity to the maximum possible extent. It is self-evident why this is the case: the third potency is that in which neither the subjective nor objective dominates, but both are expressed equally. It is the potency of relative indifference, and hence the point where indifference is most produced. The third potency manifests most reality; in other words, it is most productive of the absolute. In all things, it is equivalent to *the idea of* that thing. Because the eternal is the point of greatest productivity, it is what will be of most interest in what follows. I will be especially interested in those entities in which the eternal is dominant: organisms, art, reason, philosophy, and theology. To take the example of the organism: in the organism, the first

---

[42] See further Vater 1984, 46; Grant 2006, 174.

[43] In regard to the first two potencies, Schelling wavers between a Leibnizian position and a Spinozist position. On the former, the second, ideal potency expresses more of the absolute than the first potency (*SW* 5:306; 1966, 103). On a rigorously Spinozist position, ideal and real express the absolute to the same, parallel degree (*SW* 4:416).

[44] The potencies can thus be formulated as $0^2, 0^3 \ldots 0^n$.

two potencies of the natural world (matter and light) are made indifferent to one another. 'Matter is entirely light and light entirely matter' (*SW* 2:107; 1988a, 138). The organism is, Schelling continues, the 'highest marriage of matter and form...the production of the real indifference point in the real world' (107–8; 138). The organism takes what is emphasized in the first potency and what is emphasized in the second and makes them equivalent. For this reason, 'The organism [is] the highest expression of nature' (108; 138). As we shall see, Schelling makes very similar claims about the other entities in which the third potency predominates as well.

Bildung

As a final coda to this chapter, there is a further consequence of Schelling's *Potenzlehre* I would like to draw attention to, and that is an implicit theory of *Bildung* that the foregoing has suggested.

Crudely put, Romantic and Idealist theories of *Bildung* can be summed up in Friedrich Schlegel's fragment: 'Every good human being is always progressively becoming God. To become God, to be human, to cultivate oneself are all expressions that mean the same thing' (1971, §262). Education is a process of divinization. More concretely, this usually involves the imperative that all individual raise themselves up above the particular, thrown situation in which they finds themselves, so as to access what is universal. Moreover, it is art, religion, and philosophy that are the three most common media through which it is recommended to pass in order to annul one's particularity and access what is universal. Such is the goal of human life—a process of *Bildung*, of self-formation towards the absolute.[45]

There is a parallel demand in Schelling's *Identitätssystem*: the call to maximize one's productivity, to generate essential identity to the greatest possible extent. As Schelling puts it, 'The degree of perfection or of the reality of a thing increases to the extent that it corresponds to its own absolute idea and to the fullness of infinite affirmation' (*SW* 5:381; 1989, 29), or again, 'To strive towards blessedness = to strive as a particular to partake of absoluteness' (397; 39). And Troxler similarly mentions in his lecture notes 'the striving of the individual after absolute being' (1988, 36).[46] It is the notion of 'striving' that is important here—a dynamic process through which productivity is maximized. Schelling is most explicit in the 1804 *System*. §63 reads, 'The degree of reality held by each thing as such is in proportion to its approximation of the absolute identity' (*SW* 6:212; 1994c, 193), and in elucidating this claim, Schelling suggests that this 'approximation' is not a static state of affairs; rather,

---

[45] See Gadamer 2004, 8–17.
[46] See further *SW* 4:395; 2001b, 387—*SW* 4:233; 1984a, 134.

there 'is a *progressively* more perfect reflection of the universe' (213; 193; my emphasis). Schelling here implies a dynamic process through which each *Darstellung* cultivates its productivity. Moreover, this is made explicit in the next paragraph when Schelling adds, 'The proportion in which the particular . . . *becomes* more akin to the universe is the same as that in which the nothing or the privation *is being overcome or diminished* within the universe' (214; 194; my emphases).[47] Again, the verbs are dynamic: degree of approximation to the absolute is not set in stone; phenomena can intensify such approximation. Such is 'the endeavour of . . . all difference to return to identity' (*SW* 2:106; 1988a, 137).

In short, the imperative for *Darstellungen*, according to Schelling, is to become ideas, since ideas are those entities which most express identity. Each entity must strive to cultivate the third potency within it and to foster the eternal until it becomes its dominant potency (as in organisms and artworks). This is the Schellingian theory of *Bildung*—'a gradual intensification of all form' (*SW* 5:147; 2008, 285).[48] Form is indeed key here, for the 'amount' of essential identity produced is directly dependent on formal identity. Therefore, the form of a *Darstellung* is central to its cultivation of the third potency. Forms must approach the law of identity as closely as possible, for in so doing they approach the form of ideas. The task for all *Darstellungen* is therefore to articulate identity more intensely. 'The challenge,' the conclusion to *Bruno* states, '[is] to cultivate the sturdy seed of this principle of indifference to its fullest flower', for this will bring about 'the inevitable divinization of mankind' (*SW* 4:328–9; 1984a, 222).

The whole *Identitätssystem* is marked by quantitative differentiation. This doctrine leads Schelling to discard synthesis, antithesis, analogy, and dialectic. All differences are excesses of affirmation in either the finite, the infinite, or the eternal. Schelling's *Potenzlehre* in which each potency designates one type of excessive affirmation also follows from this theory. Reality consists, according to Schelling, in ideas and their refracted forms; all these entities are *Darstellungen*, exhibiting reality determinately, and the only way in which they are differentiated is the quantity or intensity with which they do so.

---

[47] See also *SW* 5:381; 1989, 29—384; 31.

[48] Schelling explicitly links this cultivation of identity with traditional conceptions of *Bildung* in *Über die Methode*: science provides 'training for rational thinking' and also 'guides the mind directly to the vision which in a continuous self-creating process *leads us to identity with ourselves* and thereby to a truly blessed life' (*SW* 5:238; 1966, 31; my emphasis).

6

Construction

I now turn to Schelling's epistemology. As always my task is to excavate the principles underlying his peculiar interpretation of symbolic language. In the present chapter, it is Schelling's employment of construction which is most significant for this task. The term 'construction' is a frequent one in Schelling's oeuvre between 1801 and 1805. One of the most important essays of the period is entitled *Über die Construktion in der Philosophie*, and argues at length, *pace* Kant, that construction holds a central place in the philosophical enterprise. Similarly, one of the *Fernere Darstellungen* is again entitled *Von der philosophischen Construktion*. I argue that by constantly appealing to this notion Schelling reveals the extent to which his epistemology draws on the constructive tradition of early modern philosophy. Schelling stands at the end of a long line of constructive thinkers, running through Descartes, Hobbes, and Spinoza. The role construction played in modern thought is often neglected; yet it formed (at least until 1805) a valid, irreducible alternative to more frequently stressed sources of knowledge (perception, deduction, and dialectic).

A BRIEF HISTORY OF CONSTRUCTION
FROM EUCLID TO FICHTE

The Entrance of Construction into Modernity

To claim Schelling derives construction from early modern philosophy is *prima facie* a strange claim, for the term's more famous origins are to be found in ancient Greek geometry. However, what distinguishes the modern appropriation of construction is its redeployment in philosophy: while it remains tethered to geometry in ancient Greek thought, in modernity construction is gradually set free to become an ideal for all science. In this first section, I elucidate this process.

Euclid's *Elements* repeatedly emphasizes the need to 'construct' geometrical figures; indeed, the very first three propositions of the whole work ask for constructions. Such propositions are called 'problems' (as opposed to 'theorems' which operate by means of logical deduction, not construction).[1] One of the main differences between theorems and problems is the tag which ends the proposition. Instead of the famous 'QED' (*quod erat demonstrandum*), many problems end 'QEF' (*quod erat faciendum* or, in the original Greek, ὅπερ ἔδει ποιῆσαι). Problems are to be 'done' (produced or generated[2]) so as to exhibit the required property. Problems are productive, rather than deductive. While therefore Euclid's *Elements* is usually read as an exercise in deduction (beginning from a set number of definitions and subsequently deriving the properties of figures from these definitions alone), such a reading neglects the problems. The question is therefore: why does Euclid sometimes resort to construction rather than deduction? Why is logic sometimes insufficient?

Numerous answers to this question have been given over the centuries. In early modernity, however, one solution dominated—the Menaechmean.[3] On the Menaechmean interpretation of geometry, construction is proof of existence. As one commentator puts it, 'In the geometry of the *Elements*, the existence of one object is always inferred from the existence of another by means of construction... [There is] an identification of existence and constructibility' (Mueller 1981, 15). Constructions make assertoric claims that theorems are unable to. By constructing figures, the geometer demonstrates their actuality; he exhibits the reality of the figures he is using in his work—something that theorems (which operate solely on the level of necessity) are unable to do.

With Descartes, both the 'problematic' and the 'constructive' nature of knowledge is placed centre-stage.[4] As Lachterman succinctly puts it, 'For Descartes QED is always a pendant for QEF' (1989, 156). Construction thus becomes the new ideal for knowledge in early modern thought. It is summed up in Vico's famous adage, *verum et factum convertuntur*:

> *Verum et factum convertuntur*—the identity of truth with doing, or of knowledge with construction—had been seen in the Middle Ages, at best, as the character of divine knowledge. In the seventeenth century, it became also the mark of human knowledge... A new ideal of knowledge was born—the ideal of knowledge-by-doing or knowledge-by-construction. (Funkenstein 1986, 12)

Thus, while Ficino writes during the Renaissance, 'Divine thought produces its objects according to reasons, like the spirit of geometry produces its figures

---

[1] See Heath 1926, 125.

[2] All terms originally used in this context. See Funkenstein 1986, 299.

[3] I here follow Lachterman 1989. On Menaechmeus, see Heath 1926, 125.

[4] Both Funkenstein (1986, 316) and Lachterman (1989, 4) see this as symptomatic of modernity's concern for action over contemplation. In Lachterman's words, 'The mind is first and last *poietic*.'

from itself',[5] the seventeenth century adds that humanity has access to this initial production in geometry, and this allows the practitioner to, as it were, replay in their own constructions the initial creation of things.

It is in Hobbes that the fullest appropriation of Euclidean geometry is to be found. Indeed, Hobbes even uses construction to criticize Euclid, for, he claims, the latter's definitions are not 'problematic' enough: they are inadequate because they do not rehearse the construction of the figures they define: 'If the first principles, that is to say the definitions, contain not the generation of the subject, there can be nothing demonstrated as it ought to be' (1845, 7:184). Figures must be defined in terms of what is necessary to produce them; they must be defined in terms of their cause. Such is a 'genetic definition': it is to define something by the method of its construction. Genetic definitions are *performative*: they enact the construction they describe and so 'prove' the existence of the figure they stipulate. In the process of giving a genetic definition, the very definition itself changes from one that is merely nominal to a real definition. *Verum et factum convertuntur*: by knowing the definition of a figure, the figure itself is brought into existence.

For Hobbes, genetic definitions are not merely the province of geometry; they also pertain to ethics and political philosophy—that is, everything of which man is the creator. Since we have the power to generate institutions and codes of behaviour, we are also able to construct them in philosophy:

> Geometry therefore is demonstrable, for the lines and figures from which we reason are drawn and described by ourselves; and civil philosophy is demonstrable, because we make the commonwealth ourselves. (183)

Political philosophy, like geometry, is a constructive enterprise.

However, while construction is the starting-point of philosophy, it is not the only method employed therein. Synthesis (or deduction) is also a crucial element in Hobbes' vision of philosophy: after an initial moment of construction, 'the whole method of demonstration is *synthetical*' (1:80). Philosophy proceeds from cause to effect, but in order to reach the causes in the first place, it must begin by practising genetic definitions. Such definitions construct the fundamental causes on which the rest of the demonstration rests. Philosophy requires an initial moment of construction.

Spinozan Construction

There is no doubting that Spinoza was markedly influenced by Hobbes' conception of philosophy, and especially his demand for genetic definitions.[6]

---

[5] Quoted in Gueroult 1974, 2:480.   [6] See Gueroult 1974, 2:481–5.

Just as Hobbes maintained that the whole of a science could be deduced from one cause constructed by means of a genetic definition, so too did Spinoza, as we shall see. However, Spinoza radically extends the terrain beyond what Hobbes sees as legitimate for genetic definitions: while Hobbes limited this method to geometry and moral and political philosophy, Spinoza extends it to all domains of knowledge. All causes are in principle constructible, and this is because, insofar as the idea of God is constructible, everything can be deduced from it, since everything follows logically from God's essence (Spinoza 1994, IP16). At stake in the *Ethics*, therefore, is the formulation of a genetic definition of God. In order to begin, the *Ethics* must construct God and then deduce everything from such a construction:

> Just as geometry obtains its genetic knowledge by constructing its figures and then deducing from them everything that necessarily follows, so too philosophy will construct the essence of God and, from that genetic definition, will deduce all that it is possible to deduce. (Gueroult 1974, 2:473)

However, this is not to say construction itself plays much of a role in the *Ethics*. Spinoza always employs the Euclidean tag QED, and never QEF. He takes from Euclid, more than anything else, the idea of the theorem and its deductive structure, rather than anything to do with the problem.[7] Deduction dominates the *Ethics*. There is a good reason, however, for this lack of construction: constructions exhibit how things are produced, how they follow from their cause; yet, for Spinoza, all things follow from one sole cause in the very same way—they all follow necessarily and immediately from God. It would therefore be redundant for Spinoza to continually keep offering constructions. They would be unnecessary repetitions. Once the readers of the *Ethics* have seen the way in which God is the cause of one thing, they have seen it all!

Nevertheless, there is still one construction that is absolutely necessary for the *Ethics*. This is the very beginning of the work. Here, construction is initially required in order to reach the idea of God in the first place. Deduction requires a 'prologue'—the initial construction of God as cause. In order to begin the deductive process, one initial construction is necessary that exhibits God as the absolute and unique cause of reality. The *Ethics*, that is, does not (as is usually asserted) begin with the idea of God, but rather begins with the *construction of the idea of God*. To understand Spinoza's use of construction, one must therefore look to how the *Ethics* begins.

The opening of the *Ethics* from the first definition through to IP11 provides a genetic definition of God. Spinoza had already stated in *De emendatione intellectu*:

---

[7] See König 1976, 1010.

To unite and order all our perceptions, it is required, and reason demands, that we ask, *as soon as possible*, whether there is a certain being, and at the same time, what sort of being it is, which is the cause of all things, so that its objective essence may also be the cause of all our ideas, and then our mind will ... reproduce nature as much as possible. For it will have Nature's essence, order and unity objectively. (Spinoza 1985, §99; my emphasis)

This is Spinoza's fullest programmatic statement of his method. He emphasizes deduction: from the idea of God, our mind can 'reproduce nature'; however, he also acknowledges that what makes deduction possible in the first place is acquiring the idea of 'the cause of all things' as quickly as possible. Philosophy, Spinoza makes clear, cannot begin with God, but must proceed to God in the fastest possible way. As Deleuze puts it, 'The synthetic method *invents or feigns* a cause [in order to begin] ... We should recognise [in this] a minimal regression which allows us, *as quickly as possible*, to reach the idea of God as the source of all other ideas' (1990, 161).[8] Spinoza thus proceeds in the first propositions step-by-step through a 'genesis of the divine', rehearsing the manner in which substance constitutes itself.[9] And from this one construction alone, Spinoza is in a position to deduce the whole of reality.

Kant and Construction

In the previous sections I narrated how 'problem' and 'construction' became crucial not only for mathematics, but also for how philosophy was understood in early modernity. This process continued into late eighteenth-century Germany, and only in 1780 was Kant able to halt the rise of construction. However, far from changing the constructive way in which philosophy was understood, Kant's misgivings spurred his successors on to integrate construction into philosophy even further. Construction is an indispensable element of any account of German Idealist philosophy.

What does Kant mean by 'construction'? Obviously, we already know roughly what he means: it is to make or produce a concept. He defines it as follows, 'To construct a concept means to exhibit a priori the intuition which corresponds to the concept' (2007, A713/B741). There are three aspects to construction, according to this definition: the act of exhibiting, the intuition which is exhibited, and the a priori manner in which this is done.

First, construction is a form of *Darstellung*; as such, my discussion of this concept in the previous chapter needs to be borne in mind. A *Darstellung* provides a sensible figure for a mathematical concept; what is more, this

---

[8] See further 136–7.
[9] For detailed accounts of this process, see Gueroult 1974, 1:37–8; Deleuze 1990, 75–6; Macherey 1996, 157.

concept is immediately produced in intuition through construction. There is a direct, intrinsic relation between the concept of an isosceles triangle and an exhibition of one. Mathematics makes its concepts as intuitions.

The second element of construction is intuition. In Chapters 1 and 2, I began to look at some of the properties of intuition in the eighteenth-century philosophical tradition. First, intuition is immediate (as opposed to symbolic cognition); second, an intuition is a particular (whereas concepts are universal). It follows that to exhibit a concept in intuition is to particularize it. This shift to the singular provides the geometer with information mere concepts cannot provide. Kant writes:

> I must not restrict my attention to what I am actually thinking in my concept of a triangle; I must pass beyond it to properties which are not contained in this concept, but yet belong to it. Now this is impossible unless I determine my object in … pure intuition. (2007, A718/B746)

In so doing, 'we succeed in arriving at results which discursive knowledge could never have reached by means of mere concepts' (A717/B745). So, Kant contends (in line with Euclid) that exhibition gives us access to more properties than concepts alone. Yet, Kant also points out that to 'singularize' a concept is not enough. An intuition must both be a single object, 'and yet nonetheless, as the construction of a concept (a universal representation), it must in its representation express universal validity for all possible intuitions which fall under the same concept' (A713/B741). This is the paradoxical crux of construction: the individual figure must represent the general concept. That is, here universal and particular coincide: the universal concept is fully and directly instantiated in the particular intuition.

The final element of Kantian construction is its a priori character. It is not any intuition which can exhibit a mathematical concept, but specifically an a priori one. As Kant insists, 'For the construction of a concept, we therefore need a *non-empirical* intuition' (A713/B741). Mere empirical depiction is insufficient; instead, a pure intuition is required. Mathematical construction is not an experience; it occurs in a purer, a priori medium.

Just as important as Kant's understanding of construction is his *prohibition* of its use in philosophy. The *Kritik der reinen Vernunft* rejects the assimilation of construction into philosophy (the goal which had orientated so much pre-Kantian thought). Kant's Discipline of Pure Reason thus begins, '*Philosophical* knowledge is the *knowledge gained by reason from concepts*; mathematical knowledge is the knowledge gained by reason from the construction of concepts' (A713/B742). Philosophy and mathematics are to be fundamentally distinguished and it is construction which distinguishes them: while the philosopher is unable to use this method, the mathematician has to use it. Thus, Kant rails repeatedly against the misguided appropriation of construction by philosophers:

[It is] necessary to cut away the last anchor of [philosophy's] fantastic hopes, that is, to show that the pursuit of the mathematical method cannot be of the least advantage in this kind of knowledge; and that mathematics and philosophy...[are] so completely different, that the procedure of one can never be imitated by the other. (A726/B754)[10]

The reason for this is, in short, that philosophy does not produce intuitions. It remains entirely at a conceptual level, whereas mathematics 'hastens' to intuition. Kant states, 'Philosophy confines itself to universal concepts; mathematics can achieve nothing by concepts alone but hastens at once to intuition, in which it considers the concept *in concreto*' (A715/B743). Kant emphasizes the purely analytic method of philosophy: nothing 'new' can ever be discovered by the philosopher. 'It would be therefore quite futile for me to philosophise upon the triangle...I should not be able to advance a single step beyond the mere definition' (A718-19/B746-7). The mathematician does not have this problem: through construction new information becomes evident. It is thus the inaccessibility of construction which means that mathematics 'can never be imitated by' philosophy (A726/B754).

Fichtean Autoconstruction

As with many other Kantian prohibitions, it fell to Fichte to begin to question the separation of philosophy and construction.[11] Throughout his career, Fichte places construction at the heart of the *Wissenschaftslehre* (even if often only implicitly)[12] and (more importantly for our purposes) he also proposes a new variant of the concept—self-construction. The philosopher sits back to watch reality construct itself.

This is best garnered from a letter Fichte wrote to Schelling in November 1800, just a few months before Schelling embarked on the *Identitätssystem*. Here, Fichte characterizes science as self-construction:

Science...must certainly posit nature as *absolute*, and must have nature *construct itself* by means of a *fiction*; similarly, transcendental philosophy has consciousness construct itself *through the same type of fiction*. (*SB* 2:291; Fichte and Schelling 1997, 74)

As Breazeale points out, in his reply Schelling 'enthusiastically accepted' this model for philosophical methodology (2002, 187), writing, 'I am fully in agreement' (*SB* 2:297; Fichte and Schelling 1997, 77). In consequence, what

[10] See further A712/B740, A724/B752.
[11] See Lachterman 1989, 16. Maimon's reinsertion of construction into transcendental idealism is another key precedent for Schelling's epistemology.
[12] See Ende 1973; Helfer 1996, 61-9; Breazeale 2002, 175-6.

Fichte here writes is key to understanding the role construction will play in Schelling's *Identitätssystem* and, in short, he recommends letting nature or consciousness construct itself. Construction is not a method which the philosopher imposes on reality; it is a process that reality itself is already undergoing. Something constructs itself and the philosopher charts this process. Construction therefore shifts from methodological to ontological import. Breazeale describes the role of the Fichtean philosopher thus, 'The philosopher ... sets the original I "in motion" and simply sits back to *observe it in its self-construction* and to *describe* what he thus "observes" in "inner intuition"' (2002, 192).

However, this account needs qualification, since Fichte does not pursue autoconstruction wholeheartedly. He still distinguishes between the self-construction of reality and the *reconstruction* the philosopher performs in order to recapture this original construction. In Ende's words, 'Fichte opposes the original construction of the I and of being to reconstruction in philosophy ... He designates philosophy as the reconstruction of original knowing' (1973, 43). Schelling, as we shall see, collapses this distinction, so that the self-construction of the absolute is indistinguishable from philosophical construction.

SCHELLING'S *AUSEINANDERSETZUNG* WITH KANT

Schelling's programmatic article, *Über Construktion*, begins with a manifesto commitment to construction in epistemology:

> Since philosophy can neither surpass the narrow limits of Kantian criticism, nor advance upon the path inaugurated by Fichte to a positive and apodictic philosophy without rigorously introducing the method of construction, the following text sketches and presents with the greatest clarity that central point upon which the scientific fulfilment of philosophy depends. In the future, the doctrine of philosophical construction will constitute one of the most important aspects of scientific philosophy: it is undeniable that due to the lack of a concept of construction many philosophers' participation in the advances of scientific philosophy are hindered. The drive to a rigorous construction, developed from first principles, is the most powerful means against a certain false liberality ... Construction is a powerful means against the muddle of all perspectives which confuses the true and false and makes them indistinguishable. (*SW* 5:125; 2008, 271)

Only through construction can philosophy truly claim to be a science; only through construction can the true and the false be distinguished. Construction is the *sine qua non* of epistemology and philosophical methodology in general. It is the only means, Schelling insists, of going beyond Kant and beyond Fichte. Schellingian epistemology is, in consequence, thoroughly constructive.[13]

With such an argument, Schelling explicitly and purposefully allies himself with the early moderns. Spinoza especially is the key point of reference for his understanding of construction:

> The great example that Spinoza bequeathed philosophy, through his usage of the geometrical method, instead of spurring on the perfection of that method, actually had the opposite effect...If Spinoza erred [however], it is because he did not go far enough back in his construction. (126–7; 272)

Schelling intends to reverse the anti-Spinozist—and that means anti-constructivist—tendencies of recent thought by resurrecting the constructive procedures preserved in Spinoza's geometrical method. In order to achieve this, he embarks on a detailed refutation of Kant's separation of philosophy and construction. To begin therefore, I rehearse Schelling's arguments against Kant.

Criticisms of Kant

While generally hostile to Kant on this issue, Schelling does still appropriate much from the former's understanding of construction (*SW* 5:127–8; 2008, 273). Key here is Kant's definition of construction 'as the identification of *concept* and *intuition*' (128; 273). Construction, Schelling glosses, 'must express itself, on the one hand, as an intuition that is singular and concrete and, on the other hand, as a construction of a concept that is universally valid for all possible intuitions belonging under the same concept' (128; 273). And in so glossing, he endorses Kant's definition of construction as the identity of universal and particular.

There are still three basic criticisms, however, Schelling makes of Kantian construction. First, Kant allows for the possibility of a non-empirical intuition in geometry, but this, Schelling argues, suggests that non-empirical (specifically intellectual) intuition is possible in other domains as well. Kant should, that is, draw the obvious inferences that, first, there are non-empirical intuitions corresponding to philosophy as well as geometry and so, second, construction is possible in philosophy (128–9; 273).

Second, Schelling argues that the distinction Kant draws between mathematics and philosophy is one wholly immanent to mathematics itself. He does so on the basis of one specific definition of Kant's: 'Philosophical

---

[13] In what follows, I limit myself to Schelling's post-1801 account of construction; its crucial role in his *Naturphilosophie* and *System des transzendentalen Idealismus* should not be forgotten, however. See Ende 1973, 51–3, and Verra 1979, 31–3.

knowledge considers the particular only in the universal, mathematical know-ledge the universal in the particular' (2007, A714/B742). Schelling responds:

> Arithmetic expresses the particular in the universal, geometry expresses the univer-sal in the particular. Thus it is evident that all oppositions made possible through the antithesis of the universal and the particular fall under mathematics itself and that philosophy is not in opposition to mathematics. (5:130–1; 2008, 275)

Schelling has a point. While Kant's understanding of arithmetic is the subject of much debate, many commentators agree with Schelling that Kant sees symbols, such as '7' and '+', as universals which express particulars.[14] It is on this basis that Schelling argues that Kant's above definition of the difference between mathematics and philosophy does not hold, for mathematics itself has a branch which considers the particular in the universal. The essence of philosophy, Schelling then claims, cannot lie where Kant thinks it did in either of these determinations (universal in particular or particular in universal), but rather in a third option, and the only possible third option, according to Schelling, is the complete equivalence of universal and particular. This is the standpoint which characterizes philosophy, the standpoint of indifference: 'When each side must be *either* a presentation of the universal in the particular *or* the particular *in the universal*, then philosophy is *neither* of these, but rather the *presentation of their unity in absolute indifference*' (131; 275).

Third, Schelling argues that Kant fails to discern this 'third option' (indiffer-ence), because his conceptual armoury is lacking one significant notion: 'idea'. Ideas, as we know, exhibit precisely the indifference of universal and particular Kant is searching for in his discussion of construction. Kant tries to discover a particular intuition which is the complete and immediate instantiation of its universal concept—to Schelling, he is searching for the idea. 'Concepts will not be constructed in any other way than as ideas' (133; 277), since construction is 'always the absolute and *real* equalization of universal and particular' (131–2; 276) and only ideas exhibit this identity. The 'struggle' between the universal and particular, Schelling concludes, 'can *only* be solved through the construc-tion *of the idea*' (135; 278; my emphases). By recovering the notion of an idea, Schelling is able to not only discover the archetypal construction where universal concept and particular intuition coincide, but also to show how philosophy (the study of ideas) has a construction proper to it alone.

Philosophy and Mathematics

Schelling therefore rejects Kant's dichotomy between constructive mathemat-ics and non-constructive philosophy. Philosophy is constructive too. What,

---

[14] Llewelyn (1990, 182) cites Kant (2007, B205) in support of Schelling's view.

then, is the difference between mathematical and philosophical construction? In short, Schelling conceives of a three-term 'parallelism' (Tilliette 1995, 189) in which philosophy, geometry, and arithmetic are all constructive but each in different ways. This trinity corresponds to the three potencies:

> [Arithmetic] expresses the unity of the finite and the infinite in the infinite, or the unity of pure identity, [geometry] the same unity in the finite, or the unity of difference. Philosophy, however, can have but one method, since it expresses its construction neither in the one nor in the other potency but only in the eternal, in unity considered in and for itself. (*SW* 4:399; 2001b, 390)

In arithmetic, the infinite potency dominates, in geometry the finite, and in philosophy the eternal. These are the three possible modes of construction.

This leads to a situation where philosophy and mathematics are not antithetical (as in Kant), but rather mutually inform one another. Mathematics is the science (the only science, in fact) which prepares us for philosophical argumentation. Schelling quotes with approval the Platonic dictum, 'Let none enter who is not initiated into geometry' (*SW* 7:143; 1984b, 246), and is particularly partial throughout the *Identitätssystem* to geometrical examples to illustrate philosophical points.[15] Mathematics and philosophy have a particularly close, symbiotic relationship, and this is because they are both constructive disciplines. 'The two are fully alike,' Schelling makes clear, 'in terms of their type of cognition' (*SW* 4:347–8).

As constructive, mathematics (as well as philosophy) shuns less productive ways of thinking about the world, like causality. Mathematics 'transcends the law of causality which dominates ordinary knowledge (many so-called "sciences"); it rises into the realm of pure identity' (*SW* 5:253; 1966, 47). Mathematics and philosophy are alike in the attention they give the identity of universal and particular—the realm of ideas.[16]

There is nonetheless no doubting for Schelling philosophy's superiority to mathematics: 'The peculiarity of philosophy as a science is that it is wholly and immediately itself in the absolute, whereas mathematics in general and geometry and arithmetic in particular are only the fruits of true philosophy' (*SW* 4:348). Mathematics is only 'relatively absolute, since neither space nor time is the idea of all ideas, but each is only a separate reflection of it' (*SW* 5:252; 1966, 46). Geometry deals with 'sensibly reflected' ideas (*SW* 5:128; 2008, 273) and arithmetic with 'conceptually reflected' ones—neither with ideas as such.[17] Mathematics treats absolute identity only indirectly, through the first two potencies. Only philosophy elevates itself to the third potency so as to encounter ideas directly and immediately—the ideas, that is, 'reflected purely and in

---

[15] For a justification of this procedure, see *SW* 6:165–6; 1994c, 159–60.
[16] See 248–56; 42–50.
[17] See Verra 1979, 35.

themselves' (129; 274). Philosophy takes place in the eternal, in reason, and so constructs ideas as such—free from distortion. Schelling writes:

> *Construction* is, first and in general, exhibition of the particular inside absolute form, and *philosophical construction in particular*, the exhibition of the particular within form considered without qualification—not as itself ideal or real, as in the two branches of mathematics—but form as intuited in itself or intellectually. (*SW* 4:408; 2001b, 394)

It is this specifically philosophical form of construction which I now explore.

ABSOLUTE CONSTRUCTION

For Schelling, construction is the very definition of absolute knowing, 'the sole true method of philosophy' (*SW* 4:406; 2001b, 393). As we saw above, Schelling opens his article, *Über Construktion*, claiming that a 'rigorous method of construction' is absolutely necessary for philosophy to progress, that 'the doctrine of philosophical construction' will soon be 'one of the most important aspects of scientific philosophy', and that only through the introduction of this doctrine can the true and the false be properly distinguished. 'Philosophy,' Ende glosses, 'first becomes a science through construction' (1973, 55).

The Production of Ideas

What then defines philosophical construction? It consists in the production of ideas. Construction (as we have repeatedly seen with earlier thinkers in this chapter) is a process of making, of poiesis; indeed, Schelling explicitly states (following this tradition), 'All construction is productive' (*SW* 5:150; 2008, 287). What the method of construction produces, moreover, is reality or the absolute itself. Philosophy 'produces the absolute', Schelling insists in the *Fernere Darstellungen* (*SW* 4:391; 2001b, 385). Or, more technically, reality constructs itself and it does so in the ideas. We return here to the inseparability of metaphysics and epistemology in Schelling's philosophy: the self-construction of the absolute is just one more way of describing its self-affirmation or self-knowing. Just as the absolute affirms itself in the ideas, so too it constructs itself in them. The ideas are the product of this eternal act, the objects in which the absolute constitutes itself.

Construction therefore belongs both to epistemology and ontology (*SW* 4:118; 2001a, 351). Reality constitutes itself by constructing ideas. Art provides a key example of this: it does not *re*-present the absolute, but is productive of it. Art exemplifies the poietic nature of the whole of Schellingian epistemology and simultaneously the whole of Schellingian metaphysics:

> Poesy has optimally received precisely the name *poesy*, that is, of *making* or *creating*, since its works appear as an act of producing instead of a condition of being. This is why poesy can be viewed as the *essence* of all art...Poesy is the creating agent of the *ideas*. (*SW* 5:631–2; 1989, 202)

The Indifference of Construction

Absolute construction takes place in the third potency. It is maximally productive of the absolute—that is, the absolute fully produces itself in the ideas. Yet, it must be asked: what evidence does Schelling have that this is so? Why is construction the most productive form of knowing? The answer lies in the intensity of indifference that absolute constructions produce. Indifference is discernible here in its most intense possible form. More concretely, Schelling points to four different sets of (what are normally thought of as) oppositions which are made one in construction. Enumeration of these indifferences provides the proof of the superiority of philosophical construction over all methodological alternatives.

First, there is the indifference of universal and particular. Schelling states, 'Construction as such is...always the absolute and *real* equalization of universal and particular' (*SW* 5:131–2; 2008, 275–6). This is of course the very indifference which Kant identifies as the essence of construction in the first *Kritik* and likewise it is what defines construction for Schelling. The universality of the concept and the particularity of the intuition are not to be distinguished. In geometry this identity is subordinated to a preponderance of the particular intuition and in arithmetic it is subordinated to the surplus of the universal concept, whereas 'in philosophy it achieves a point of absolute indifference' (131; 275). As such, 'To identify...the universal and the particular is the spirit of true philosophy' (*SW* 7:143; 1984b, 245).

Second, Schelling also stresses the identity of thought and intuition in constructions. This again follows quite simply from Kant and Schelling's definition of construction. In construction, an a priori intuition becomes equal to its concept, for the intuition fully and immediately manifests this concept.[18] Hence, Schelling praises Kant for 'consistently describ[ing] construction as the identification of *concept* and *intuition*' (*SW* 5:131; 2008, 273).

Third, Schelling points to the indifference of constructing activity and constructed product. Absolute knowledge occurs at 'the point at which constructing and constructed, thinking and thought come together as one. Only

---

[18] This also results in the identity of form and matter (*SW* 5:126; 2008, 272).

this point can be called the *principle* of construction' (134; 277).[19] This is another way of speaking of the identity of the subjective and objective in construction: 'Absolute knowing is not one in which subjective and objective are united as opposites, but one in which the entire subjective is the entire objective, and *vice versa*' (*SW* 2:61; 1988a, 46). Or, as Schelling puts it even more explicitly, 'Subjectivity and objectivity are absolutely one, and there is no construction in which they are not one' (*SW* 4:363; 2001b, 378).

Fourth, construction brings about the identity of possibility and actuality. For early modern exponents of construction, construction is a proof of existence: what is possible (i.e. without contradiction) becomes actual in construction. For Schelling too, possibility and actuality are one in construction: 'The mind recognizes…what it knows as *absolute* possibility to be absolute reality as well' (*SW* 2:202; 1988a, 162). Moreover, Schellingian construction also exhibits the necessity of its object: what is constructed has to be so constructed.[20] Possibility, actuality, and necessity are all indifferent in construction.

And yet not all binaries are necessarily made indifferent in constructions. There is one binary which need not be so indifferentiated—the ideal/real relation. There are preponderantly real and preponderantly ideal constructs and this will become absolutely crucial in the coming chapters.

Construction and the Absolute

Construction therefore produces the complete and immediate *Darstellung* of the absolute in one determinate form. It produces an idea, for in absolute construction the third potency (that of the eternal and the ideas) dominates. Construction maximally produces the indifference of the absolute in an idea. Moreover, of course, such ideas are for Schelling the building-blocks of reality; hence, 'The absolutely One is constructed in the absolute point of indifference, and this construction is presented in the *reflex* as the totality of a real universe and as the totality of an ideal universe' (*SW* 4:420). The absolute constructs itself as reality.

This reality is (in essence) one, and so therefore is all knowledge. Knowledge is monistic just like being, therefore Schelling insists on 'the identical absolute-ness of all constructions in philosophy' (*SW* 4:410; 2001b, 395). All constructions are constructions of the absolute by the absolute, and so (no matter what idea is constructed) they are all ultimately identical. Schelling emphasizes this point in his correspondence with Fichte:

---

[19] See Ende 1973, 53–4; Verra 1979, 34.   [20] See further Verra 1979, 34–6.

> Both of us admit but this one and only absolute knowledge, which is the same and ever recurring in all cognition, and which it is our common task to present and to reveal in all knowledge ... Once this knowledge is formally established and rooted as the sole theme and principle of philosophical speculation ... [philosophy] will repeat and bring to light in infinite forms and shapes only the one, the absolute. (*SB* 2:326; Fichte and Schelling 1997, 80)

All knowledge is of the absolute, and, while there are infinitely many forms this knowledge can take on, its essence will be forever the same: identity. In consequence, what constructions construct is not at issue, rather the degree to which they construct it is; in other words, while the essence of every construction is identical, its form is not—and this form crucially is the cause of the intensity with which the essence is generated. Philosophy no longer has an issue with subject matter; its overriding concern is the form in which that one subject matter is produced. This will become increasingly clear in the coming chapters.

We must remember here Schelling's metaphysical commitment to the fact that the absolute can be formed and become determinate without thereby losing any of its absoluteness. Construction is a case in point: the constructed idea 'receives the entire absolute into itself and even in uttermost particularity it becomes entirely absolute again' (*SW* 4:405; 2001b, 392).[21] What is constructed is a particular idea; however, this idea manifests the identity of subject and object, universal and particular, matter and form, and it does so in the fullest and most complete possible way. The construction maximally produces the identity of the absolute. Thus, Schelling writes in the *Fernere Darstellungen*, 'The particular [idea] is itself exhibited within the absolute only insofar as it contains the *entire absolute* exhibited within itself' (393; 386). Essence always exists in determinate forms; the absolute always exists in determinate constructions. This, as I have repeatedly stressed, is the heart of Schellingian thought.

Construction is a form of absolute knowing. In other words, in construction form—knowing—is equivalent to essence—what is known—and both are the absolute. Schelling insists upon this point in *Fernere Darstellungen*:

> The absolute unity of thought and being ... is the absolute's eternal form, the absolute itself ... Consequently, formally absolute cognition is necessarily a knowing of the absolute in itself. Thus there is an immediate cognition of the absolute and this is the first speculative cognition, the principle and ground of possibility of all philosophy. (368; 381–2)

---

[21] In consequence, Schelling sees no contradiction in affirming a plurality of formally differentiated absolutes (see Wanning 1988, 38). It is for such reasons that Szondi is wrong to claim that 'construction [is] destruction ... the negation or sublation of formal oppositions' (1974, 2:225), continuing, in construction 'the particular is thought in its universality and thereby dissolved as particular' (229), thereby 'devaluing the reality of concrete beings' (246). On the contrary, construction exhibits the absolute *as* particular: it is the affirmation of the particularization of the absolute.

There is nothing above or beyond philosophical constructions, for the form of knowing is equal to what there is. There is nothing that such constructions do not comprehend—no remaining mystery. And this is because reality is first produced in construction; it does not pre-exist construction, but comes to be through it. Essence does not exceed form; reality does not exceed constructions.

INTELLECTUAL INTUITION

One concept noticeably absent from my description of Schellingian epistemology thus far is intellectual intuition—the most controversial and notorious element of the *Identitätssystem*. Partly this is a rhetorical strategy: so many prejudices are bound up with this concept, it seems better to elucidate Schelling's epistemology without it. Partly my reasons are substantive: it is my contention that during the *Identitätssystem* intellectual intuition was subordinated to the method of construction, and this implies Schelling's rejection of his own previous 'ecstatic' notion of it.

The Redeployment of Intellectual Intuition

Intellectual intuition is the concept most associated with Schellingian philosophy and is usually seen as its greatest weak-point (from Hegel's criticisms of intellectual intuition proceeding 'like a shot from a pistol' (1977b, §27) to Lukács' claim (1980, 147) that, through it, irrationalism first entered modern philosophy).[22] It must be admitted that Schelling is committed to a form of intellectual intuition throughout the *Identitätssystem*. 'Intellectual intuition is the beginning and first step to philosophy,' Schelling writes at the beginning of the *Fernere Darstellungen* (SW 4:348), and in *Über die Methode*, he goes even further claiming, 'Without intellectual intuition no philosophy!' (SW 5:255; 1966, 49). However, what is at issue here is not Schelling's continuing commitment to the term, but rather its meaning.

The first thing to note is the *break* which occurs between Schelling's classic use of intellectual intuition in *Vom Ich* and its deployment in his later philosophical work. In the former, intellectual intuition falls foul of all the criticism to which it is often subjected: it is a mystic experience of creative freedom beyond concepts and language, an experience of the noumenal which transcends everyday phenomenal experience. Schelling seems at times to conceive it as an 'intellectual vision of the noumenon', a perception beyond

---

[22] See also di Giovanni 1987, 657, 661; Groves 1999, 26, 33. Beiser (2002, 579) offers a much-needed corrective.

ordinary sense perception (1:181; 1980b, 85). In Chapter 4, I discussed the 'two-world' metaphysics on which this use of intellectual intuition is grounded and I also charted the manner in which after 1795 this 'two-world' metaphysics is discarded by Schelling on the back of the poor reception of *Vom Ich*. The same is true of the mystical interpretation of intellectual intuition offered in that work (although this process of discarding was less clear-cut).

That there was a break in Schelling's view is evident from the 1801 *Darstellung*. In it, the term 'intellectual intuition' (or anything remotely resembling it) does not occur at all.[23] As Tilliette has claimed, 'This remarkable absence is probably part of his latent—or nascent—rupture with Fichte, an indirect means of distinguishing himself' (1995, 176). Tilliette continues:

> Are we right to underline the exclusion of intellectual intuition from the *Darstellung*? Yes, if one is making clear that intellectual intuition has finished its Schellingian career as transcendental intuition and productive intuition [the forms it takes on in the *System des transzendentalen Idealismus* and the *Naturphilosophie* of the late 1790s]. No, if one observes that it continues to appear in neighbouring texts where it is synonymous with absolute knowledge; but it undergoes an eclipse in others, and in general begins its decline. (186)

Hence, as Tilliette implies, when intellectual intuition does reappear in Schelling's writings in the summer of 1802, it is in a much subdued and faded form.[24]

Schelling reinterprets intellectual intuition during the *Identitätssystem*. At the very moment it re-enters his philosophy in the *Fernere Darstellungen*, he is emphatic that it does so as a reformed concept, one no longer open to the charge of mysticism:

> Most people understand by 'intellectual intuition' something incomprehensible, mysterious, but with no more reason that one would have in thinking the intuition of pure space something mysterious, disregarding the fact that all outer intuition is possible only *in* and through this intuition. (*SW* 4:369; 2001b, 382)

In short, his new version of intellectual intuition is not the same concept as appeared in *Vom Ich*. It has now been shorn of its ecstatic and transcendent characteristics—'divested of its mystical resonance', in Tilliette's words (1987, 117).[25]

---

[23] The same is true of Schelling's next major work, *Bruno*, although this may well be due to its avoidance of epistemology altogether (*SW* 4:221; 1984a, 123). Ironically, it is probably the influence of Hegel that led Schelling to reintroduce the term back into his philosophical vocabulary in the *Fernere Darstellungen*. In his *Differenzschrift* published in late 1801, Hegel had stated (posing as Schelling's disciple), 'Intellectual intuition is the absolute principle of philosophy, the one real ground and firm standpoint in Fichte as well as in Schelling' (1977a, 173). The irony of course is that Hegel later became famous precisely for his critique of Schelling's adherence to intellectual intuition.

[24] See further Tilliette 1970, 1:258–9; 1995, 188.

[25] White claims more generally that Schelling's work between 1801 and 1804 is 'a concerted, even single-minded attempt...to banish from his system the spectre of mysticism' (1983, 73).

The question then becomes, of course: having described what it is not, what is intellectual intuition during the *Identitätssystem*?

The Priority of Construction

A common interpretation[26] sees intellectual intuition as an original, epiphanic moment of insight which is then translated into systematic form through the process of construction. Schelling himself lends credence to this view in his popular presentation of the *Identitätssystem*, *Über die Methode*: 'Philosophical construction interprets what is grasped in intellectual intuition' (*SW* 5:255; 1966, 49). On this view, intellectual intuition is a primary insight, which employs construction as a secondary means of clarifying and communicating this insight.

However, to subordinate construction in this way (as merely a means to elaborate systematically the insight attained in intellectual intuition) is to misinterpret the significance construction has not just for Schelling, but also for the whole modern philosophical tradition on which he draws. Construction is not posterior to intuition but the overarching methodology within which intuitions are produced. Let me quote once more Kant's definition of construction: 'To construct a concept means to exhibit a priori the intuition which corresponds to the concept' (2007, A713/B741). Construction is the means by which intuition is produced and it determines the type of intuition so produced and its relation to the concept. Intuition is not prior to construction; rather, it is a component part of the process of constructing. This is the view Schelling adopts in *Über Construktion* and *Fernere Darstellungen*: the self-construction of the absolute is the means by which it knows itself; it is not secondary to an initial act of self-intuition. Indeed, the grandiose claims Schelling makes for construction in the opening lines of *Über Construktion* make little sense on the above view.

Perception and Production

Schelling's post-1801 concept of intellectual intuition can further be determined in terms of its productive and hence non-perceptual character. This property will play a crucial role in the next chapter when I chart the differences between the Schellingian symbol and 'the romantic symbol'.

Intellectual intuition is open to being interpreted as something perceptual. It is easy to think of it as a form of perception directed no longer at the sensory realm, but at the archetypical realm. Intellectual intuition perceives

---

[26] For example, Beiser 2002, 585–6.

archetypes, just as sensory intuition perceives sensible objects. Again, Schelling does encourage this manner of interpreting intellectual intuition; he calls it 'a faculty for seeing things solely as they are in the idea' (*SW* 5:256; 1966, 50) or 'the capacity to see the universal in the particular' (*SW* 4:362; 2001b, 377). Moreover, commentators have often drawn on these remarks: Beiser defines Schellingian intellectual intuition as 'the capacity to perceive archetypes' (2002, 586) and Tilliette suggests (in a discussion of Schellingian construction) that 'to think is to see' (1995, 188).

However, this language of perception misrepresents the thoroughly *productive* nature of intellectual intuition in the *Identitätssystem*. Intellectual intuition does not perceive ready-made ideas; it produces those ideas in the first place. Schelling insists, 'Intellectual intuition... produces the absolute' (*SW* 4:391; 2001b, 385). In Vater's words, intellectual intuition 'name[s] the supplier of reality, the creative force, the fact of ontological foundation... Intellectual intuition is the self-realization of the idea of God in reason' (2000, 228–32). This is about as far from a model of perception as one could get.

This is in many ways an obvious point. Scholars of Fichte's work have been stressing the corresponding non-perceptual nature of Fichtean intellectual intuition for decades. However, in light of the above, it does seem necessary to emphasize that the ideas are not perceived by the absolute in its self-knowing, but produced by it. There is no eternal heavenly realm to contemplate (as a crude version of Platonism would have it). We saw this in Chapter 4 in respect to Schelling's Platonism: while Schelling may talk in terms of a distinction between archetype and copy, they are in fact identical—the act of 'copying' is the very same act which constitutes the ideas in the first place. Ideas only come into being by being known by the absolute (and, we must remember, only the absolute knows).[27]

OVERVIEW: THE NATURE OF SCHELLINGIAN CONSTRUCTION

To conclude, it is worth summarizing what construction means for Schelling. Kant's definition of construction reads, 'To construct a concept means to exhibit a priori the intuition which corresponds to the concept' (2007, A713/

[27] It is surprising that scholars have not made more of Hintikka's work (see 1969). While his conclusions for Kant's philosophy of mathematics remain controversial, the comments he makes concerning the meaning of 'intuition' in late eighteenth-century Germany seem to me invaluable. Earlier in the book, I discussed Hintikka's contention that, in the late eighteenth century, intuition is *not* perception. The following conclusion can be drawn from this: intellectual intuition is not a mutated version of sensory perception, it is not modelled after it in the slightest.

B741). Schelling reinterprets this definition through his adherence to early modern traditions of philosophy. He holds on to Kant's conviction that intuition is the product of construction, while *Darstellung* names the process; however, following early modernity and *pace* Kant, Schelling insists philosophy can construct. Moreover, following Spinoza, Schelling contends that what is exhibited in each construction is not merely a concept (as Kant thinks), but is God. God (or the absolute or identity or indifference) is the content of all construction. The multiplicity of different constructions is not therefore a consequence of a multiplicity of contents, but rather a multiplicity of different forms and so different intensities of identity.

What is at stake in the difference between constructions (for example, between mathematical and philosophical constructions) is the intensity of production. However, an obvious question arises here: how does a construction guarantee a high intensity of production? How can one be sure that one's philosophical construction is truly philosophical and so truly absolute? We have seen that once the construction is generated, one is able to assess its absoluteness by means of the amounts of indifference it manifests. Yet, the question remains: how does one guarantee absolute construction in the first place? This is a variant of the question many have asked of Schelling: how does one begin? As Hegel famously wrote, the *Identitätssystem* proceeds to the absolute like a shot from a pistol without justifying how or why it gets there (1977b, §27). Later critics have been just as concerned with such questions: Schelling is seen to fall 'head over heels into the absolute' (Beiser 2002, 588).[28] Indeed, as we have seen, Schelling insists that philosophy begins in the absolute and remains there. How can this be the case? In other words, how can philosophical constructions guarantee their own absoluteness from the very beginning?

In the months leading up to the *Identitätssystem* and most famously in his essay, *Über den wahren Begriff der Naturphilosophie*, Schelling gives a very clear answer to this question. *Abstraction* is the necessary condition for philosophizing: one must begin by abstracting from all potentiated phenomena to reach the unpotentiated starting-point from which all proceeds:

> One must *reduce the object of philosophy to a lesser potency* and to begin once more to construct with this object reduced to its first potency... By this abstraction, I arrive at the concept of the pure subject-object, from which alone I can raise myself to the conscious subject-object. (*SW* 4:85–6)

Once such a process of abstraction has taken place, the philosopher is then in a position to chart the self-construction of reality. The problem, however, is that despite a half-hearted appearance at the beginning of the 1801 *Darstellung* (*SW* 4:114–15; 2001a, 349), abstraction plays little part in the *Identitätssystem*,

---

[28] See also Challiol-Gillet 1996, 29; Fischbach 1999, 219–24.

and indeed by the 1804 *System* the term has solely negative connotations (*SW* 6:192; 1994b, 178). What, therefore, does Schelling substitute for abstraction as the means of guaranteeing absolute philosophy? The answer to this question will only be given at the end of this book—much more needs to be elucidated before I am able to show the practice needed (in place of abstraction) to guarantee absoluteness.

This, therefore, is Schelling's epistemology. There is no sharp line to distinguish where it stops and metaphysics begins; rather, the two fields are merely two ways of describing the same thing: the self-construction or self-production of the absolute. As in geometry, this process of construction results in figures which exhibit the absolute; however, unlike geometry (and arithmetic), such figures are not reflected in space or time, but exist as pure ideas in the realm of the third potency, the eternal. Ideas are the maximal self-constructions of the absolute.

Part III
Symbol

7

§39 of the *Philosophie der Kunst*

In the first two parts of this book, I considered the two contexts in which Schelling's construction of symbolic language should be located: first, efforts by other contemporary thinkers to theorize symbolic language; second, Schelling's own philosophical system of the period. Both contexts are crucial to what follows and I return to them repeatedly. In Part III, I now turn to what Schelling actually has to say about symbolic language. This part comprises three chapters: in the present chapter, I first provide a commentary on Schelling's remarks about the symbol in general—how it is defined, the role it plays and the peculiar interpretation he gives it. Chapter 8 is an intermediary chapter in which I consider some common misconceptions of Schelling's attitude to language. I argue that a construction of symbolic language is both possible and necessary for the *Identitätssystem*. Finally, in Chapter 9, I provide a commentary on §73 of the *Philosophie der Kunst*, bringing all the previous material to bear on the claims Schelling makes about symbolic language.

The present chapter, then, treats Schelling's more general comments on the symbol, especially his introduction of the term in §39 of the *Philosophie der Kunst*. In the first section, I analyse his definition of the symbol; in the second, I provide a specific example of symbolic form—mythology; finally, I elucidate the ways in which this definition differs from 'the romantic symbol'.

SCHELLING'S DEFINITION OF THE SYMBOL

The Symbol as *Darstellung* of the Absolute

The proposition defended in §39 of the *Philosophie der Kunst* reads, '*Darstellung* of the absolute with absolute indifference of the universal and the particular *within the particular* is possible only symbolically' (*SW* 5:406; 1989, 45). A page later, Schelling goes on to state, the symbol 'constitutes the absolute form' (407; 46). In making these two claims, Schelling brings the symbol into contact with two crucial elements of his *Identitätssystem*: his doctrine of formation and notion of construction. In terms of the latter claim, the symbol is defined as the absolute (or most productive) mode in which the absolute is exhibited: the absolute constructs itself most fully in the symbol. This is obviously a key claim; however, initially, I want to concentrate on the former point—that the absolute forms itself into a symbol.

The metaphysics of the *Identitätssystem* posits two elements to reality— essence and form. There is one essence, so whatever exists does so by express- ing this essential identity to a greater or lesser extent. All there is is this one essence in quantitatively different amounts. What determines these different amounts is form, and the idea of the necessary formation of the absolute is, as we have seen, a lynchpin of the *Identitätssystem*. Reality (or the absolute) always exists in a determinate form; moreover, this form is in no way a diminution of its being; nothing is lost here. Instead, formation is an intensifi- cation of essential identity. There is no apophatic beyond which is lost in the becoming-formed of the absolute. This formation can also be articulated in epistemological terms: each form constitutes a specific cognition the absolute has of itself. It is for this reason that 'form' is synonymous with *Darstellung*, for it is the way in which the absolute exhibits itself as knowledge. Finally, it is necessary to remember that there are numerous (in fact, infinite) quantita- tively different forms the absolute can take on and all these forms intensify the indifference of the absolute to various degrees. Schelling categorizes the different types of intensity into three groups which potentiate reality to different extents—the finite, the infinite, and the eternal potency. The eternal or idea is the maximal intensification of the absolute. By calling the symbol 'absolute form', Schelling obviously aligns it with the final, eternal potency— and we will flesh out this correspondence in detail in what follows. Even more significant is the mere fact that Schelling designates the symbol a 'form' or 'mode of *Darstellung* [*Darstellungsart*]' (407; 45) at all. 'Symbol' names, one must conclude from this, one way in which the absolute forms itself, a way in which reality is potentiated and essential identity produced.

Before moving on, it is necessary to note a distinction. The term 'symbol' only appears in the *Philosophie der Kunst* in a discussion of how art can be conceived as the self-formation of the absolute. That is, when he introduces the concept of the symbol, Schelling is clear that it applies only to indifference manifest within the *particular* or (what is the same thing) to the idea as it exhibits itself *really*. In this respect, 'symbol' occupies a very specific place in Schelling's aesthetics. Yet, in Chapter 3, I insisted on the symbol as a leitmotiv for the *Identitätssystem* as a whole. 'Symbol' is one name out of many, but it is a name which is particularly revealing about the inner workings of the *Identitätssystem*. And, in fact, Schelling himself does also make this claim. He explicitly draws his readers' (or listeners') attention to the fact that symbol, allegory, and schematism 'are also universal categories' (410; 48). In this way,

Schelling admits the term 'symbol' can be applied more universally than to just art; indeed, the series allegory/schematism/symbol can designate any tripartite manifestation of entities whatsoever:

> One can say that nature merely allegorizes in the corporeal series... In light, in contrast to the corporeal series, nature schematizes, and is symbolic in the realm of the organic... Similarly, thinking is simply schematism; all action, in contrast, is allegorical; art is symbolic. This distinction can also be applied to the sciences. Arithmetic allegorizes... Geometry can be said to schematize... Finally, philosophy is the symbolic science among these. (We will return to the same concepts during our construction of the individual forms of art. Music is an allegorizing art, painting schematizes, the plastic arts are symbolic. Similarly, in poesy lyric poetry is allegorical, epic poetry demonstrates the necessary inclination to schematization, and drama is symbolic.) (410–11; 48)

Organisms, artworks, philosophies, sculptures, and dramas are all specifically symbolic ways in which reality forms itself. Not only art, but also natural objects and scientific discourse can be labelled symbolic. It is for this reason that in what follows I will switch interchangeably between sculpture, drama, or philosophy (to name but three) as examples of the symbol. I am not particularly interested in why Schelling selects these particular phenomena; my concern is far more with how these examples illustrate the more general theoretical structure of the Schellingian symbol.

Thus, Schelling argues, since symbol, allegory, and schematism name the three modes in which the absolute exhibits itself, they can therefore be applied to all kinds of phenomena (just like the potencies on which they are based). For this reason, we must distinguish between a narrow application of the symbol and a broader one, both of which Schelling sees as legitimate. It is of course the latter, broader version with which the following is primarily concerned.

Allegory, Schematism, and the Magnetic Line

To demonstrate his definition of the symbol as absolute form, Schelling constructs a three-term series comprising schematism, allegory, and symbol. Each of these terms designates one specific form of the absolute, one particular mode of *Darstellung*. Here is how Schelling introduces them:

> That *Darstellung* in which the universal means the particular or in which the particular is intuited through the universal is *schematism*. That *Darstellung*, however, in which the particular means the universal or in which the universal is intuited through the particular is *allegory*. The synthesis of these two, where neither the universal means the particular nor the particular the universal, but rather where both are absolutely one, is the *symbolic*. (SW 5:407; 1989, 46)

In allegory, Schelling writes, 'the universal is intuited through the particular'—that is, the indifference between universal and particular is masked, and the particular rises to prominence (as that on which the universal depends). The particular is immediately accessible and only through it is knowledge of the universal attained. The particular dominates and contains the universal within it. The example Schelling gives of this mode of exhibition is the allegorical interpretation of myth in which the particular events of the story are read as referring to entities of more universal significance: the behaviour of Eros in *Eros and Psyche*, for instance, is meant to represent the capriciousness of love (409–10; 47–8). The universal is not exhibited but only reached by means of an act of interpretation through the particular. Allegory signifies 'ideas by means of real, concrete images' (549; 148).

While the particular predominates in allegory, the opposite is true for schematism—indeed, the two forms are 'the reverse' of each other (409; 47). In schematism, 'the particular is intuited through the universal'; hence the universal dominates ('the dominating element in the schema is the universal' (407; 46)). This predominance again conceals indifference. The universal is what is immediately given and the particular only mediated through it.[1] The example Schelling gives is 'the mechanical artist' who produces particulars only according to their type (that is, mediated through a universal concept):

> The schema is the rule guiding his production, but he intuits in this universal simultaneously the particular itself. First he will produce only a rough outline of the whole according to this intuition; then he develops the individual parts completely until the schema gradually becomes for him a fully concrete image. (407–8; 46)

The particular (the image) is contained within the universal and is a product of it.[2]

Finally, in the symbol, 'neither the universal means the particular nor the particular the universal, but rather...both are absolutely one' (407; 46). Universal and particular exist here in a state of indifference in which both are immediately and directly expressed to the same extent and neither predominates.

Two things require note. First, one should be extremely wary of the use of the term 'synthesis' in this connection. Schelling is fond of it in the *Philosophie der Kunst*, and he even goes on to label the symbol 'the synthesis of two opposing modes, the schematic and the allegorical' (407; 45–6). However, this was a lecture course not written for publication, and Schelling's published writings should always have the last word. In these, as we saw at length in the

---

[1] Here, Schelling explicitly acknowledges the influence of Kant's definition of schematism (although Goethe's definition of allegory was presumably no less influential) (407; 46). See my discussion in Chapter 3.

[2] Elsewhere, Schelling gives the example of numbers (576; 165).

previous three chapters, there is no such thing as synthesis for Schelling: to speak of synthesis is to speak from the standpoint of reflection—a minimally expressive mode of philosophizing. The rule, 'What is third for reflection (i.e. the product of synthesis) is first for reason (i.e. the point of indifference)' is a basic one for Schelling at this period.[3] Thus, it seems more in keeping with the *Identitätssystem* as a whole to employ the term 'indifference point' instead of 'synthesis'. Indeed, later Schelling makes clear in reference to mythology, 'Its essential nature is neither allegorical nor schematic, but *the indifference of both*: the symbolic' (410; 47–8; my emphasis).[4]

Second, as I began to argue in Chapter 3, schematism, allegory, and symbol can only be thought of as qualitatively distinct (and so capable of being synthesized together) from the viewpoint of reflection. From a genuinely philosophical point of view, on the contrary, there is no such thing as qualitative opposition, but only the 'preponderance' or 'surplus' of certain elements. Hence, strictly speaking, the modes of *Darstellung*—schematism, allegory, and symbol—are different intensities of absolute form. In schematism the universal predominates, in allegory the particular, but symbol is the most intense form, in which the indifference of universal and particular is manifest to the maximum possible extent. The symbol produces essential identity most intensely because it approximates most closely to formal identity.

From these qualifications, it follows that allegory, schematism, and symbol correspond to the three potencies in Schelling's *Identitätssystem*—finite, infinite, and eternal, respectively. Schelling stresses this point, 'One can view the succession of the three forms of *Darstellung* also as a succession of potencies' (410; 48). In consequence, just like the potencies, they can be depicted on Schelling's magnetic line (Fig. 2).

Allegory, schematism, and symbol name the three potencies. They correspond to the three different types of self-formation of reality: the one which expresses the finite element of reality disproportionately (allegory), the one which expresses the infinite element of reality disproportionately (schematism), and the one which produces reality as indifference (symbol).

Yet, this is not the full picture, because Schelling goes on to distinguish a fourth category in §39 (and this strongly implies a fifth as well):

> We also must distinguish each of these three from the *image* [*Bild*]. The image is always concrete, purely particular, and is determined from all sides such that only the definite factor of the space occupied by the original object prevents it from being identical with the object itself. (407; 46)

---

[3] See Chapter 5, also Wanning 1988, 91–3.
[4] Similar language can be found in many other passages (for example, 571; 162).

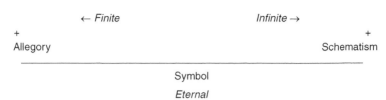

Fig. 2. *The symbol on the magnetic line—first version*

The image is a *Darstellung* which is particular to the greatest possible extent. In it, all trace of universality (and, in consequence, of the particular's identity with the universal) is seemingly erased. Indeed, Schelling claims the only thing distinguishing a particular object from its image is the different area of space each occupies. The image is therefore allegory taken to such an extreme that the universal element drops out of view. It is for this reason Schelling calls the image 'mere *meaningless being*' (411; 49). One must be careful here to remember Schelling's insistence on the composite nature of all things: everything is a mixture of the three potencies, and in nothing do any of the potencies disappear entirely; however, having said that, the image exhibits the infinite and eternal potencies to the minimal extent possible. Hence, to all intents and purposes, they are erased.

Moreover, although Schelling does not make it explicit, this entails a corresponding notion which designates that in which universality predominates to the greatest possible extent, and thus in which the finite and eternal potencies are only minimally present. This, we can infer, is the concept, 'mere meaning' as Schelling describes it (412; 49). The concept is that which stresses universality at the expense of particularity to such a great extent that many previous philosophers assumed it did not contain any reference to particularity whatsoever. The concept is an exaggerated form of schematism.

Thus, a five-term series is created which can be depicted on the magnetic line as shown in Fig. 3. What both these versions of the magnetic line have in common is the symbol's position as the centre or point of indifference between the two poles of allegory/image and schematism/concept. It is the most intense mode in which the absolute can exhibit itself. In the next section, I discuss why this is the case.

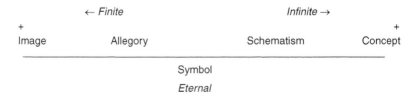

Fig. 3. *The symbol on the magnetic line—second version*

The Symbol and Indifference

What evidence is there for locating the symbol at the point of indifference between schematism and allegory—that is, what evidence is there for its definition as 'absolute form'? The answer to this (in parallel to the answer given in the previous chapter concerning absolute construction) is that the symbol manifests indifference most fully. It is a *'Darstellung* with *complete indifference'* (*SW* 5:411; 1989, 49). This has a twofold aspect—indifference is produced both *intensively* and *extensively* to the maximum extent: there are extensively numerous indifferences which the symbol manifests and it manifests them all intensely. As we have seen, 'syntheticism' or the positing together of opposites is a primary characteristic of all varieties of the symbol during the *Goethezeit*; it is therefore not surprising that Schelling locates the point of indifference of binaries in an entity termed 'the symbol'.

The first and foremost indifference which the symbol manifests is that between meaning and being—that is, (what I have called in this book) the symbol's tautegory. The symbol is the point of indifference between meaning and being; neither predominates: 'Meaning here is simultaneously being itself, passed over into the object itself and one with it' (411; 49). It is for this reason Schelling resurrects the previously forgotten name for the symbol, *Sinnbild*: 'The German language renders the word *symbol* [*Symbol*] excellently with the term *Sinnbild*' (412; 49). For the symbol is an image (*Bild*) whose meaning (*Sinn*) is one with it; it is 'as concrete and self-identical as the image, and yet as universal and significant as the concept' (412; 49). Image and concept should therefore be added to the list of elements made indifferent in the symbol, as too should their corollaries, objective and subjective.

Another crucial indifference equally stressed by Schelling is that between universal and particular. This follows directly from the previous indifference: the being of the symbol (its image-element) is particular, whereas its meaning is universal; hence, just as the symbol manifests the indifference of meaning and being, so too it expresses the indifference of particular and universal: 'The universal is completely the particular and the particular the universal' (411; 48). For Schelling, therefore, the universal does not exceed the particular in any way, but is entirely identical to it. From this also follows the indifference between finite and infinite, as well as (more obliquely) that of possibility and actuality (623; 196).

This, then, is the evidence for the absolute nature of symbolic form. First, the symbol exhibits numerous indifferences—being and meaning, image and concept, subjective and objective, particular and universal, finite and infinite, possibility and actuality. Second, it exhibits each indifference completely and immediately. That is, both extensively and intensively indifference is made manifest in the symbol to the greatest possible extent, i.e. absolutely. It is an absolute exhibition of the absolute. Symbols are indifferent forms of reality; they consist in formal identity. This is the very ideal to which all forms in the Schellingian cosmos aspire, because formal identity is maximally poietic—it produces essential identity as intensely as possible.[5]

However, as with absolute constructions, a qualification is necessary. There is one indifference the symbol does not *necessarily* manifest—the indifference of real and ideal. That is, Schelling conceives the possibility of predominantly real and predominantly ideal symbols. Mythology (as we shall soon see) is an example of the first kind: it is symbolic, but still rooted very much in the real. The extent to which symbols identify real and ideal thus becomes the criterion by which to differentiate and assess them. In fact, Schelling claims, there is only one symbol which identifies the real and the ideal fully, and this is symbolic language. It is a claim to which I return in Chapter 9.

Schematism, Allegory, and the Operation of Reflection

One name for reality in the *Identitätssystem* is indifference; in other words, Schelling is a rigorous monist, and so there is one thing and one of its names is 'indifference'. Therefore, only what manifests indifference is real. Conversely, any entity in which such indifference does not pertain at all is impossible. In short, Schelling's position is that *everything is symbolic*. All reality is indifferent, and so must be (to that extent) symbolic. What does this mean for allegory and schematism? Basically, they merely name lesser degrees of symbolism. Allegory and schematism are not distinct modes of presentation in their own right in which no indifference pertains between being and meaning; instead, they are less intense forms of symbolic exhibition, in which being and meaning are indifferent in a lower intensity.

Lower intensity (as we have seen in the previous chapters) is a result of reflection. Reflection is a mode of thinking or being in which the indifference of the absolute is not produced to a very high degree, and hence the symbolic nature of all things is concealed. Reflection designates the less intense ways in which reality manifests itself. Allegory and schematism are therefore products of reflection. When the universal predominates in schematism or the particular in allegory, this predominance implies imbalance between the two terms— as well as a partial separation of them. This imbalance lessens the intensity of the schema or allegory's production of essential identity.

Implicitly criticized here is the concept of signification. As we saw above, in the definition both of schematism and of allegory, signification (or the process of one thing 'meaning' another) is emphasized: the universal signifies the

---

[5] In consequence, as we know, essence and form are thus identical (575; 165), for they are both identity.

particular or the particular signifies the universal. For one thing to signify or mean another, Schelling implies, there needs to be a disequilibrium and a partial separation between them: for the universal to mean the particular, the universal must be something different from the particular. The two cannot be identical if signification is to make sense. Three statements Schelling makes concerning allegory are pertinent here: first, the allegorical image 'is actually nothing in and for itself, but is significant only in its relationship to [its referent]' (*SW* 5:453; 1989, 79); second, 'The particular *only* means or signifies the universal *without being it itself*' (410; 48; my emphasis); third, 'What is actually portrayed signifies or means something other than itself, and suggests something different from itself' (549; 148). The non-identity between being and meaning which Schelling draws attention to in each comment is a failure to produce identity. Non-identity—and therefore the notion of signification based upon it—is a less productive way of understanding reality.

A connected criticism is that signification requires some form of causality. If the particular signifies the universal, there is implicitly a causal relation between them: the particular is the cause of the universal's appearance. However, as we have seen, causality is an inappropriate concept by which to describe reality, according to Schelling. It is a misdescription, a minimally productive manner of conceiving the way the world works. Since signification relies on causality (however minimally), it must be a relatively useless way of describing what is. Signification articulates reality badly.

In short, the problem is that allegory and schematism (as well as signification in general, their common presupposition) both retain traces of a representational paradigm. As we have seen in Chapter 4, representation is premised on the separation of subject and object, and moves causally from one to the other. As such, it relies on a view of the world governed by qualitative opposition (between subject and object) and by casual explanation. Schelling is adamant in his rejection of both these tenets. Moreover, allegory and schematism—since they both separate (to some extent) subjective meaning from objective being and move from one to another in a causal chain— share common ground with representation.[6] Unlike the symbol, they both distort what really is.

One concept that is remarkably absent from both §39 and §73 of the *Philosophie der Kunst* is *the sign*. Indeed, one has to wait until the 1810s to find Schelling make explicit the critique of the sign which is already implicitly present in the *Identitätssystem* (*SW* 8:439–54). Such an implicit critique can be reconstructed because the sign is a composite of two elements that are important to §39—the image and the concept. The sign is that entity which

---

[6] Allegory and schematism, it must be emphasized, are not particularly severe cases of representation, since meaning and being are here only partially distinguished, and the causal connection between them is only implicit.

moves causally from pure image to pure concept by means of signification. Unlike the symbol, allegory, or schematism, there is no intrinsic connection here between meaning and being, but a purely extrinsic one. The sign combines in a causal (hence non-productive) manner the least productive way of conceiving being (the image) with the least productive way of conceiving meaning (the concept). It is thus the most distorted or reflective way of exhibiting reality.

On the contrary, the symbol does not signify:[7] 'The finite is simultaneously the infinite itself, and does not merely signify it' (*SW* 5:453; 1989, 79). Elsewhere, Schelling repeats, 'It does not merely mean or signify its objects' (707–8; 261). Indifference is immediately manifest and there is no need for a causal relation to be instantiated. Everything necessary for the symbol's meaning is immediately evident in its being—signification and indeed all forms of reference and representation are discarded. Schelling's ontologization of the semiotic makes meaning immediately evident. Hence, one can conclude that both sign and symbol exhibit some sort of identity between being and meaning, but, whereas the sign's identity is the most extrinsic and mediated connection between image and concept conceivable, the symbol presents the two in their primordial indifference. It is 'at once completely idea and completely thing' (621; 195).[8]

Symbol, Philosophy, and Ideas

The symbol is one name for the absolute mode in which the absolute exhibits itself. As we saw at length in the previous chapter, this absolute mode of exhibition also bears the name 'construction'. Hence, the symbol describes the self-construction of the absolute. We can see this in §39 itself: what Schelling here dubs symbolic ('*Darstellung* of the absolute with absolute indifference of the universal and the particular') closely resembles his definition of construction (discussed in the previous chapter). Symbolic exhibition is thus a construction of the absolute in a particular *Darstellung*.

It is at this point, moreover, that the differences between the Schellingian and Kantian theories of the symbol become most apparent. For Kant, there are various modes of *Darstellung*: the most expressive is construction, the least expressive the symbol. That is, construction is that form of *Darstellung* in

---

[7] *Pace* Niklewski 1979, 77–87.

[8] 'Idea' is here being used non-technically by Schelling. The above reading depends heavily on the theory of quantitative differentiation. If one were to give more weight to the dialectic of *Ineinsbildung*, on the other hand, a slightly different picture (in emphasis at least) would emerge, in which allegory and schematism become *component parts* of symbolism—the moments of *Einbildung* and *Wiedereinbildung* in the overall process of *Ineinsbildung*. 'Synthesis' would indeed be a more appropriate term for Schelling to use in this context. See Barth 1991, 154–9.

which the concept is directly and immediately manifest in intuition, whereas the symbol is that form of *Darstellung* in which such manifestation is most indirect and mediated. On the other hand, for Schelling, all forms of *Darstellung* are constructions and the symbol names the most expressive form of construction. Thus, instead of being at the bottom of the pile as the *Darstellung* most opposed to construction, symbol for Schelling is the highest peak of exhibition and names a particularly intense form of construction.

This is made clear in the manner in which Schelling lines up arithmetic, geometry, and philosophy with allegory, schematism, and the symbol. He writes,

> Arithmetic allegorizes, since it signifies the universal through the particular. Geometry can be said to schematize, to the extent that it designates the particular through the universal or general. Finally, philosophy is the symbolic science among these. (*SW* 5:411; 1989, 48)[9]

There are (as we saw in the previous chapter) three forms of construction, depending on whether the intuition generated in the constructive process is reflected through space, time, or not at all. Schelling here aligns these three constructive sciences with allegory, schematism, and symbol.

The symbol is therefore proper to philosophy. Symbolism is the genuinely philosophical way of exhibiting the absolute.[10] It is for this reason Schelling concludes the first part of his essay, *Über das Verhältnis der Naturphilosophie zur Philosophie überhaupt*, as follows:

> What *abides* is only what supersedes dichotomy...From it alone can a true universe of knowledge evolve, an all-encompassing structure. Only what proceeds from the absolute unity of the infinite and finite is immediately capable *per se* of symbolic presentation. (*SW* 5:115; 1985, 373)

As Schelling elsewhere puts it, philosophy is 'the symbolic science' (*SW* 5:576–7; 1989, 166).[11]

As the most intense form of construction, the one which corresponds to philosophy, symbolism is construction in the third potency—in the eternal. We have, of course, sufficiently demonstrated this already; what needs adding here is that this is a construction of ideas. To exhibit the absolute symbolically is to exhibit ideas, to construct 'the eternal in visible form' (364; 13). The

---

[9] The details of this quotation are extremely problematic. If number operates schematically (see note 2), why is arithmetic allegorical (indeed, elsewhere, Schelling does seem to think arithmetic schematic (576; 165))? Moreover, if a geometer constructs spatial diagrams (which are particular) to represent universal truths, how can such diagrams be schemata?

[10] This applies to the broad notion of the symbol alone. Schelling explicitly opposes the narrow notion to philosophical *Darstellung* (406; 45).

[11] I will return to the relation between philosophy and symbolism at length in the next chapter.

symbol of a thing is its idea. This is crucial: symbolism is not an abstraction from reality or an embellishment of it; it is the only means of attaining what is as it is.[12] Symbolism is real like nothing else is. Thus, in Robinson's lecture notes on the Jena *Philosophie der Kunst*, we read the following: 'The symbolic is the absolute in itself' (1976, 161).

THE EXAMPLE OF MYTHOLOGY

In this next section, I explore further the main example Schelling gives of symbolism: mythology. This brief discussion is not meant to exhaust Schelling's extensive reflections on mythology from the *Älteste Systemprogramm* to the *Vorlesungen über die Philosophie der Mythologie*;[13] indeed; it is not meant even to exhaust these ideas as they are presented in the *Philosophie der Kunst*. Rather, my concern is with using Schelling's conception of mythology as an illustration of the previous, rather abstract discussion of the symbol.[14]

The theory of the symbol in §39 is embedded within the section, 'Construction of the Content of Art', which is in turn devoted to a discussion of mythology as the proper content of art ('Mythology is the necessary condition and first content of all art' (*SW* 5:405; 1989, 45)). The link between symbolic exhibition and mythology is made explicit by Schelling in the following bald statement, 'Mythology as such and every poetic rendering of it in particular are to be comprehended neither schematically nor allegorically, but rather *symbolically*' (411; 48). Indeed, Schelling writes with respect to the construction of the symbol in §39: 'This proposition is thus the principle of construction of mythology as such' (406; 45).[15] From such comments, it is clear why an examination of mythology provides an aid to understanding Schelling's theory of the symbol.

---

[12] For anyone who has not raised himself to the level of the symbol, 'reality' '*is* no true reality at all, but is rather in the true sense non-reality' (390; 35).

[13] Certainly, the socio-political role of mythology would need to be emphasized for the purposes of an adequate presentation of Schelling's views on mythology. On this point, see especially the discussion of 'constant two' ('Artistic production has a socio-political task') in Shaw 2010.

[14] My discussion of 'speculative transformation' in Chapter 3 is again pertinent here: there are many ways in which Schelling's discussion of mythology is dependent on Goethe, the Schlegels, and Moritz (indeed, with respect to Moritz Schelling says as much (412; 49)); however, this should not deflect us from the main *philosophical* purpose of Schelling's construction of mythology.

[15] See further Hennigfeld 1973, 71.

What is Mythology?

The first question that needs to be asked is what Schelling means by 'myth-ology'. Indeed, in his correspondence with Fichte, he makes much of the peculiarity of his use of this term: 'If I make the claim that there are myths in the Old Testament and someone responds by asking how that could be if it teaches the unity of God, would it be my fault if this person cannot hear the word "mythology" without associating it with the trivial notion of a theory of the gods?' (*SB* 2:353; Fichte and Schelling 1997, 88). Likewise, in the *Philoso-phie der Kunst*, Schelling provides a comprehensive history of myth beginning with Homer, passing through the Christian sacraments and ending with *Naturphilosophie*. In what follows, however, I will focus merely on Greek mythology for this serves as Schelling's paradigm.

Yet, Schelling's concern is not with Greek mythology as a whole: he has no interest in the stories of heroes or even in the concrete detail of the *Iliad* or *Odyssey*; instead, he limits myth to exhibitions of 'the gods'. §37 reads, '*The entirety of the poetic renderings of the gods*, by acquiring complete objectivity or independent poetic existence, *is mythology*' (*SW* 5:405; 1989, 45). However, this is no mere arbitrary limitation, for Schelling designates as 'god' anything which manifests indifference absolutely. This becomes clear in §28: 'These same syntheses of the universal and particular that viewed in themselves are ideas, that is images of the divine, are, if viewed on the plane of the real, the *gods*' (390; 35). The term 'god' is the correlate of 'idea': both are constructions of the absolute in the third potency.[16] What is more, such a definition of 'god' should not surprise us. I pointed out at the very beginning of my exposition of Schelling's metaphysics that 'God' is one of the names Schelling gives reality. Just like 'the absolute' or 'identity', 'God' is a way of designating what is. Therefore, it seems natural that Schelling gives such significance to the gods and mythology—mythology treats what is, just as philosophy, theology, or natural science does.[17] Thus, Schelling comments, myths 'were more real for the Greeks than every other reality' (391; 35). To exhibit the gods is the very same task as to exhibit identity, reality, or the absolute. Gods are synonymous with ideas, so mythology is analogous to philosophy.

Schelling is most explicit on this point with respect to sculptural presenta-tions of mythology:

> Sculpture in and for itself...must portray gods, for its particular task is precisely to portray the absolutely ideal simultaneously as the real, and accordingly to portray an indifference that in and for itself can be found only in divine natures.

---

[16] Schelling claims in *Philosophie und Religion*, 'The true mythology is a symbolism of ideas' (*SW* 6:67), and in so doing neatly brings together my three foci: ideas, mythology, and the symbol.

[17] See Dietzsch 1975, 399.

> One can thus say that every higher work of sculpture in and for itself is a deity, *even if no name yet exists for that deity*. Furthermore, sculpture, if left only to itself, would have portrayed as realities all the possibilities residing in that highest and absolute indifference, and thereby quite independently would have filled the entire circle of divine figures and even invented the gods if they had not already existed. (621–2; 195; my emphasis)

Schelling is not interested in the named Pantheon of Greek gods, but in any absolute *Darstellung*, even those which are as yet nameless.[18] Mythology is the presentation of symbols already named and still to be named.

Ideas Intuited Really

In its narrower sense, the symbol is the absolute exhibited *in the real*; in parallel, mythology is a presentation of the ideas *within the real*. Mythology is synonymous with the ideas, but from the perspective of the real—that is, mythology intensifies the real element of ideas at the expense of their ideal element. Schelling writes,

> The universal symbolism or universal *Darstellung* of the *ideas* as real is thus given in mythology ... Indeed, the gods of mythology are nothing other than the ideas of philosophy intuited objectively or concretely. (*SW* 5:370; 1989, 17)

Myths are therefore *real* symbols: they exhibit the indifference of meaning and being, but through an excess of the real. They still exhibit other indifferences (and so are symbolic); however, they do not exhibit the indifference of real and ideal as an indifference, but rather stress the real over the ideal (hence, are real symbols).

We should be careful here to remember the qualifications to which I subjected Schelling notion of intuition in the last chapter. Myths are the ideas 'intuited' in the real, Schelling claims. However, to intuit the absolute really in mythology is not to perceive something already there; it is to construct the absolute. Mythology is therefore not a conglomeration of already existing works of art; it is an *activity* by which the absolute exhibits itself absolutely. This is what Schelling means when he speaks of mythology as 'absolute poesy' (406; 45)—the poeisis of the absolute as it forms itself into particulars. He writes, 'Mythology is nothing other than the universe in its higher manifestation, in its absolute form, the true universe in itself, image or symbol of life and wondrous chaos in the divine *Einbildungskraft*' (405–6; 45). The reference to 'divine *Einbildungskraft*' is key: mythology is part of the manner in which the absolute manifests itself through the informing of finite

---

[18] *Pace* Jähnig 1969, 2:191.

and infinite. Mythology is one moment of the absolute's self-formation, and a particularly absolute moment at that (since it is symbolic). I will return to this 'productive reading' of mythology when I consider Schelling's interpretation of heautonomy below.

Limited Absoluteness

Mythology also makes particularly clear one key tenet of Schelling's *Identitätssystem* as a whole: in myths, the absolute limits itself without thereby diminishing its absoluteness in any way. §30 of the *Philosophie der Kunst* reads, 'The determining law of all gods is pure limitation on the one hand, and undivided absoluteness on the other' (*SW* 5:391–2; 1989, 35). In other words, 'Within...limitation every form receives into itself the entire divinity' (392; 36). Elsewhere, Schelling dubs this 'the essence of all art' (639; 207) and 'the law of beauty' (Robinson 1976, 160). It is this, Schelling insists, which gives rise to 'the enormous significance of the gods', for this law is 'the means by which art acquires separate, self-enclosed figures for portrayal, and yet within each figure simultaneously the totality, the entire divinity' (*SW* 5:392; 1989, 36). Mythology as such is defined as '*Darstellung* of the absolute within limitation without suspension of the absolute' (405; 45).

The gods therefore exemplify a key aspect of Schelling's *Identitätssystem*: that formation is an intensification of the absolute, not its diminution. He writes:

> [The gods] are possible only through fantasy [*Phantasie*] which brings the absolute and limitation together and forms into the particular the entire divinity of the universal...According to the same law the universe forms and moulds itself...[Its] consistent and pervading law is absoluteness in limitation. (393; 37)

Schelling elsewhere states baldly, 'The mystery of all life is the synthesis of the absolute with limitation' (393; 36). 'Absoluteness in limitation' is a key phrase for mythology, the symbol, and also the *Identitätssystem* as a whole: it summarizes the fundamental process which all reality undergoes—and mythology and symbols undergo in an exemplary manner.[19] This is the process by which the absolute in-forms itself (*sich einbilden*) into ideas, which do not inadequately hint at an absolute beyond, but which are the absolute itself in an intensified form.

Of course, from the point of view of a theory of correspondence which privileges the original over the copy, this may look like a paradox (for example, when Schelling writes of a 'simultaneously limited and unlimited intuition of the absolute' (*SW* 5:394; 1989, 37)). Yet, from the perspective of a constructive

---

[19] See Barth 1991, 149.

epistemology, it is not. It is worth remembering Euclid and Kant's claim that through constructing a triangle one knows more of it than through its concept alone. Construction is a generative procedure, and this model lies at the basis of the law of 'absoluteness in limitation': to determine the absolute is generative. Myth is not an imperfect reproduction of reality, but an intensification or potentiation of it.[20]

It is because mythology exemplifies the law of absoluteness in limitation that Schelling conceives it as the most intense exhibition of the absolute possible in art. Mythology is symbolic—it exhibits the absolute absolutely in determinate forms.

The Indifference of Mythology

Mythology is symbolic—an absolute exhibition of the absolute—and, as one would expect, it thus displays the same properties as the symbol: heautonomy, syntheticism, and tautegory.

The heautonomy of mythology follows directly from the law of absoluteness in limitation. Each mythological *Darstellung* is absolute; each is a universe or self-enclosed world; that is, each god, according to Schelling, is a totality—sufficient unto itself and requiring nothing external. Hence, each god should exist 'first of all for its own sake . . . [It] should be absolute according to its own nature and should not exist for the sake of any purpose external to it' (*SW* 5:411; 1989, 49). Or again, 'Each is in and for itself what it is . . . None is there for the sake of another or in order to signify the other' (402; 42). This is what Jähnig dubs 'the *Totalitätscharakter* of Greek mythology' (1969, 2:184).[21] Each god in itself is ultimately heautonomous.

The syntheticism of mythology also follows directly from the law of absoluteness in limitation. Since every god is an absolute *Darstellung*, it produces the requisite indifference of opposites. Myths combine universal and particular (*SW* 5:403; 1989, 43); finite and infinite (453; 79), and possibility and actuality (391; 35). Indifference is expressed—as in the symbol—both extensively and intensively to the maximum possible extent.[22]

Finally, and obviously, since mythology stands at the point of indifference of all the above oppositions, so it does too in terms of the indifference between meaning and being. Myths are therefore tautegorical. Indeed, Schelling's most famous remarks about meaning passing into being occur in reference to

---

[20] See Wanning 1988, 77–83.

[21] Furthermore, as a collective as well the gods also exhibit heautonomy: they form 'a second *world*' (*SW* 5:414; 1989, 51). See Hennigfeld 1973, 78.

[22] Except in the case of the real and the ideal already discussed.

mythology in particular (although, of course, in the context of his discussion of the symbol):

> [It is] *not* that Jupiter or Minerva *means* or *signifies* this or *is supposed* to signify it. This would completely destroy the poetic independence of these figures. They do not *signify* it; they *are* it themselves. (400–1; 42)

The gods are '*real* beings that *are* simultaneously that which they signify' (410; 48). Schelling continues (as I have repeatedly quoted in this book):

> Each figure in [mythology] is to be taken as that which it is, for precisely in this way is each also taken as that which it means or signifies. Meaning here is simultaneously being itself, passed over into the object itself and one with it. (411; 49)[23]

The gods of mythology are symbols par excellence.

SCHELLING'S INTERPRETATION OF THE SYMBOL

It is now time to turn explicitly to a sustained comparison between the Schellingian and 'the romantic symbol'. To do so, I discuss in turn the three 'first-order' properties set out in Chapters 1 and 2 of this book (heautonomy, syntheticism, and tautegory).

Heautonomy

Just like 'the romantic symbol' and indeed all other theories of the symbol during the *Goethezeit*, Schelling envisages the symbolic image as heautono-mous. That is, it is self-enclosed and self-sufficient. It is *ab-solute* in the original meaning of the term—absolved from all relations.

The major respect in which Schelling makes this point (as we have seen) is in terms of signification and reference. The symbol does not signify anything outside itself; it does not have an external referent. Its meaning is self-suffi-cient. Art in general, for example, is 'a construction of a world as self-enclosed and as perfect as nature itself' (*SW* 5:351; 1989, 8). As such, the symbol is to be valued for its own sake and contains its own telos. It is 'without any external purpose' (357; 9). This is precisely the meaning of heautonomy: the symbol

---

[23] As Challiol-Gillet puts it (summing up nicely why I have dubbed this property of the symbol 'tautegory'), 'The god does not signify the universal, it is itself the universal. This is what Schelling will later name the tautegorical aspect of mythology, which is here its symbolic aspect' (1996, 41).

sets its own rule for itself and is thus incomparable to anything external. Schelling thus calls attention to 'the independent life' of the symbol: all symbols 'acquire a life within themselves' (461; 85), they have 'independent poetic existence' (405; 45). The symbol 'is something that exists and endures on its own power, a being *in itself* that does not merely mean or signify something else' (461; 85).

To this extent, of course, the Schellingian symbol displays the very 'first-order' properties which are also manifest by 'the romantic symbol' and all other symbols of the *Goethezeit*. However, differences appear when we begin to consider *how* the Schellingian symbol exhibits these properties—that is, for what reason and by what means it is heautonomous.

At stake here is the distinction between rationalist and empiricist interpretations of heautonomy introduced in Chapter 2—is heautonomy a result of construction or perception? Does the symbol manifest heautonomy like a blade of grass or a logical argument? It should be clear from the foregoing that I consider Schelling to come out firmly on the side of the rationalists: his is a constructive (not a perceptive) heautonomy. Perhaps the best place to get a handle on this is an early discussion of the notion of construction. In the Appendix to his 1798 *Abhandlung*, Schelling compares philosophical practice to the mathematical construction of a straight line in intuition. Schelling contends that both philosophy and mathematics are valid a priori because they produce their own objects:

> [The geometer] will be concerned only with his own constructions. This line, the object of this primordial construction, *exists* nowhere *outside* of this construction but is only *this construction itself*. The same is to be the case in philosophy... Whatever originates for [the philosopher] by means of [the initial] construction is *nothing outside* of it, and it *exists* only to the extent that he constructs. (*SW* 1:447; 1994b, 134–5)

Schelling conceives of philosophy's constructive procedure as one which generates a form of heautonomy—that is, the constructions are self-enclosed, without external reference. The construction does not refer to anything outside of it, but has validity only within the process of construction. Schelling continues:

> By virtue of this primordial construction, the philosopher obtains a product; however, this product exists nowhere *outside* of this construction, just as the straight line postulated by geometry exists only to the extent that it is primordially constructed and is *nothing outside* of this construction. (448; 135)

That is (translated into the language of the *Identitätssystem*), the absolute constructs itself and in so doing exists solely within its constructions. The *Darstellungen* which are products of this process of self-construction are completely self-sufficient; they form an absolute whole in themselves, with no reference to anything outside.

We see here how closely the experience of heautonomy is tied to that of construction in Schelling's philosophy (as well as his insistence on immanence). In consequence, the similarities to the rationalist, rather than the empiricist, tradition of heautonomy should be clear. Just like Spinoza, Schelling models the wholeness of construction on a process of geometrical reasoning in which the conclusion is wholly immanent to the act of postulating—it is not a form of immediate vision.

The issue can be further elucidated in terms of the respective theory of the organism presupposed by empiricist and rationalist heautonomy. All theories during the *Goethezeit* liken the symbol to an organism;[24] however, while, for theorists of 'the romantic symbol' (like Goethe) the organism is something encountered ready-made, for Schelling the organism is the product of a process of potentiation. Whereas theorists of 'the romantic symbol' consider the organism as a given, Schelling treats it genetically as one way in which the absolute exhibits itself absolutely. In short, heautonomy is experienced as a making, not as something already made.

The productive nature of symbolization is emphasized by Schelling. We have already seen this in the connection he draws between mythology and poiesis. In Robinson's lecture notes, it is stressed further:

> In art the mystery of creation becomes objective, and art is for this reason absolutely creative or productive. For the absolute in-formation which is objective in the production of art is the source of everything, and the production of art is thus a symbol of divine production. This principle of the absolutely immanent power of creation is that which produces. (1976, 158)

Art is one mode of the self-affirmation of the absolute. The absolute forms itself and this process of construction is also art and symbolization. In this regard, Schelling draws attention to the etymology of poetry as a form of poeisis—a productive or constructive activity.[25]

In a similar vein, Adams stresses symbolizing activity over the symbolic product in his discussion of the Schellingian symbol: it is this constructive procedure which is important to Schelling, not the entity produced. Helpfully, Adams criticizes Copleston's interpretation of Schelling as a 'two-world' Platonist (1975, 7:123–5):

> [Copleston] implies that the absolute in Schelling is somehow Platonically previous to nature, where it would be better to state the absolute is generated as idea...This is a fundamental difference between Schelling and Plotinus, for Schelling emphasises always...the living *process* as the source of reality. (Adams 1983, 59)

---

[24] Schelling, for example, speaks in this vein of 'the organism of art' (*SW* 5:357; 1989, 9).
[25] See Chapter 6.

This is a view that we have seen borne out at length in Chapter 4, and Adams goes on to apply it to Schelling's concept of the symbol:

> For the development of a theory of the symbolic, a dynamic rather than a Platonic or Plotinian Schelling is the important one. The dynamic Schelling finds in the intercourse of subject and object, rather than a window into a Platonic sort of archetype, the actual construction in each instant of a particular reality *behind* which there is nothing. The act of consciousness [or, more precisely, the self-cognition of the absolute] is a making. (62)

The Schellingian symbol is an act. It thus fits into Adams' category of the 'second type' of symbol in which 'the universal becomes not something previously there to be contained but something *generated by* the particular as the seed generates the plant' (19).[26] Drawing on Blake, Adams labels this form of symbol, 'prolific' (23)—a productive and creative process, rather than something encountered passively ready-made.

The above therefore provides some indications that Schelling subscribed to a rationalist, not an empiricist, version of heautonomy and that this makes his interpretation of the symbol peculiar (compared to 'the romantic symbol'). However, these indications are by no means conclusive, and we will return repeatedly to this issue in the forthcoming chapters. Indeed, it is only in the final chapters when I argue that Schelling presupposes symbolic practices (not symbolic objects) that it will ultimately be demonstrated that Schelling's interpretation of heautonomy is constructive.

Syntheticism

We should now be in a position to understand just how inappropriate Todorov's term 'syntheticism' is when applied to the Schellingian symbol. There is no synthesis in Schelling's *Identitätssystem*, and this is just as true for the symbol as for anything else. Synthesis is a minimally productive mode of reflection—one not adequate to describe the self-formation of the absolute (especially not in its symbolic mode). Of course, this is not to deny that there is much in Schelling's theory of the symbol reminiscent of syntheticism—the positing together of what are conventionally considered as opposites. As we have already seen at length, universal and particular, subjective and objective, infinite and finite, actuality and possibility are all posited together in the symbol. What Schelling says of Dante's *Divine Comedy* is valid of art as a whole (and, indeed, all things): 'It is the most indissoluble mixture, the most complete interpenetration of everything' (*SW* 5:686–7; 1989, 239). However, the symbol is a point of indifference rather than a synthesis. This is what is

---

[26] See further my discussion of Adams' work in Chapter 1.

key—and what differentiates the Schellingian symbol so fully from 'the romantic symbol'.

Synthesis presupposes an already existing opposition between two terms (whether universal and particular or real and ideal); yet, this is precisely what the *Identitätssystem* denies.[27] No qualitative opposition exists in the Schellingian cosmos: all there is is indifference expressed in different intensities. Universal and particular are originally indifferent, and are only seen as oppositional from a limited, minimally productive perspective. 'What is third for reflection is first for reason' is the guiding motif here: the identity of opposites is not the derivative result of a process, but what already is. Thus, Schelling conceives the identity of opposites in a manner very different from conventional syntheticism and so from 'the romantic symbol'.

Schelling versus 'the Romantic Symbol'

For 'the romantic symbol' (as I discussed in Chapter 1), the sign is primary; the symbolic mode of signification is only sometimes grafted onto it. That is, the symbol is precisely the result of a synthesis, the endpoint of a process in which the sign is the initial given state. Such is what I dubbed its 'additive model'. Schelling, however, completely departs from such a model. For him, the symbol is primary, and the sign a 'derivative' product of a process of distortion. The symbol is the norm and the sign the exception—this distances the Schellingian symbol decisively from the 'occasionality' of 'the romantic symbol'.

Indeed, according to Schelling, all there is is the symbol, and sign, allegory, and schematism (even image and concept) are merely less intense forms of the symbol. Thus, the symbol is not just the norm, it is the only state in which meaning and being can exist. There can be no purely extrinsic or causal connection, no relation of signification; only indifference which masks itself relatively under these different labels. Again, the complete divergence of such a model from 'the romantic symbol' (for which indifference is a state of exception) must be insisted upon.

Another aspect of 'the romantic symbol' Schelling rejects is partial tautegory. Theorists of 'the romantic symbol' remain enthralled to a view of meaning which conceives it as (partially at least) external to the image. This is the significance of the synecdochical metaphysics on which 'the romantic symbol' is grounded: the particular image participates in meaning, yet, at the same time, meaning always exceeds the particular. It is always both inside and outside the symbolic image. Synecdoche is, however, not a legitimate figure for Schelling's

---

[27] Although, again, this is not quite true if one stresses the dialectic of *Ineinsbildung*.

metaphysics: here, meaning and being primordially exist in complete and utter identity. Any claim that this identity is even partially incomplete is a falsification of reality. Meaning cannot exist separate to being in any way whatsoever; there is only complete identity between them. Thus, Schelling writes, being and meaning 'are absolutely one' in the symbol (*SW* 5:407; 1989, 46)—something neither Goethe (who conceives the universal as exceeding the particular) nor any other theorist of 'the romantic symbol' could claim. Synecdoche is not an option for Schelling. Niklewski sums this up as follows:

> [In the 'romantic symbol', there remains] the idea that symbolic embodiment can only succeed imperfectly, that [there is] an 'allegorical remainder', an ultimate discrepancy... [But this] is vigorously disputed by Schelling by means of the figure of identity. (1979, 87)

Another way of phrasing this divergence is that theorists of 'the romantic symbol' remain tethered to the category of signification. Thus, the symbol's participation in a universal meaning is still conceived along the lines of a form of signification. Schelling, however, rejects signification as a model for the relation of being and meaning. The relation between them is one of indifference, not signification. It is for this reason Schelling is so keen to reclaim the term *Sinnbild*—meaning and being are here represented as fully identical (412; 49).

Finally, what of the analogous evocation of the ineffable so dear to theorists of 'the romantic symbol'? Todorov envisions 'inexpressibility' as one of the basic features of all theories of the symbol during the *Goethezeit* (1982, 221), as do many other scholars.[28] We are now, however, in a position to see the falsity of this claim, because Schelling (at least) did not subscribe to symbolic inexpressibility. His symbol does not evoke the ineffable and there is no model of analogy on which it is based. Indeed, we have seen at length that there is no such thing as the ineffable or analogy in the Schellingian cosmos. The absolute fully exhibits itself in determinate forms; nothing is lost. Moreover, Schelling's rigorous commitment to monism means no dialectic of sameness and difference is to be found either ontologically or epistemologically in his philosophy. He is committed to univocity and construction, which both dispense with relations of analogy. These tenets are rigorously repeated by the Schellingian symbol. The absolute is completely present in each symbolic *Darstellung*—there is nothing outside the symbol.

What is more, while Schelling does equate symbolic meaning with the concept of infinity, his interpretation of the symbol is not in any way irrational or suprarational; indeed, the presence of the infinite in and as the finite is the very definition of *reason* for Schelling![29] For many, there may still remain a

---

[28] See also Müller 1937, 6; Sørensen 1972, 264; Titzmann 1979, 652; Halmi 2007, 93. For further criticisms of this view, see Hayes 1969, 280–1.
[29] See Barth 1991, 160.

question concerning the discursiveness of the symbol; however, I will argue in the next two chapters that the symbol in fact provides the very paradigm for Schellingian discourse. Hence, the meaning present in the symbol exceeds neither reason nor language; it is fully expressible. Jähnig makes this point clearly (emphasizing—as I have not—its relevance to Schelling's discussion of art in the *System des transzendentalen Idealismus*):

> This consideration of Schelling's notion of the symbol in the *Philosophie der Kunst* should serve to ensure the keeping apart of Schelling's definition of the fundamental character of art in the *System* as an 'unconscious infinity' from any irrationalist misconceptions. The property of 'infinity'... here has the sense for Schelling of the resoluteness and determinateness of *form* in Greek and all 'Classical' art. 'Infinity' and 'unconsciousness' do not imply a Romantic condition of nocturnal dreams or obscure-mystical premonitions... but the mystery of daylight clarity. (1969, 2:193)

Jähnig continues, art's 'meaningfulness [occurs] *within* clarity, *within* the determinate' (352). There is nothing inexpressible about Schelling's symbol. It is for this reason that the evocation of the ineffable by analogy so fundamental to 'the romantic symbol' is foreign to Schelling both generally in his metaphysics and specifically in his interpretation of the symbol.

Tautegory

All I have written above concerning Schelling's rejection of 'the romantic symbol' applies in turn to tautegory. According to Schelling, meaning and being are identical prior to separation, and, indeed, they never truly separate. The sign is a distortion and a tautegorical relation of meaning and being is the norm. In Chapter 2, I discussed the radicality of the idea of identity between meaning and being in the history of theories of language; yet, Schelling goes one step further than most proponents of tautegory: he does not just envisage the possibility and occasional actuality of tautegory, but claims there is only tautegory. He thus takes up a far more radical position than any other theorist of the symbol. He utterly rejects the 'occasionality' of conventional theories of the symbol, in which language (or art in general) is for the most part a sign but occasionally attains the status of symbol. Instead, the symbol is the basic—and, in the end, sole—mode in which language or art can exist. In short, unlike theorists of 'the romantic symbol', Schelling makes the symbol *the essence of language*. In §73 of the *Philosophie der Kunst*, language is not presented as incidentally symbolic on occasion, but is defined by the symbolic. Language, he writes, 'is the most appropriate symbol of the absolute or infinite affirmation of God' (*SW* 5:483; 1989 100)—an absolute *Darstellung* of the absolute in essence.

Again, it needs to be stressed just how much of a departure this is from the norm. I described in Chapter 2 the extent to which theorists of 'the romantic symbol' struggle with the idea of symbolic language. Not only do they fail to find much evidence of it,[30] they have conceptual difficulty conceiving of its very possibility. The idea of symbolic language for Goethe, especially, is a contradiction, for the symbol is defined in an anti-linguistic manner. Symbolic language becomes a paradox. For Schelling, this is not the case. Language is not only problematically or paradoxically symbolic; it is symbolic in essence. Language is defined as a fundamentally symbolic phenomenon. Indeed, Schelling goes one step further still: language is the most symbolic phenomenon—the phenomenon which fits most snugly with his theory of the symbol. Symbolic language is not the most problematic, but the paradigmatic manifestation of the symbol.

At the moment this is merely a claim. It will be the purpose of the next two chapters to show both how symbolic language is possible for Schelling and what it actually looks like. In what follows, I therefore interrogate Schelling's claim that the essence of language is symbolic in order to flesh out his radical interpretation of tautegory.

[30] See Halmi 2007, 3–4, 133.

8

Language in the *Identitätssystem*

In the previous chapter, I began to consider Schelling's radical interpretation of tautegory (the identity of being and meaning) and the consequences this has for his theory of language. One of the most important consequences, I argued, is that language is essentially symbolic, and this differentiates Schelling completely from other theorists of the symbol of his time. While theorists of 'the romantic symbol' define the symbol in a manner which makes it very difficult to reconcile with linguistic processes, this, I claim, is not the case for Schelling. Yet, for the moment this is merely a claim. The prejudice of contemporary critical theory is that to define language as symbolic is to define it in a manner antithetical to language's operations. The onus is therefore on me to demonstrate the necessity, the possibility, and the actuality of symbolic language in Schelling's *Identitätssystem*—and this is the task of the next two chapters. In the present chapter, I outline Schelling's need for a construction of rational language and also why his philosophy of this period does not fall foul of the anti-discursive criticisms usually levelled against it. I demonstrate that Schelling's treatment of language and his philosophy as a whole allows for a properly symbolic language. In the next chapter, I look at Schelling's construction of symbolic language itself by giving a detailed commentary on §73 of the *Philosophie der Kunst*.

In the first section, I focus on the practice of philosophy as a key example of a language that produces the absolute. In the second section, I consider a number of objections concerning the possibility of a specifically discursive *Darstellung* of the absolute on Schelling's philosophical premises. My task here is negative: to undermine objections usually made against the status of language in Schelling's philosophy.

THE NECESSITY OF SYMBOLIC LANGUAGE

My aim in this chapter is to consider in detail the role language plays in Schelling's *Identitätssystem* in general. With this aim in mind, it is first necessary to elucidate the reasons why I claim Schelling's construction of symbolic language is so crucial to the project of the *Identitätssystem* as a whole—that is, why Schelling needs his theory of symbolic language and needs to remain committed to it. In short, the reasons why this is so are the absolute status of philosophy and the absolute status of poetry—two tenets central to Schelling's enterprise. Schelling needs a theory of symbolic language otherwise he cannot justify the superiority of philosophy to mathematics or the pre-eminent position given to poetry as an expression of the absolute. In what follows, I focus solely on the example of philosophy, but a parallel exposition could also be given for poetry.

The Absoluteness of Philosophical Language

In the previous chapter, I examined Schelling's adherence to the idea that some *Darstellungen* by which the absolute exhibits itself are maximally productive—in other words, are symbolic. I also considered Schelling's claim that philosophy is one example of this. This commits him to the view that phenomena, like philosophy, which occur in language (and therefore operate discursively) can and do maximally express the absolute. Language, that is, is no obstacle to the absolute's self-exhibition.

Obvious examples of Schelling's commitment to such an argument are the very titles of the 1801 *Darstellung* and the 1802 *Fernere Darstellungen*. They do not employ this key term from Schelling's philosophy (*Darstellung*) for nothing. Schelling believes his philosophy is one of the modes in which the absolute exhibits itself, and, more than this, he believes it is one of the modes in which the absolute's self-exhibition is most intense. The *Identitätssystem* is *the* system of philosophy—a philosophy that has become absolute and, in consequence, is a maximal *Darstellung* of the absolute. In other words, it is a symbol. Schelling writes:

> Philosophy, then, is the presentation of the self-affirmation of God in the infinite fertility of its consequences ... Philosophy is the presentation of totality as it emanates immediately from God's self-affirmation as His own, eternal identity—hence it is presentation of totality as the One, and all philosophical and rational cognition is grounded in *this* identity of totality and oneness. (SW 6:176–7; 1994c, 167)

In the *Philosophie der Kunst*, Schelling is even more explicit: 'Philosophy is merely reason that has become or is becoming aware of itself ... Philosophy is the immediate or direct *Darstellung* of the divine' (SW 5:381; 1989, 29). Philosophy is therefore a paradigmatic example of a linguistic symbol (or symbolic language): a discursive yet maximal *Darstellung* of the absolute.

Schelling departs here from some of his contemporaries. As I noted in Chapter 6, for Fichte, philosophy is a *re*-construction of the absolute's original constructions. The absolute I constructs itself primordially in the individual I and it is the task of the philosopher to reconstruct this primordial activity. This was also Schelling's view of the role of the philosopher in his 1800 *System des transzendentalen Idealismus*: philosophy is a derivative enterprise concerned with replaying or re-presenting what has already taken place. This is not, however, Schelling's view after 1801: philosophy here is one more original *Darstellung* of the absolute; it is just as primordial as the absolute's exhibition in the self, in art, or in nature. Philosophy is part of the absolute's self-exhibition, rather than a derivative redescription of this process or its results.[1] To repeat Schelling's words from the *Philosophie der Kunst* (quoted above), 'Philosophy is the immediate or direct *Darstellung* of the divine.' The *Identitätssystem* is therefore a symbol of the absolute, in the technical sense I explored in the previous chapter—and so it requires a form of language that can be symbolic as well.

In Chapter 6, I rehearsed Schelling's claims for the superiority of philosophy over mathematics. Geometry exhibits the absolute allegorically, arithmetic schematically, but philosophy does so symbolically. As such, its constructions are reflected neither into space nor into time, but occur as intellectual intuition. Such assertions of philosophy's superiority depend, however, on the ability of its medium (language) to exhibit the absolute symbolically (as pure, unreflected intellectual intuition). Language needs to be capable of bearing symbols.[2] Schelling's description of 'divine philosophy' in his correspondence with Fichte makes this clear:

> It will...bring to life in infinite forms and shapes only the one, the absolute. Whatever it touches will immediately become holy by virtue of its touch, and this knowledge will transform everything into the divine itself...Yet it will be only a presentation, in thought and in works, of the One. (*SB* 2:326; Fichte and Schelling 1997, 80)

Philosophy produces 'the one, the absolute' in 'infinite forms and shapes'—such 'forms and shapes' are the articulated concepts and expressions which constitute the language of philosophy. Language *as the form of philosophy* must allow the one essence of all thought to be produced in ever more intense and potentiated ways. The *Identitätssystem* itself is no exception, and as my argument progresses, it will become increasingly clear that one of Schelling's overriding concerns at this period is to fashion a scientific language (or form) maximally productive of the absolute, a symbolic language that does justice to philosophy's subject matter.

---

[1] I here diverge from a number of critics who conceive Schellingian philosophy as a 'repetition' or 'reflection' of divine self-affirmation (Courtine 1990, 120–1; Fischbach 1999, 239). Schelling's originality is to have rejected this derivative status of philosophy.

[2] Moreover, one could infer, language also needs to be identified with intellectual intuition—a suggestion I make in the next chapter.

Ultimately, the question of philosophy's superiority reduces to the question whether there is a form of language (and so a form of philosophy that employs this language) appropriate to reason rather than mere reflection.

The *Identitätssystem* therefore requires a theory of symbolic language in order to justify its own possibility as philosophy. It is for this reason that, just prior to his construction of symbolic language in §73 of the *Philosophie der Kunst*, Schelling comments on the significance of this proposition to all of philosophy (not just aesthetics):

> We must remind ourselves here that the philosophy of art is actually general philosophy itself, except presented in the potency of art... [Therefore] we can assume here only certain propositions as being given by general philosophy, and not prove them ourselves. In this respect we preface our discussion with the following borrowed propositions. (*SW* 5:480; 1989, 98)

Such 'borrowed propositions', Schelling goes on to stipulate, include §70, §71, and §73—this last paragraph being Schelling's construction of symbolic language. Such a construction (although it occurs within the *Philosophie der Kunst*) belongs to philosophy in general. Indeed, in §73 itself, Schelling explicitly states, 'The proof of this proposition also belongs in general philosophy' (482; 99). The task of constructing symbolic language is a basic requirement for philosophy as such (not one restricted to aesthetics). For philosophy as a whole to get off the ground, Schelling needs to prove that there is symbolic language and that philosophy employs it to exhibit the absolute absolutely.[3]

However, all these reasons for the necessity of Schelling subscribing to the idea of symbolic language run up against obstacles. Many critics see the metaphysics and epistemology of Schelling's *Identitätssystem* as prohibiting the very idea of a rational or symbolic language. There are a number of tenets of Schelling's philosophy at this period (like his commitment to intuition) which stop him, it is claimed, from being able to entertain a symbolic language or in fact any discourse about the absolute at all. In order therefore to demonstrate the possibility of exhibiting the absolute in language, it is necessary to put paid to these misconceptions concerning what is perceived to be the anti-discursive set-up of Schelling's *Identitätssystem*. Therefore, in the second half of the chapter, I analyse and refute objections along these lines often levelled at Schelling.

---

[3] It should also be noted that the same is true for theology. For theology to gain its proper stature, i.e. for it to become 'absolute theology' (discussed in Chapters 10 and 11), it requires a discursive medium which does not hinder its exhibition of reality—that is, theology too needs symbolic language.

LANGUAGE AND INTUITION

One common misconception of Schelling's *Identitätssystem* is that his recourse to the notion of intellectual intuition excludes language and discourse. Tilliette expresses a typical, critical view: Schelling's 'philosophy of intuition is constantly menaced by the work of discursivity' (1970, 1:368). In the *Fernere Darstellungen* (in which intellectual intuition makes its reappearance), Tilliette continues, 'traces of discursivity... are energetically swept away' (372). Likewise, Beierwaltes claims that Schellingian intellectual intuition 'works in an immediate—non-discursive, non-objectifying—way' (1983, 82). He continues:

> For Schelling, it is true... that [the absolute] is inconceivable and difficult to express, for language... is inadequate to the expression of indifference... [Indifference] requires an intellectual intuition congenial to unity or the mystical *ekstasis* as the medium of evidence which, it is true, is prepared by discursive thought, but which stands above this. (1983, 99)[4]

We have dealt with this characterization of intellectual intuition as anti-discursive at length in Chapter 6. There I argued that, although this anti-discursive interpretation might well be true of Schelling in 1795 when mystical intuition seemed to transcend all discursive forms, it is not at all true of Schelling's employment of the concept between 1801 and 1804. Schelling here appeals to intellectual intuition in muted form as a component of the process of construction. There is no need to consider this an anti-discursive move.

The Critique of Jacobian Intuition

One way of charting Schelling's shift away from an anti-discursive interpretation of intellectual intuition is through his growing hostility to Jacobi. At the turn of the nineteenth century Jacobian 'faith' was the very epitome of an immediate awareness of reality that bypasses any form of mediation (whether syllogistic or discursive). Faith is the paradigm for all attempts at that period to escape from 'the prison of language'. Moreover, it is certainly true that Schelling's conception of intellectual intuition in *Vom Ich* is modelled closely on Jacobi's epistemology. Its subtitle (*Über das Unbedingte im menschlichen Wissen*) is Jacobian in inspiration, and Jacobi receives a number of glowing references within the work as well (1:156; 1980b, 67–216; 109). More importantly, Schelling follows him closely in rejecting concepts, argumentation, and all forms of language as expressive of the absolute. Schellingian intuition *at this period* is an act that transcends words. However, after the turn of the century, Schelling became increasingly sceptical about, and then outright

---

[4] See also Halmi 2007, 148–53.

hostile to, Jacobi's thought.[5] While many of Jacobi's problems remained crucial to Schelling, after 1801 the answers Jacobi provided were deemed incorrect.

It is in the publications of the *Kritische Journal* that Schelling's vitriol against Jacobi is most often vented. Schelling lists 'the preaching of Jacobi' as one particularly virulent form of contemporary 'dogmatism' (*SW* 5:109; 1985, 368–9). Faith, Schelling and Hegel write more specifically, 'has no scientific significance and has no interest either' (5:6; Hegel and Schelling 1985, 277). As Tilliette contends, throughout the *Identitätssystem* Schelling stresses 'the problems ... issuing from Jacobean mysticism' (1970, 1:313), continuing, 'The irrational ... and the suprarational are foreign to this epoch' (411). Behind all these attacks lies Jacobi's anti-conceptual, anti-discursive interpretation of faith. Schelling rejects it: from 1801 onwards, he is after something different—an interpretation of intellectual intuition compatible with language.

The Critique of Fichtean Seeing

Another way of articulating Schelling's distance from anti-discursive interpretations of intellectual intuition is by means of his thesis that all entities are composite. Everything is a mixture of the three potencies (finite, infinite, eternal) in different amounts, and so all things express both particular and universal, finite and infinite, and concept and intuition (except that in different things the stress falls on one aspect). This is as true of intuition as it is of anything else. Intellectual intuition is not merely perceptual, but a compound of perception and concept. Genuine intuition, Schelling insists, 'is all at once the finite, the infinite, and the eternal' (*SW* 4:293; 1984a, 189–90). Intuition of the absolute is not merely a 'seeing' (as it is commonly conceived), but the indifference of 'seeing' and concept.

This becomes clear in Schelling's critique of Fichtean epistemology. By philosophizing through 'seeing', Fichte begins with something impoverished and even fictional. Hence, when Fichte writes to Schelling (in criticism of the 1801 *Darstellung*), 'One cannot start out from *being* ... rather, one must start out from seeing' (*SB* 2:341; Fichte and Schelling 1997, 82), Schelling responds by claiming that to begin with seeing means one can never attain anything more than mere seeing: 'The necessity to proceed from seeing confines you and your philosophy to a thoroughly conditioned series in which nothing of the absolute remains' (348; 85). In contrast, Schelling insists, 'The identity of ideal and real ground = the identity of thought and intuition. [This is] the

---

[5] See *SB* 2:239.

highest speculative idea: the idea of the absolute, where intuition is thought and thought is intuition' (348; 85).

Philosophy presupposes that intuition is not merely intuitive in a limited sense (in which it is opposed to what is conceptual and discursive). Intuition must rather designate something absolute: not mere seeing, but the indifference of seeing and thinking. There is therefore no reason why Schelling's appeal to intuition would exclude language; instead, there is every reason to conjecture it includes language. To emphasize subjectivity and the process of seeing over thinking (as Fichte does) is to relegate being 'to the realm of belief', and Schelling asks Fichte, 'Is this not sufficient proof that your notion of knowledge is not the absolute, but rather that it remains in some way conditioned knowledge?' (348–50; 85–7). By stressing the perceptual, 'seeing' element in cognition, Fichte traps himself in subjectivity and is unable to attain the absolute.

In *Bruno*, Schelling expands on this critique. Intuition 'can only be that truly real element wherein thought and being are forever indistinguishable'. It is 'the absolute identity of thought and being'. Whenever Fichte conceives reason as a mere 'seeing', he 'distort[s]' it. Fichtean seeing, Schelling continues, 'is not truly intuition, but only a distorted and confused reflection thereof' (4:292–3; 1984a, 189–90). Intuition, for Schelling, is not something merely perceptual and anti-discursive, but a compound entity that encompasses discursive elements.

Hegelian Discourse

One means by which many commentators criticize Schellingian intuitionism for excluding discourse is by stressing Hegel's supposed 'improvements' on Schelling. While Schelling remained in thrall to an anti-discursive intuitionism, the story goes, Hegel managed to introduce discursiveness back into philosophy. For example, di Giovanni writes, the Hegelian 'kind of discursiveness has nothing to do with the intuitionism of Schelling' (1987, 663). Schelling is forced to construct reality by means of intuition, di Giovanni claims, 'that is to say, not *discursively*' (661). By rediscovering the labour of the concept and the negation which motors thought, Hegel transformed philosophy back into something capable of being presented in language.

In order to realize how false (or, at least, oversimplistic) such a picture is, one need only look at Schelling's own response to the *Phänomenologie*. He writes to Hegel in 1807 after having read the Preface:

> I admit that as yet I do not comprehend the sense in which you oppose 'concept' to intuition. By concept you can mean nothing other than what you and I have

called 'idea' whose nature it precisely is to have one aspect whereby it is concept and another whereby it is intuition. (*SB* 3:471–2; translated in Vater 1984, 96)

Schelling insists that his notion of the idea is *already discursive*. Hegel's recourse to the concept adds nothing to what is already present in his *Identitätssystem*; it is in fact a regressive move which establishes a dualism between intuition and concept where previously there had been identity. The idea—as the indifference of concept and intuition—already contains a universal, conceptual, and so discursive element, as well as a particular element. There is no need to separate the concept out from this to provide a necessary supplement. 'The idea' is sufficient and contains within it all the properties that the Hegelian concept could ever exhibit, including discursiveness.

The Discursive Understanding

A similar criticism is often made by means of the term 'the discursive understanding' and this is again meant to show Schelling's philosophy to be anti-discursive. 'Discursive understanding' is contrasted to 'intuitive reason', implying that Schelling valorizes a form of thought (reason) which leaves no room for language. Language belongs to the subordinate understanding alone. During his *Identitätssystem*, Schelling is meant to have associated the low level of cognition engendered by the understanding with the epithet 'discursive': discourse is thus disparaged along with the understanding. Lukács, for example, writes that 'the antithesis of discursive and intuitive plays a downright crucial role in Schelling's philosophy', implying that intuition here occupied the superior position at the expense of discourse (1980, 140). 'Language is the tool of the understanding and dependent on images', as Vater puts it (1984, 60).[6]

However, the phrase 'discursive understanding' does not occur in Schelling's works between 1801 and 1805 (apart from one minor exception which I discuss below). It is an invention of later commentators and is just not Schellingian. It is the term 'reflection' which Schelling associates indelibly with the understanding and disparages as a minimally productive form of cognition. Of course, the rejection of reflection is also a rejection of a certain type of discourse, one based on signification and the qualitative opposition between image and concept in the sign; however, symbolic language is precisely what is left unscathed by this, for symbolic language belongs to reason, not the understanding. To therefore dub the understanding 'discursive' is to have too narrow a conception of discourse. Schelling conceives of a form of discourse (opposed to the conventional sign) which is not a product of

---

[6] See further Vater 1984, 58, 60; Llewelyn 1990, 184; Barth 1991, 152.

reflection or the understanding, but is a genuinely expressive *Darstellung* of the absolute.

SCHELLING'S OTHER REFERENCES TO LANGUAGE

Another reason why Schelling's philosophy is often taken to be anti-discursive is the fact that—apart from a few crucial exceptions—Schelling's passing remarks about language between 1801 and 1805 are very often negative and slighting.[7] Such remarks are often used as evidence for Schelling's inability to account for language as a positive means of exhibiting the absolute.

Bruno and *Philosophie und Religion*

In *Bruno*, for example, Schelling makes two negative remarks about the capacity of language. First:

> No mortal discourse, however, is capable of adequately praising this heavenly wisdom or of measuring the profundity of the intelligence that is perceived in [the celestial] motions. (*SW* 4:272; 1984a, 171)

Second:

> It is difficult to express the inner essence of the eternal in mortal words, since language is derived from images and is created by the understanding. (302; 199)

It is of course this second quotation which has led critics to speak of the 'discursive understanding' in Schelling's philosophy. However, both of these quotations are rather non-technical in their evocation of 'heavenly wisdom' and 'mortal words', and we must remember that the *Bruno* as a whole mimics Platonic dialogues, often at the expense of faithfully transcribing Schelling's own thought of the time. We should not take some of its rhetorical flourishes too seriously. Schelling, however, also makes a very similar point in *Philosophie und Religion*:

> Whoever has encountered this force of evidence which resides in the idea of the absolute and it alone and which no human language has the power to express will consider that all [Eschenmayer's claims concerning faith] do not belong to such an idea. (*SW* 6:27)

---

[7] It is worth emphasizing that I am only interested in Schelling's references to language between 1801 and 1805. There are of course plenty of other discussions of language in his work both before and after these dates, but these lie outside the remit of this book. For surveys of Schelling's philosophies of language, see Hennigfeld 1984; Surber 2000; Whistler 2010.

It is necessary to stress here that I am not claiming that Schelling subscribed to symbolic language consistently throughout his *Identitätssystem*: discussion of it and of the symbol in general belongs almost exclusively to the *Philosophie der Kunst*, and Schelling seems oblivious of the potential these concepts offer him both before[8] and after this period. It may well be, therefore, that other statements from within the *Identitätssystem* gainsay it.

Nevertheless, Schelling's emphasis on 'mortal' or 'human' language in the above passages from *Bruno* and *Philosophie und Religion* should give us pause for thought. Such phrases are obviously meant to be contrasted with the language of the gods. 'Gods' here is both a Platonic rendering of the Schellingian absolute, but also should recall Schelling's definition of the gods discussed in the previous chapter. 'Gods' in this latter sense are *Darstellungen* which exhibit the indifference of the absolute to the highest possible extent: the divine is for Schelling what is most indifferent in reality. The gods name those entities which express the absolute most fully. To speak of 'mortal words' is therefore to implicitly leave open the possibility of divine or absolute language. Indeed, this is precisely what commentators who dub the understanding discursive forget: the understanding is discursive only in a mortal, human or non-absolute manner. Schelling certainly does not rule out a higher, more productive form of discourse.

What is more, there are passages scattered through the *Identitätssystem* where Schelling does write of language positively and in a manner very reminiscent of §73 of the *Philosophie der Kunst*. In *Über die Methode*, for example, Schelling designates language a 'spiritual medium' (SW 5:225; 1966, 19), and goes so far as to speak of 'language as a direct expression of reason and, as such, an object of scientific construction' (246; 39). The 1804 *System* also makes positive claims about language's capabilities in a short, but highly suggestive passage. Language is designated the proper expression of reason (SW 6:491) and 'the highest in nature' (492). 'It is,' Schelling continues (employing obvious Christic overtones), 'the Word which has become flesh, the infinite, eternal affirmation which resounds in the universe' (492).

§39 of the *Philosophie der Kunst*

A bigger problem for my purposes is a passage from the *Philosophie der Kunst* itself where Schelling seems to relegate language as such to a low level of significance. Here one can neither counter that these remarks belong to a different period of Schelling's thinking nor that they are merely rhetorical flourishes. This demotion of language occurs in §39 of the lecture course—the

---

[8] For example, in his 1801 lectures on metaphysics, Schelling calls language 'a product of reflection' (Troxler 1988, 40).

very section in which Schelling constructs the symbol and which I discussed at length in the previous chapter. When defining his notion of schematism (which, we remember, is a less productive mode of *Darstellung* than symbolism), Schelling gives a number of examples of schematic exhibition, one of which is language:

> Our act of thinking the particular is actually always schematization of that particular, we really need only reflect upon that perpetually active schematism at work even in language in order to secure an intuition of it. In language, too, we make use of merely universal designations even for the designation of the particular. To this extent even language itself is nothing more than a perpetual schematization . . . Language itself is, of course, completely schematic. (*SW* 5:408; 1989, 46–7)

Schelling here asserts categorically—and in complete opposition to his construction of language later in the lecture course—that language never attains the level of a symbolic exhibition of the absolute, but remains purely and perpetually a schematic *Darstellung*. Indeed, on this view, philosophy itself— as a linguistic description of the absolute—becomes merely schematic and equivalent (not superior) to arithmetic in its ability to express the absolute. This characterization of philosophy (and the same could be said for all forms of linguistic art) seems to refute Schelling's own pronouncements on its superiority to arithmetic and other schemata. Schelling here rules out the possibility of symbolic language, and in so doing rules out the possibility of a maximally expressive philosophy (and also, by extension, theology and poetry).

   Yet, one can well understand Schelling's temptation to define language as merely schematic. Schemata apply universal designations to particulars indifferently. It seems plausible to understand language along the same lines: the universal term 'house', for example, applies to particular houses, no matter what their idiosyncrasies. The universal here predominates, operating *at the expense of* the particular. Particulars are subsumed under universal terms. This is of course a view of language based on a model of representation, where a universal term stands for or represents a group of particular images—and such a representational conception of language is incompatible with Schelling's definition of the symbol. Language, according to §39, is a less productive (that is, reflective) mode of being. Symbolic language is here ruled out, for language is understood as incompatible with the symbol. This schematic determination of language is another resource therefore for those critics who see Schellingian philosophy as incompatible with language. It is also the passage in which the Schellingian symbol resembles other theories of the symbol (especially the 'romantic' interpretation) most closely.

   From these considerations, it should be clear that this cannot be Schelling's final word on the nature of language. And indeed it is not: Schelling returns to the question of language in §73 of the lectures and there embarks on a full construction of language. It is here that he realizes the need for a far more positive construal of language than he has heretofore given—that is, he realizes the need for a construction of symbolic language. It should also be noted in this regard that the *Philosophie der Kunst* was never intended for publication; it is therefore unsurprising that there are contradictions between different parts of the lecture course, and rather than attempt to reconcile them, it is perhaps more helpful to treat such inconsistencies as evidence of Schelling's philosophical development—his gradual realization of the necessity of a theory of symbolic language, and so the gradual abandonment of his characterization of language as schematic.[9]

THE INEVITABLE MUTISM OF
THE *IDENTITÄTSSYSTEM*

Finally in this chapter, I want to consider one more set of arguments which are meant to demonstrate Schelling's dismissal of language and his commitment to an anti-discursive philosophical position. Two very similar arguments have been proposed by Tilliette and Beiser, both purporting to show how the presuppositions of the *Identitätssystem* force Schelling into a dilemma between either (a) remaining consistent to these presuppositions and so abandoning any talk about the absolute whatsoever or (b) talking about the absolute but reneging on some of these central presuppositions. I contend, on the contrary, that this is a false dilemma, born out of a mistaken interpretation of the *Identitätssystem*. I wish to refute the suggestion that Schelling commits himself to an inescapable mutism.

The problem Beiser and Tilliette both locate in the *Identitätssystem* arises out of Schelling's commitment to talking about the absolute and so his consistent refusal to resort to apophatic practices. To talk about the absolute is to determine it or (at the very least) to apply predicates to it. Yet, to say 'A is p' (a statement of predication) is precisely not to say 'A is A' (a statement of the law of identity), and, since identity alone defines the absolute, such a statement of predication falsifies and distorts the absolute identity which defines the essence of the absolute. In short, (A is p) ≠ (A is A), and so language is an inappropriate medium to express Schelling's absolute. At stake is thus the possibility of any form of predication from the Schellingian viewpoint.

Beiser, for example, writes:

---

[9] For an attempt to reconcile §39 and §73, see Hennigfeld 1984, 21–4.

Schelling's Parmenidean vision...forbids the possibility of all intellectual discourse about the absolute. The proper conclusion to draw from it is that we cannot say anything at all about the absolute, because to do so would be to ascribe some property to it, which is to posit some difference within it. To attribute some property to the absolute is to divide it, because any property has its determinate meaning only in contrast to its negation. *Omnis determinatio est negatio*, Spinoza said, and Schelling agreed. But if this is so, then the sum and substance of absolute wisdom should be nothing more than A = A. After uttering this empty tautology the philosopher should, like all better mystics, observe a strict silence. (2002, 568)

In a similar passage, Tilliette remarks:

Absolute identity is determined only negatively... 'Pure unadulterated identity' is, so to speak, withdrawn, inaccessible. It is above definitions and predicates. At the moment of utterance, philosophy of identity seems sworn to a fixed mutism. (1970, 1:328)

Tilliette later concludes, 'The dilemma is patent: either mutism and the sterility of the absolute or an impure melange of contrasts' (366). That is, either Schelling remains committed to his rigorous monism of absolute identity (in which case language becomes impossible) or he relaxes the rigour of his metaphysics and so language become possible.[10]

There are two reasons why I object to these arguments: in both cases, it is a case of the critics not realizing the significance of crucial tenets in Schelling's *Identitätssystem*—in the first case, the importance of the form/essence distinction, and, in the second, the importance of quantitative differentiation.

First, the role of form. Having argued that Schelling is forced through the consistency of his monism into a mystic silence, Beiser continues:

But Schelling never had the makings of a Trappist. True to his prodigal and prolific nature, he provides a rather elaborate account [in the 1801 *Darstellung*] of the various potencies of the absolute... How could Schelling justify such a theory in the face of his vision of the absolute as pure oneness, utterly undifferentiated unity? His response to the difficulty is to distinguish between the *essence* and the *form* of absolute identity... All knowledge of the absolute, and so all discourse about it, belongs to its form rather than its essence. (2002, 569)

It is, Beiser suggests, the form/essence distinction which can ultimately save Schelling from mutism. However, crucially, Beiser finds this distinction 'tenuous and artificial' (569). Hence, Schelling is (or at least should be) cast back into mystic silence. The problem with Schelling's theory of form, according to Beiser, is that if form is determinate it once again falsifies the essence of the absolute and, in consequence, is in no way adequate to the absolute's

---

[10] See similar arguments in Knittermeyer 1928, 316; Beierwaltes 2002, 397.

indeterminate essence. Predication falsifies identity once more, and so again talk about the absolute becomes impossible. Beiser writes,

> Any form whatsoever—even the very sparse form limited to the distinction between the subject and predicate of A = A—involved some distinction and so could not grasp, but only falsify, absolute identity itself. The main problem is that the absolute, as pure indifferentiated unity, cannot have any form at all, any specific manner of being, given that all determination involves negation. This means, however, that all discourse about the absolute must stand outside it, so that it has a purely imaginary status, consisting in nothing more than arbitrary and artificial abstractions of the understanding. (569)

In his conclusion, Beiser returns to this problem which he considers unresolved within the *Identitätssystem*: 'Schelling places the discursive knowledge of the finite subject *outside* the absolute, and even condemns it to the realm of illusion' (592–3).

One of the problems with Beiser's criticisms is his comparison of Schelling's thought to the mystical and apophatic traditions. More apt would be a comparison to Spinoza or Bruno. The assessment Beiser makes of Schelling's philosophy that 'the absolute, as pure indifferentiated unity, cannot have any form at all, any specific manner of being, given that all determination involves negation' seems absurd in the context of early modern metaphysics: is Spinozist substance hindered from existing in specific modal forms merely because it is monistic? For Spinoza, there is no contradiction between a monistic conception of substance and substance existing determinately in its attributes and modes—and the same is true of Schelling.

We must remember two things: first, Schelling's complete rejection of representation and, with it, correspondence and adequacy. Form in no way needs to correspond to or adequately represent essence. This is not how the two are related. Beiser and Tilliette both conceive of the absolute as an entity existing behind appearances, to which language tries vainly to adequately correspond. We have seen at length in this book, however, that this is not the case: Schelling rejects a transcendent absolute, the model of correspondence, representation, and so the criterion of adequacy. Second (and relatedly), it is necessary to recall Schelling's commitment to 'absoluteness in limitation'—to the fact that formation is a generation of absoluteness, not a diminution of it. Forms are merely more or less intense productions of absolute indifference; they do not fail to represent correctly some transcendent entity named 'the absolute'. Nothing exists above, beyond, or outside of form. Determination, in this respect, is a production of absoluteness, not its falsification. As forms approach indifference, they generate more and more absoluteness, until the idea or symbol is attained. To speak of forms falsifying identity misses the point that this identity exists only in forms.

This is only half the story, however, and does not fully refute Beiser and Tilliette's claims. The full picture only emerges with the introduction of Schelling's theory of quantitative differentiation. Twice in the above passages Beiser has recourse to the Spinozist maxim, *omnis determinatio est negatio*.[11] Yet, in Chapter 5, I rehearsed Schelling's rejection of this principle at length. Beiser assumes that to determine is to negate, but this is precisely what Schelling's theory of quantitative differentiation rejects. In consequence, he reconceives determination as a type of affirmation. Differences in determination depend on the intensity with which this affirmation is made. To determine the absolute is not to negate its absoluteness, but to affirm this absoluteness to a certain generative extent. As late as 1807, for example, Schelling insists, 'Definiteness of form in nature is never a negation, but always an affirmation' (7:303; 1953, 334). All determination is quantification: this is the Schellingian principle which replaces its Spinozist forebear. Schelling replaces the binary of affirmation or negation with a quantitative scale of different degrees of affirmation of identity.

In *German Idealism*, Beiser is overhasty in his dismissal of Schelling's doctrine of quantitative differentiation (2002, 568); he does not realize the extent to which it alters the very structure of determination and predication. On this model, 'A is p' is not a negation of a pre-existing absolute, but an affirmation and intensification of it. Language can talk about the absolute without falsifying it, because language (as a determinate form) is one of the ways in which the absolute is produced in the first place.

From all these considerations, it should be clear that Schelling was able to readily admit the possibility of talk about the absolute, that this was a perfectly coherent admission on his metaphysical tenets. This is because the *Identitätssystem* is founded on two metaphysical principles which critics have seriously neglected: the ineluctable formation of the absolute and quantitative differentiation. It is these two principles which make possible Schelling's construction of symbolic language. The absolute is necessarily formed and this is an intensification of its absoluteness, rather than a diminution; moreover, determination of the absolute (which is a necessary consequence of discoursing about it) does not falsify identity, but rather affirms it in a specific intensity. These principles provide the reasons why any *Darstellung* can be symbolic and not merely reflective: it can fully produce the absolute in limited form. Although all *Darstellungen* are determinate, this is in no way a loss of absoluteness; instead, 'absoluteness in limitation' structures the *Identitätssystem*. What is more, there is no reason why such considerations concerning *Darstellungen* in general should not apply to linguistic *Darstellungen* in particular.

---

[11] Beiser is not the only commentator to claim Schelling subscribes to this dictum during the *Identitätssystem*. See also Frank 1985, 124; Bowie 1993, 63, 71.

To understand precisely how symbolic language operates, however, it is necessary to turn to §73 of the *Philosophie der Kunst*, where Schelling provides a detailed construction of a language of the absolute. This forms the subject matter of the next chapter.

9

§73 of the *Philosophie der Kunst*

§73 of the *Philosophie der Kunst* puts paid to a common critical prejudice. It is a widely held assumption that Schelling and the other German Idealists have nothing interesting to say about language at all, that they ignore language. However, this is just not the case. While Kant, it is true, does seem oblivious to questions of language (as I argued in Chapter 2), Fichte, Schelling, and Hegel all devote small but significant passages of their philosophical output to interrogating the nature of language. §73 of the *Philosophie der Kunst*, Fichte's essay on the origin of language and the sections devoted to language in Hegel's *Enzyklopädie* (and more implicitly 'The Religion of Art' section of the *Phänomenologie*), all demonstrate German Idealist engagement with language. Indeed, Surber has plausibly argued that it is later commentators on German Idealism (rather than the Idealists themselves) who are guilty of neglecting language. 'None of the standard histories of German Idealism itself,' he writes, 'make any significant mention of linguistic issues either as figuring in Idealist thought or as impacting prevailing interpretations of it in any significant way' (2000, 305). What is more, all studies that do discuss philosophies of language in German Idealism 'have generally remained at the margins of the scholarly mainstream and have as yet had little significant impact on it' (305).

This point is nowhere more true than in Schelling scholarship. Only a handful of scholars[1] have engaged at all with Schelling's construction of language in the *Philosophie der Kunst* and, as Bär points out, the baleful state of critical awareness of his philosophy of language is further evidenced by the fact that these scholars are ignorant of each other's existence.[2] Schelling's engagement with language in the *Philosophie der Kunst* deserves better treatment than it has so far received. Only by paying attention to §73 will critical ignorance of German Idealist philosophy of language begin to be overturned.

---

[1] Coseriu 1977; Hennigfeld 1984; Wanning 1988; Rosenau 1990; Bär 1999; Surber 2000.
[2] 'Schelling's philosophical and philological significance remains scarcely acknowledged. The fact that Henningfeld obviously does not know Coseriu's essay and Wanning is ignorant of them both appears symptomatic' (1999, 144).

In this chapter, I therefore provide a commentary on Schelling's construction of symbolic language in §73 of the *Philosophie der Kunst*. Here we discover how in fact symbolic language is constituted. The previous eight chapters have prepared the way for our understanding of this construction: we are now in a position to appreciate its contemporary context, the metaphysical and epistemological principles underlying it, the general theory of the symbol out of which it derives, and finally its systematic necessity and possibility. All that is now needed therefore for §73 to make sense is a statement of the additional twists Schelling provides in the section itself.[3]

FROM IDEAL SYMBOL TO SYMBOL OF SYMBOLS

§70 presents the context in which Schelling's construction of symbolic language takes place. It returns to the subject matter of §39 (Schelling's construction of the symbol in general), and recapitulates some of the conclusions reached in the earlier section. Like §73, §70 is also a 'borrowed proposition', demonstrating (as I argued in the previous chapter) the importance of Schelling's theory of the symbol to his *Identitätssystem* as a whole. §70 reads:

> The absolute becomes objective in the phenomenal realm by means of the three unities to the extent that the latter are... [taken] in their relative difference as potencies, thereby becoming symbols of the ideas. (*SW* 5:480; 1989, 98)

Schelling goes on to maintain (summarizing his earlier argument in §39) that the absolute 'produces itself' as 'a particular unity' which thereby 'becomes a symbol of [itself]'. Each symbol is an 'image' or 'objectification' of a 'primal idea', and Schelling defines such objectification as follows, 'The essence of all particularity *is* within the absolute itself, but this essence manifests itself through the particular' (480–1; 98). From all this, Schelling concludes that there are entities within the real world (organisms, for example) and entities within the ideal (like art) which—as particular—still maximally express the absolute (i.e. the eternal predominates in them). They are real and ideal symbols, respectively. Nothing is lost in so becoming particular, rather absoluteness is generated in limitation. Schelling has thus summarized his theory of the symbol from §39.

In the next two propositions, Schelling turns to the *material* forms which act as real symbols of the absolute. These real symbols constitute the forms of the formative arts, especially sculpture. It is because matter can become symbolic and maximally express the absolute that sculpture can also be a

[3] Unless otherwise stated, all quotations in this chapter are from *SW* 5:482–6; 1989, 99–102.

symbol. Sculpture expresses the absolute so well, precisely because its medium is able to bear symbolic expression. Having thus dealt with 'the real side of the world of art', Schelling turns to the verbal arts and their medium, language, to produce a parallel construction. This therefore is the context to Schelling's construction of symbolic language: having summarized the significance of symbolic *Darstellungen* for his philosophical project, Schelling attempts to construct a form of language that is able to permit the verbal arts to be symbolic in the same way as sculpture is.

However, in §73 itself, Schelling goes a step further than this context would suggest. He does not merely show that language is an ideal symbol in parallel to matter as a real symbol; he, in fact, demonstrates that language is a symbol situated at the point of indifference between ideal and real. Language is not just an ideal symbol; it is *the* symbol which overcomes any distinction between real and ideal—and so it expresses the indifference of the absolute to an even greater extent than any other symbol. It is the symbol of symbols—the 'indifference of indifference...the identity of identity' (Bär 1999, 165).[4]

Language becomes a more paradigmatic symbol than matter, and this forms the basis for Schelling's conjecture that poetry and linguistic symbols are generally superior to material symbols. Language replaces nature as the paradigm for Schelling's philosophy.[5] Yet, language's superiority is merely quantitative, for Schelling here dissolves any qualitative difference between real and ideal (or formative and verbal) arts—all art forms are in fact quantitatively different manifestations of symbolic language (Wanning 1988, 159–61). Indeed, language forms 'the structure of the absolute' (163), so all symbols (including all artworks) are ultimately linguistic. Language is not (as for theorists of 'the romantic symbol') the most problematic symbolic phenomenon, but the most exemplary symbol. In what follows, I chart this shift in more detail.

THE INDIFFERENCE OF REAL AND IDEAL

Language as Symbol

The proposition defended in §73 reads, 'The ideal unity, as the resolution of the particular into the universal, of the concrete into the concept, becomes objective in *speech* or *language*.' The task of the section is thus to construct language as ideal symbol of the absolute; moreover, Schelling here indicates that he will do so by showing how language unifies particular and universal, concrete image and concept. He continues, 'Language constitutes the...resolution of the concrete

[4] See also Wanning 1988, 160–1, 166.   [5] I discuss this further in the final chapter.

into the universal, of being into knowledge.' Language, that is, is symbolic: as the indifference of particular and universal, it exhibits syntheticism; as the indifference of image and concept, it exhibits tautegory. Language, Schelling insists, is a symbolic phenomenon and this is why it is an appropriate medium for poetry.

How does language exhibit these indifferences? Such is the question which dominates §73. That is, why does the eternal predominate in language, or how does language exhibit both particular and universal, image and concept as indifferent? The answer is that language is both ideal and real to exactly the same extent: it is not just an ideal symbol, but *the* symbolic form (and the only symbolic form) which indifferentiates ideal and real. Schelling writes:

> Viewed from the one side, language is the direct expression of something *ideal*...
> in something *real*, and is to that extent itself a work of art. Yet viewed from the
> other side it is just as definitely a work of nature, since it is the one necessary form
> of art that cannot be conceived as being invented or generated by art. Hence, it is
> a natural work of art.

Language is equally real and ideal—a work of nature and a work of art. To this extent, the context surrounding §73 is (as I argued above) misleading: language is not a purely ideal phenomenon to be contrasted with matter which is real. What is more, language should not even be confined to the *Philosophie der Kunst*: while art (the subject matter of the *Philosophie der Kunst*) is predominantly ideal, language is not. Philosophy of language is more than just philosophy of art; it treats a more indifferent and hence more productive domain of being, situated at the very heart of the *Identitätssystem*.

Language is the absolute in-formation of real and ideal. This guarantees its status as symbol. It manifests, rather than conceals, indifference and so in it the eternal predominates. Language is thus an entity of the third potency, an idea; it is, in short, a symbol.

The fact that language is the only symbolic form to fully indifferentiate real and ideal has the further consequence that *language manifests reality most*. In Wanning's words, 'Nothing more intense is possible within the *Identitätssystem*' (1988, 166). In language, the third potency dominates, so to describe something in language is to produce it in the most intense possible manner. Entities exist most intensely in words, or put differently, the idea or symbol of an entity is its name. Such a striking conclusion strengthens Schelling's claims for the superiority of philosophy, theology, and poetry: as discursive forms of thought, they are able to produce reality more intensely than anything else.

Language and Reason

The importance of Schelling's description of language as both a work of nature and a work of art should not be overlooked. This is a remarkable statement. As we know, according to Schelling, reality can be divided into two series of potencies: the series of real potencies runs matter, light, organism; the series of ideal potencies runs knowledge, action, art. Although Schelling's construction of language occurs in his *Philosophie der Kunst*, he here makes clear that (as I have just mentioned) language should not be subsumed under the potency of art; indeed, it should not be restricted to the ideal series of potencies at all. Language is not just a work of art; it is also a work of nature: unlike any other phenomenon (with one exception), it must be considered both ideally and really:

> From a finite point of view... language shows itself as belonging to either nature or the ideal world, and can thus be designated... as either organism or artwork. Considered absolutely, it exhibits more than any other phenomenon the unity of the real and the ideal and thus is considered as a direct consequence of absolute identity itself. (Bär 1999, 165–6)

Language is not limited to one series of potencies or the other, but transgresses the very potency-determinations that constrict all other phenomena. Language operates *trans-potency*. Bär graphically depicts this situation as in Fig. 4.

In fact, the only other phenomenon given a comparable status in the *Identitätssystem* is *reason*. Reason, like language, cannot be constrained within one potency (or even one series of potencies) alone (5:378–9; 1989, 27). Language and reason are the two exceptions to Schelling's *Potenzlehre*. It is therefore unsurprising that Schelling makes much of the similarities between the two in §73.

Language moves beyond both the predominance of the real found in matter and the predominance of the ideal in art to the third, eternal potency (where real and ideal are indifferent), and, in so doing, it attains the same status as reason. It is 'for this reason', Schelling infers, 'language and reason (which is precisely absolute knowledge, the knowing of the ideas) have one and the same expression in most languages'. Schelling here draws attention to the linguistic (and presumably conceptual) identification of language and reason in most thought-forms. He insists forcefully on the need to see language as not only occupying a status equal to that of reason, but as existing in identity with reason. Rational language is a tautology: reason is necessarily linguistic and, what is more, this language in which reason necessarily and universally occurs

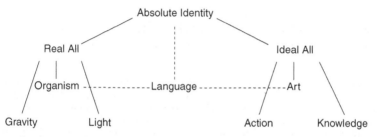

Fig. 4. *The place of language in Schelling's system* (Bär 1999, 166)

is the symbolic language Schelling constructs in §73. It is not only the case therefore that Schelling lays claim to a language adequate to reason, he sees reason itself existing *as* this form of language.

Language as Intellectual Intuition

It is worth pausing here to make a conjecture which, although nowhere explicitly endorsed in Schelling's writings, seems a natural consequence of this construction of language: intellectual intuition is, for Schelling, to be identified with symbolic language.

Let us recall the role intellectual intuition plays in Schelling's *Identitätssystem*: knowledge is construction and this construction involves 'laying out' a idea in pure intuition—indeed, the very notion of 'idea' itself implies that knowledge exists simultaneously as both conceptual and 'laid out'. In geometry and arithmetic, the intuition is reflected through space and time, respectively; however, philosophy is superior to mathematics, because its ideas are constructed in pure, unreflected intellectual intuition. Yet, what precisely is this intellectual intuition? Geometry, for instance, is spatial because it is a *Darstellung* of mathematical concepts in space; the 1801 *Darstellung*, on the other hand, 'lays out' its ideas in language. On such evidence, it seems plausible to suggest that language is here synonymous with the unreflected intellectual intuition in which philosophical constructions take place.[6] The medium in which philosophy is performed is symbolic language.

This is, however, extremely surprising considering the prejudices of most commentators. As I discussed in the previous chapter, Schelling's intuitionism is supposed to bar him from discourse; his commitment to intuition is to be opposed to Hegel's reintroduction of discursiveness into philosophy. We have seen this to be false. In fact, we now discover that Schelling seems to consider intuition as a form of discourse!

THE GENESIS OF SYMBOLIC LANGUAGE

In the following paragraphs of §73, Schelling attempts to construct the real and the ideal elements of language separately, before bringing them together. To

---

[6] Again, it is important to emphasize the limited connotation of *Anschauung* in Schelling's era. *Anschauung* does not mean perception, but merely an immediate and particular form of knowing. Language too is non-perceptual for Schelling, but is an immediate and particular *Darstellung* of the absolute. It does not seem strange to conclude therefore that language is the highest form of intuition (in this restricted sense); it is the medium in which the absolute constructs itself most intensely.

summarize Schelling's argument: he points to the shortcomings of phenomena in which the real predominates (nature) and of phenomena in which the ideal predominates (art), in order to show how language combines both real and ideal so as to avoid such limitations. Whereas pure matter and pure concept fail to produce the absolute fully, language—as the indifference of the two—succeeds.

Schelling begins with a summary of his metaphysics: 'The absolute is by nature an eternal act of producing. This producing is its essence. Its producing is an absolute act of affirming or of knowing, where two sides constitute the two postulated unities.' Reality produces itself, and such production generates the indifference of two terms—for example, the indifference of the universal and particular or of the ideal and the real. Each of these terms is equivalent to the absolute and to all the other terms.[7] However, the entities which are produced by the absolute can still exhibit a surplus of one of these terms—that is, the absolute's indifference is always expressed in a specific intensity. If the real predominates, then, 'as a particular unity, [the absolute] no longer appear[s] as idea or as self-affirmation, but rather as something affirmed, as matter'. Schelling concludes therefore that matter can act as a *Darstellung* of the absolute: 'The real side as a particular unity becomes the symbol of the absolute idea.'

Yet, Schelling is quick to insist that, while matter is a symbol, it is still not fully productive of identity. This is because matter does not maximally exhibit the indifference of one pair of terms in particular—the real and ideal. He depicts this relative failure as a form of 'concealment': matter is only an allegory of the absolute; its surplus of the real *masks* maximal indifference. Matter lacks an ideal element; it lacks meaning, and so subsists as relatively meaningless being. In consequence, the eternal potency, in which indifference is most intensely manifest, fades into the background, hidden behind the prominent real aspect of matter. This excess of the real therefore becomes a 'husk or covering' hindering meaning from becoming manifest. Hence, Schelling writes, 'The real side as a particular unity becomes the symbol of the absolute idea here, *which only through this husk or covering becomes recognized as such*' (my emphasis). The predominance of the real in matter lessens its ability to produce the absolute; identity must be recognized somehow *despite* this concealment.

In the next paragraph, Schelling goes on to show how a similar failure of expression occurs in predominantly ideal phenomena, like paintings. This time, however, it is not due to concealment that the absolute is not maximally expressed. Thus, unlike matter, there is no husk: 'Wherever the ideal unity itself, as a particular unity, functions as the form for the idea—in the ideal

---

[7] Hence, Schelling specifies that the real 'is the entire idea, the entire infinite self-affirmation'.

world—it is not distorted into something else.' However, ideal phenomena are still only 'relatively ideal', for the real stands outside of and opposed to such pure ideality. It is still only the second potency which predominates (still not the third potency of the eternal). In consequence:

> It remains ideal, yet such that it leaves the other [real] side behind and thus does not appear as something absolutely ideal, but rather merely as something relatively ideal that possesses the real outside of itself—standing over against it.

The real is partially excluded.

Having pointed out the shortcomings of matter and art, Schelling then turns to the genesis of symbolic language. What the predominantly ideal entity lacks, Schelling makes clear, is a means of objectivization. It remains caught at the subjective pole of the magnetic line and requires some form of 'body' in order to shift towards indifference. We should remember in this regard Schelling's notion of the *Bildung* of all *Darstellungen*: everything that exists strives to maximize its productivity and so strives towards indifference. Schelling writes:

> As purely ideal, however, [the ideal entity] does not become objective, but rather returns to the subjective and is itself the subjective. Thus it necessarily strives *yet again* toward a covering, a body, through which it may become objective without detriment to its ideality. It integrates itself again through something real.

The ideal must take up the properties of the real within itself without thereby annulling its ideality. The *Darstellung* strives to manifest the indifference of ideal and real, to be simultaneously universal meaning and particular body. This striving thus culminates in a meaning which objectifies itself without thereby concealing itself behind its objective form. It takes on an appropriate body which does not obscure the ideal, but is precisely what allows the ideal to reveal itself. A 'transparent' (or even translucent) material form now bears the concept.

Absoluteness in limitation is thereby achieved. Schelling concludes:

> In this integration the most appropriate symbol of the absolute or infinite affirmation of God arises, since this affirmation *here* represents itself through something real without ceasing to be ideal (which is precisely the highest requirement), and *this* symbol is language, as one can easily see.[8]

Schelling here resumes his theory of the symbol. The symbol is 'the most appropriate' or most productive *Darstellung* possible—it exhibits the absolute in a particular to the maximum possible extent. Such is 'the highest requirement'

---

[8] A similar summary is given later in the lecture course, 'Regarding the basis and significance of language itself, let me refer you to §73 where we proved that it is the most appropriate symbol of the absolute cognitive act, for this act appears in language on the one hand as *ideal*, not real, as in being, and yet integrates itself on the other hand through something real without ceasing to be ideal' (635; 204).

(what Schelling elsewhere calls 'the law of beauty')—absoluteness in limitation. Yet, now Schelling claims, this highest requirement is achieved most completely in language, and language alone. Only language exhibits the absolute in a determinate form to such an extent that the real and ideal are thereby manifest as indifferent: 'Language [is] the infinite affirmation that expresses itself in a *living* fashion.' The ideal is expressed or objectified in language, but in a way that does not encase it behind meaningless being. It is expressed in language in a way which intensifies its meaning. Such is 'the sublime significance of language'.

Therefore, Schelling here goes beyond what was intimated in §39 and so contends that not only that language can be symbolic, but that language is the very paradigm of the symbol. That is, symbols are linguistic! Language here names the only entity which attains the point of indifference between real and ideal, and which in consequence becomes 'the most appropriate symbol of the absolute'. Language is the symbol par excellence.[9]

Again, it needs emphasizing how far Schelling's views are from those of his contemporaries. Kant distanced the symbol decisively from all 'mere characteristics'; for Goethe also language was the most problematic symbolic phenomenon (his use of sculpture as the paradigm for the symbol made it very difficult for him to envisage how language could really be symbolic). We are not in a position yet to claim that Schelling fully overcomes these difficulties; however, what is clear from this passage is the extent to which Schelling thought he had overcome them. His system culminates in language. It is for this reason critics have claimed: 'Language must appear as the very crux of his *Identitätssystem*' (Surber 2000, 322), Schelling 'gave language a special place and function' (Bär 1999, 167), or 'Schelling's philosophy of art ends in a philosophy of language' (Seidel 1976, 111).

Moreover, we also see here the extent to which Schelling repudiates those critics who see no room for language in the *Identitätssystem*. Language can be symbolic, an absolute *Darstellung* of the absolute, Schelling here asserts. It is 'the most appropriate *symbol* of the absolute'—neither allegorical, nor schematic. This construction of language makes possible the superiority of philosophy to mathematics and the pre-eminence of poetry.

THE ORIGIN OF LANGUAGE

Yet, this is still mere assertion. Schelling does claim that 'one can easily see' the symbolic nature of language, for it does indeed seem uncontroversial to define

---

[9] See Bär 1999, 167.

language as the real embodiment of ideal meaning, concepts conveyed in images. However, this is to say very little, since everything in the Schellingian cosmos is some mixture of real and ideal; there are no purely real or purely ideal entities. A further claim is still possible, though: as the above argument implies, language is the indifference of ideal and real, of concept and image. The evidence for this further claim seems lacking, however: the sign, for example, possesses image and concept in equal amounts, but these are related extrinsically and causally (rather than through indifference). Schelling, of course, claims language is a 'symbol', but we need to discover how exactly it is symbolic.[10] Why is language founded on the symbol, rather than the sign?

Unfortunately, Schelling does not provide a single explicit argument to demonstrate this. As I mentioned in Chapter 7, it is only after 1809 that one can find Schelling explicitly criticizing the sign in favour of another model for language. However, it is clear from §73 of the *Philosophie der Kunst* that Schelling does also hold a similar view at this earlier date, as can be seen most explicitly in his intervention in the controversy over the origin of language. At the end of §73, Schelling appends some comments on this question:

> At this point I would like to make some brief remarks concerning the variously posed question concerning why reasonable beings opted specifically for language or voice as the immediate body of the inner soul.

Schelling immediately articulates his disagreement with the premise of the whole debate as it had been carried out throughout the eighteenth century: 'Yet even the question itself views language as an arbitrary choice or invention...Yet language is not that accidental. There is a higher necessity.' In consequence, 'Both assertions—that it arises as an invention of human beings, through freedom, and by divine instruction—are false'—that is, Schelling rejects both the typical answers to the question of the origin of language. The theological response of Süssmilch that language is a result of divine instruction and the Condillacian solution that it is a product of human freedom are both wrong. They form a false dilemma, an antinomy resting on an incorrect presupposition—arbitrariness.

The arbitrary nature of the sign, and so any unmotivated relation between signifier and signified, is therefore categorically rejected by Schelling. There is a 'higher necessity' to how language operates. The conjectures of earlier linguists do not exhibit 'the absolute idea of language', but treat the question

---

[10] The problem is compounded when Schelling appeals to the following as an illustration of the identity of meaning and being in language: 'Concrete and nonconcrete elements are one here; the most palpable element may become the sign for the most abstract.' This use of the term 'sign' demonstrates that what Schelling here claims concerning symbolic language is also true of language founded on the sign. They both unite meaning and being—the sign does it extrinsically, the symbol intrinsically. The question therefore becomes more insistent: what evidence is there that language identifies the two intrinsically rather than extrinsically?

of the origin of language from a limited standpoint, the standpoint of reflection: 'The whole question concerning the origin of language, at least as it has been treated until now, is merely an empirical one with which the philosopher accordingly has nothing to do.'[11] The philosopher must look to the eternal, to 'the idea itself' of language, free from the distortions of reflection: 'In this sense, language, just as the universe itself, still emerges in an unconditional fashion through the eternal effect of the absolute cognitive act.' Hence, all previous philosophy of language has not been speculative enough.

Schelling here announces the need for a speculative transformation of linguistics that would transform pre-existing empirical and psychological theories into a genuinely philosophical account—language according to its idea, rather than according to reflection: 'The controversy over a divine or human origin of language is in the *Identitätssystem* sublated into a "construction of language"' (Hennigfeld 1984, 16). Such a speculatively transformed philosophy of language would provide an adequate account of its 'higher necessity' and so of its symbolic essence. Such a philosophy of language would rigorously demonstrate the incorrectness of presupposing arbitrary signs, and, in consequence, the cogency of a language of symbols.

Frustratingly, however, it is at this point Schelling closes the section with the following remark:

> An exposition of the particular model of reason and reflection within the structure and inner conditions of language belongs to a different sphere of science than the one with which we are here concerned and in which language itself functions merely as a medium.

This is tantalizing, precisely because at no other place in his *Identitätssystem* (nor indeed in his philosophy as a whole) is such an exposition given. The reader is left wondering what detailed linguistics was lurking behind these tantalizing glimpses.[12]

THE HEAUTONOMY OF LANGUAGE

What then of Schelling's claims for symbolic language? In his remarks on its origin, Schelling gestures towards 'a higher necessity' to language without

---

[11] 'Contemporary theories of the origin of language remain inadequate because they have no ontological-metaphysical basis' (Hennigfeld 1984, 21).

[12] Perhaps further details of the workings of Schellingian symbolic language could be inferred from his theory of music which provides a much fuller 'model of immanent meaning' (Biddle 1996, 35). Here, Schelling sketches how quantitative differences in intensity give rise to rhythms. In Biddle's words, 'The sign... carries within itself the immanent code, the very "signness" of its designation' (35). See further Biddle 1996; Spitzer 2004.

explicitly describing in what this higher necessity consists; however, what these remarks do tell us is that Schelling certainly thinks the relation between image and concept, being and meaning in language is not an 'accidental' one, but is instead symbolic. Therefore, it seems fair to conclude that their identity is an intrinsic one—a relation of indifference—rather than an extrinsic or causal one. In consequence, language is based on symbols not signs.

There is further, indirect evidence for this view within §73 itself, and this can be inferred from the extent to which language exhibits all three first-order properties of the symbol. We have seen at length that Schelling conceives language as displaying syntheticism and tautegory: it unifies the real and the ideal, image and meaning. Language does not conceal its meaning behind a husk, nor does it retreat into the subject; in language, meaning takes on sensuous form without thereby reducing any of its meaningfulness. Language is meaningful being: it is tautegorical (and therefore synthetic).

Schelling also demonstrates the extent to which language manifests heautonomy or self-contained unity. Indeed, it exhibits heautonomy at various levels: first, on the level of language as a whole ('Language viewed absolutely or in itself is unified or *one*'); second, on the level of individual languages ('Each language is a universe if taken by itself'); third, in individual utterances (different tones and sonorities 'are all blended in human language, which accordingly does not particularly resemble any one sonority or tone, since all reside within it');[13] finally, even individual words possess a form of heautonomous wholeness through the interplay of vowels and consonants that occur within them. The word forms an organic whole of soul and body. Even in the individual word, real and ideal, body and soul, are intermingled to form a self-sufficient whole which generates its own meaning internally: 'Each new word is a particularisation of the absolute' (Coseriu 1977, 5).[14]

Language is therefore one on many levels: 'Everything resides as one in language, regardless of the perspective from which one views it.'[15] As a result, language mimics the identity which constitutes reality or, more technically, it produces absolute identity most intensely. 'Absolute identity is expressed in language to an even greater extent...Language itself thereby becomes the symbol for the identity of all things.' Language is maximally productive of reality, because it exhibits formal identity. It is completely indifferent—'indifference exhibited objectively' (Coseriu 1977, 6)—and this is what makes it a symbol, the most productive *Darstellung* possible.

[13] 'Speech is the material of all tones and sonorities reduced to indifference,' he later writes (*SW* 5:635; 1989, 204).
[14] See also Schelling's discussion of the heautonomy of rhythmic, poetic language (*SW* 5:635–8; 1989, 205–6—*SW* 6:491–2).
[15] Language is therefore an organism (Hennigfeld 1984, 20).

This, therefore, is Schelling's response to the need for symbolic language—a construction of the ways in which language is symbolic. Language is the indifference of meaning and being; it is the indifference of ideal and real; it possesses a 'higher necessity' than the mere sign, and it exhibits heautonomy on many levels. Schelling has demonstrated that there is a language appropriate to reason, not reflection—a language that can faithfully articulate symbolic forms of thinking. Philosophy can therefore be superior to mathematics, because its discursive medium is also superior. Schelling is not trapped in a mute prison, unable to utter the intuitions of the absolute he has attained; instead, he has shown how language articulates the absolute in the most intense possible way.

Part IV

Metaphilosophy

10

Science Without Reference

Following the metacritical attacks mounted by Hamann and Herder, it became impossible for *Goethezeit* philosophers to ignore the close relationship between philosophies of language and metaphilosophical practice. One could no longer coherently both consign all languages to inadequacy and claim to be writing an adequate philosophical text. In this vein, Maimon engages in a rhetorical analysis of the vocabulary of the transcendental philosopher in his *Versuch über die Transzendentalphilosophie* (2010, 139–72), while Fichte's *Von dem Sprachfähigkeit und dem Ursprung der Sprache* justifies the arbitrary sign through transcendental argument as an implicit response to metacritical attack.[1] Schelling's pre-1809 work, however, seems on first glance to hark back to an age of linguistic innocence. Compared with Fichte and Hegel who like nothing better than to discuss their own practice of philosophy, Schelling is often reticent about metaphilosophical themes in general.

In this final part of the book, I contend that such appearances are misleading. I employ Schelling's construction of symbolic language in §73 of the *Philosophie der Kunst* as the key to elucidating his metaphilosophical practice. Schelling takes seriously the demand to write in a symbolic language, a language suited to the productivity of the *Identitätssystem*. He also criticizes previous philosophical attempts to live up to the rigour of symbolic language. This gives rise to the enumeration of a set of practices by which such failure can now be avoided. In short, I argue that Schelling recognizes the need to articulate a metaphilosophy that integrates his philosophy of language.

I proceed in these final two chapters by focusing on the example of theology as a means of bringing out Schelling's metaphilosophical presuppositions. As we shall see, not only does this concentration on theology immediately flag up the relationships that should hold between the different sciences (and in particular between philosophy and theology), theology is also integral to Schelling's account of the failures of modern thought to live up to the demands of symbolic language and rationality in general. It is precisely by dethroning theology from its

---

[1] See Chapter 2 and Surber 1996.

privileged position in modernity and thereby democratizing the sciences that Schelling believes symbolism will again be achieved in thought.

In the present chapter, I draw some conclusions from my analysis of §73 of the *Philosophie der Kunst*, concentrating especially on the significance of this theory of language for scientific practice. I argue that the elimination of reference stands at the heart of Schelling's construction of symbolic language. This results from his commitment to absolute tautegory and rationalist heautonomy. Instead of functioning referentially, language is defined by the degree to which it produces reality (or identity or God), and this is furthermore dependent on the indifference of being and meaning language attains. That is, what matters is the structure or form of language, rather than its content. Implicit in this idea of language, I go on to argue, is a critique of Christian theology which typically confuses God with meaning, or the eternal with the infinite. Schelling thus sees the need to reform theology, so that its form (i.e. its language) can become symbolic and so that it can manifest God (or reality) in its words to the maximum possible extent.

It is here therefore in Part IV that discursive practice takes centre stage in my argument. Having built up a picture of Schelling's thought and its place in his contemporary context over the previous nine chapters, I now draw out its consequences for forming an absolute system.

FROM THE INFINITE TO THE ETERNAL

To begin therefore, I return to Schelling's construction of symbolic language to draw out its most important and contentious aspects.

The Elimination of Reference

There are two overriding elements to the Schellingian interpretation of symbolic language which distinguish it from the standard 'romantic' interpretation: the commitment to absolute tautegory and rationalist heautonomy.

First, Schelling is committed to an absolute interpretation of tautegory: meaning and being are not partially identified in some kind of synecdochical structure (in which being is the part and meaning the whole). Rather, meaning is utterly identical to being—there is nothing to distinguish them. Schelling thus goes far beyond his contemporaries on this point. No distinction can be drawn between meaning and being; they exist equally and indissociably in a state of indifference.

Second, Schelling's rejection of the representational paradigm is thorough. And it follows from this that words cannot represent something in the world; in fact, there is no outside to words. Language, that is, is heautonomous. Here we arrive at the second major element of Schelling's interpretation of symbolic language: his rationalist interpretation of heautonomy. For theorists of 'the romantic symbol', meaningful being is to be perceived; this is a passive encountering of a ready-made object whose properties are self-evident. Schelling rejects this view. Meaningful being, according to him, is not to be perceived but constructed. It is not seen but made.

On both the above points, Schelling rejects the interpretation of symbolic language offered by his contemporaries. The Schellingian symbol is based on a very different interpretation. Moreover, all the criticisms Schelling implicitly makes of 'the romantic symbol' have the same end in view: the annihilation of any residual elements of signification from symbolic language. For Schelling, there is no more signification. First, absolute tautegory denies the transcendence (or even otherness) of meaning in any form. Meaning does *not* (even partially) exist separate from being—and so no process or activity (including signification) is required to transfer from the latter to the former. Second, rationalist heautonomy asserts the production of meaning *as* being (rather than the pre-existence of meaning). Language remains completely immanent to itself. Reference is no longer a valid category.

This is a conception of language that is 'acratylian'. Cratylism, as I explored in Chapter 2, designates those theories of language which make the signifier/signified relation a motivated one. I am here asserting, however, that to call Schelling's theory of language cratylian would be incorrect (he does not think the signifier/signified relation is motivated), so too would be naming it non-cratylian. Schelling criticizes theories of both motivated and unmotivated signs for presupposing that signifier and signified are distinct. Cratylian theories of the motivated sign assume the two exist separately (so as to be related naturally); non-cratylian theories of the unmotivated sign assume the same (for the purpose of an arbitrary relation). According to Schelling, this separation distorts the truth, i.e. it distorts the absolute indifference of meaning and being. There is for Schelling no longer any signifier or any signified, solely the symbol. While it is due to a broadly cratylian impulse that Schelling makes this move, he goes beyond Cratylism: there is no longer a motivated relation at the heart of language; there is in fact no relation at all. All reference and signification is eliminated. This makes Schelling's theory of language as radical as anything offered in Western linguistics before or since. The elimination of reference also means that Schelling avoids the more pernicious aspects of Cratylism: there can be no 'naturalization' of one referent above all others,[2] because there is no referent whatsoever.

Again, this shows the extent to which Schelling goes beyond 'romantic' theories of the symbol. In cratylian conceptions of language, a motivated

---

[2] Again, see Chapter 2 for this problem for Cratylism.

relation between sign and reference (being and meaning) holds, but theories of the symbol take this conventional cratylian interpretation of language one step further by subscribing to tautegory: the cratylian correlation between sign and referent is here radicalized into some form of ontological sameness between them. An identification of meaning and being (however partial) occurs, and this moves theorists of the symbol beyond the category of motivation. Schelling takes up a more extreme position still—not only does he go beyond Cratylism as normally understood, he also takes up a position more radical than any other theorist of the symbol. He identifies meaning and being absolutely. In consequence, like cratylian theories, there is no unmotivated relation between sign and referent, but, unlike cratylian theories, there is no motivated relation either. And this is because there is no longer any sign nor any referent, but just immediately and fully meaningful being. All relations of reference—even cratylian ones—are revoked.

The Two Relations of Language

What is the point of acratylian language? Language is typically defined by its referential function, so then what is left of language after this has been eliminated? In order to obtain a preliminary answer to such questions, I first need to distinguish between two relations in Schellingian symbolic language: the relation of the finite to the infinite and the relation of the finite/infinite to the eternal.

In Chapter 5, I introduced Schelling's *Potenzlehre*: all phenomena consist in three elements—the finite, the infinite, and the eternal. The different amounts of each element distinguish one thing from another. This three-term series needs to be borne in mind when considering language too. Language has a finite element (its image or sound), an infinite element (its meaning), and an eternal element (its idea). Therefore, language does not consist merely in a relation of finite being to infinite meaning, but in a more complex interplay of three elements. That is, Schelling adds an extra, third term to the typical view of language: language is not merely defined by the relation of the finite to the infinite, but also by a supplementary relation that both the finite and the infinite have to the eternal. So, in order to genuinely comprehend Schelling's conception of symbolic language, both relations need to be noted.

First, as we have seen, Schelling interprets the relation of finite to infinite or being to meaning in a radical way—as pure identity. The finite is the infinite and the infinite is the finite. In symbolic language, the first two potencies are in a state of complete indifference and, whenever this is not the case (even partially), this marks the deterioration of symbolic language into schema or allegory—the slide of rational language into reflective language. This idea of the identity of meaning and being may seem somewhat difficult to grasp in the abstract, but there is an obvious illustration of such identity in everyday language: performative statements. The statement 'I promise' does not refer to anything external to itself, but creates the very state of affairs which is its meaning. Meaning is generated as the words are formed—this is a constructive procedure. Performative statements thus exhibit the very rationalist heautonomy Schelling demands of all language: meaning and being are constructed simultaneously and identically. Meaning is performed in and as being; it is thus wholly immanent to, and ultimately identical with, being.

Yet, this is not the only (or even the most important) relation out of which Schellingian symbolic language is established. This honour falls to the second relation of the finite and the infinite *to the eternal*—a relation which is unique (at least in its specifics) to Schellingian language. This is the additional element that sets Schelling's construction apart from many other linguistic theories in Western modernity. Language is not constituted by the relation of being to meaning alone, but also by the way both being and meaning relate to a third element—the eternal.

How then do the first two potencies relate to the third potency in symbolic language? The answer is: through *production*. We have repeatedly seen the central role production has for Schelling in Part II and it is no less important here. The being and meaning of language produce the eternal (or the idea or reality). Just as all individual *Darstellungen* are defined and differentiated by the degree to which they produce the absolute, so too language. Language is defined by the extent to which it produces the absolute, and symbolic language does so to the maximum extent. This is a repetition of the form/essence distinction within language: meaning and being together constitute the form of language and this form is the condition for the production of essence. Language is not only defined by the indifference of meaning and being, but also by its generation of the absolute.[3]

Absolutely crucial here is the relation that holds between these two defining linguistic relations (meaning to being and meaning/being to the eternal). In short, the second relation is completely dependent on the first. The extent of the indifference pertaining between meaning and being is the sole criterion for the intensity of the reality that is thereby generated. Indeed, this can be put much more strongly: the extent of the indifference pertaining between meaning and being *is* the intensity of the reality thereby generated—and this is because indifference is another name for reality. Construction of indifference and construction of reality are identical procedures. The two relations therefore collapse back into one: productivity is synonymous with indifference.[4]

---

[3] This is ultimately the same thing, as we shall see in the next paragraph.

[4] Again, the form/essence distinction is helpful: the amount of essential identity produced is dependent on (or is) the formal identity of the *Darstellung*. So, the more the form of language is indifferent (i.e. the more meaning and being are identical), the more essential identity is generated.

Symbolic language is the absolute maximally potentiated in language (and Schelling even contends, as I discussed in the previous chapter, it is the absolute maximally potentiated *tout court*).

This then is the point of Schellingian symbolic language; this is what remains after the elimination of reference. What matters is not the referent (for there is none), but the product. What is more, this product is dependent on there precisely not being a referent—that is, it is dependent on meaning and being entering into a relation of indifference and so excluding all forms of signification and reference altogether. Symbolic language does not refer to reality; it produces reality, and does so only on the condition it does not refer.

Is Symbolic Language Still Language?

An obvious response to the preceding is scepticism concerning not only the viability, but even the conceptual coherence of Schelling's account of symbolic language: is it not incoherent to conceive of a non-referential, non-signifying language? We here return to the criticisms de Man and Titzmann make of symbolic language which I rehearsed in Chapter 2: language is just not like that. Schelling, it could be argued, rejects a number of fundamental features of language and so has no right to call symbolic language 'language' at all. The problem that such a criticism immediately faces, however, is the fact that questions such as 'what counts as an essential property of language?' and 'what makes language language?' are deeply controversial. To assert that Schellingian symbolic language is not language presupposes a clear definition of language—and the latter is not available.

A debate within contemporary philosophy of music illustrates this point nicely. Music evidently communicates to us; the musical notes of a Beethoven sonata (for example) convey meaning of some sort. This gives rise to the following questions: is music a language? Does music function in a way that is structurally identical to or at least resembles linguistic signification? The philosophical stakes are clear: by what set of criteria can one assess whether music is a form of language—and, indeed, are there any such criteria? Such questions have divided philosophers of music. On the one hand, Stephen Davies has notoriously asserted that 'music fails to meet most of the conditions crucial to something's being, and functioning as, a language... [This] is to deny that music says anything at all' (1994, 24). Among the conditions Davies sets out are reference (29), the separation of signifier and signified (11), and arbitrariness (34). On this set of conditions, it is clear that Schelling's conception of a non-referential symbolic language in which meaning and being are identical could not count as linguistic either.

However, Davies' argument has received much criticism. Most significantly, Ridley and Bowie (from very different philosophical presuppositions) both criticize Davies for presuming an uncontroversial definition of language. Davies 'assume[s] that we already know what a language is, and can just apply the theory of language to music' (Bowie 2007, 17).[5] Indeed, Bowie (who, it must not be forgotten, is an eminent Schelling scholar) goes on to insist that Davies' focus on representation and reference in his definition of language is particularly question begging (4); in contrast, Bowie focuses on theories of language as world-making or productive (77–9)—theories which are, of course, much closer to Schelling's own.

The point here is not to claim that Schelling defines language correctly and Davies wrongly; it is rather to indicate the difficulty in deciding this question decisively.[6] Circumspection is required when answering the question, 'Is symbolic language still language?'

To further develop the idea that Schelling's conception of symbolic language is not immediately implausible, it is worth comparing it with the linguistics of Paul de Man, the great twentieth-century critic of symbolic language. To compare Schelling and de Man's conceptions of language is thus to pit Schelling against an adversary, but also to test his idea of language against the presuppositions and prejudices of late twentieth-century linguistic thought.

De Man's criticisms of symbolic language centre on the category of aesthetic ideology. Aesthetic ideology designates the ideological falsification of the nature of language that took place under the name of aesthetics during the eighteenth and nineteenth centuries. 'Aesthetics', de Man writes, 'is a phenomenalism of a process of meaning and understanding' (1986, 7), the making perceptible of linguistic meaning. This is, for de Man, the very definition of ideology: 'What we call ideology is precisely the confusion of linguistic with natural reality, of reference with phenomenalism' (7).[7] Words, on this view, become flowers (as Hölderlin put it): they are ready-made objects passively encountered, and *not* produced.[8] The 'aesthetic *aura* of the symbol' (de Man 1996, 104) is precisely that it too participates in this phenomenalization of meaning: symbolic language reduces conventional reference to the perceptibility of natural objects. Theories of symbolic language ignore, suppress and neglect those 'factors or functions that cannot be reduced to intuition' (1986, 13). At stake here—as I have emphasized throughout this book—is the distinction between empiricist and rationalist heautonomy. De Man claims that all theories of symbolic language must be committed to the

---

[5] See Ridley 2004, 22–4.
[6] See further Bowie 2007, 48–9. It is also worth noting that one contribution to this debate (Spitzer 2004, 299–319) directly appeals to Schelling's *Philosophie der Kunst* and his symbol/schema/allegory distinction for solutions.
[7] Culler describes this ideological process of phenomenalization as follows, it is the process 'when something—words, meanings, affects, effects—would simply be given to perception rather than produced by reading' (1988, 132).
[8] See further de Man 1984, 3–7.

empiricist interpretation, and so conceive the symbol as an empirical object. As we have seen, however, this is not true. Schelling interprets symbolic language constructively; he thus does not fall foul of de Man's criticisms or even of the more general label of 'aesthetic ideology' (at least on this issue). Schelling does not phenomenalize meaning; he constructs it.

Therefore, while the Schellingian symbol could superficially be seen as close to 'the romantic symbol' on this point, it is in fact quite distant from it. Schelling (like other theorists of the time) does hold on to terms like 'organic', but he reinterprets them. In short, the symbol and its properties undergo a speculative transformation in Schelling's thought: the 'naturalness' of the symbol, far from being a result of phenomenalization, is reconceived as a form of poiesis. The term 'organic', for example, is interpreted by Schelling as a name for the mode in which the absolute produces and constructs itself. It is the name for a process of creating meaningful being. This is very different from theorists (like Goethe) who consider language a natural object to be encountered passively in the world.

To this extent therefore there seems no reason why Schelling's conception of language should be thought of as problematic on de Man's terms. Language is the mode in which the absolute exhibits itself in its most intense form; it is the maximal production of the indifference of meaning and being. Yet, this is not to say that there are not massive divergences between Schelling's view of language and that of de Man (and for that matter any theorist of language of the twentieth century); there obviously are. In what follows, I want to consider four such differences and tentatively suggest that they do not necessarily undermine the plausibility of Schelling's conception of language; they merely flag up its untimeliness.

(a) Metaphysics

There is no doubting the strangeness of Schelling's philosophy of language from a post-Saussurean standpoint. Even from the 1830s onwards, linguistics took on an empiricist methodology, taking the concrete speaking subject or the determinate existence of a body of language at a particular time as its starting point. Schelling's linguistics, however, is unashamedly metaphysical. Indeed, he explicit criticizes the empiricist and subjective foundations of earlier theories of language: 'The whole question concerning the origin of language, at least as it has been treated until now, is merely an empirical one with which the philosopher accordingly has nothing to do.' More specifically, Schelling opposes the arbitrary nature of the sign as one pernicious manifestation of this empiricism: previous theories 'view language as an arbitrary choice or invention... Yet language is not that accidental. There is a higher necessity' (SW 5:485; 1989, 102). To discern this higher necessity, Schelling insists, philosophizing must begin from the 'idea' of language. Schelling's question is always 'what connection exists between language and the absolute' (Hennigfeld 1984, 19).

It is no understatement, however, that Schelling's argument has had no influence; indeed, the eighteenth-century theories which Schelling here labels too empiricist come to be seen by later linguists as still too metaphysical. Schelling's speculative account of language goes against the grain of the majority of modern Western thinking about language.

Philosophically, what is at stake is the legitimacy of Schelling's practice of speculative transformation. As we saw in Chapter 3, Schelling makes use of the material of empirical aesthetics so as to transform it into a metaphysics of art; in the process, art as a particular, temporal object is cast aside in favour of the eternal idea of art. The same operation is at work here: Schelling surveys previous philosophies of language and transforms them into a metaphysics of language. It is precisely the legitimacy of such an operation which is implicitly questioned by later nineteenth- and twentieth-century theorists. Their assumption is that to transform phenomena speculatively is to falsify them, and language is no exception. To attempt to metaphysically construct a theory of language irrespective of its empirical properties is to misunderstand the nature of language itself.

Of course, there is little hope of asking linguists to reconsider the validity of the Schellingian view of language; however, two points might be made in order to stop us immediately discarding Schelling's viewpoint. First, Schelling belongs to a long and well-established philosophical tradition (indeed, his work is in many respects the culmination of this tradition) in which to think adequately is to think *sub specie aeternitatis*. It is the eternal idea—not the mutable phenomenon—which is the proper subject of philosophy, and this is no less true of language. While it is certainly the case that much of this tradition has today fallen out of favour, it is important to acknowledge how compelling such an assumption was for generations of philosophers. Second, what modern linguistics and philosophy of language seem to discourage is any interrogation of the *ontology* of language—the philosophical basis of our everyday employment of language. And to interrogate the ontology of language requires more than just empiricism.[9] While, of course, Schelling's metaphysical explanation is not the only (or even most compelling) account of this ontology, its pursuit of a philosophical justification of language as such is certainly valid.

(b) Immediacy

Language is a productive process for Schelling; yet this process is free of any form of mediation. This is true for both of the relations which constitute

---

[9] See Surber 2000, 335.

Schellingian language. In terms of language's relation to the eternal, all *Darstellungen* are immediate exhibitions of the absolute, so no form of mediation is required to access the absolute through language.[10] In terms of the finite/infinite relation, meaning is also immediately present in language. Neither any hermeneutic activity of uncovering concealed meanings nor any process of signification (in which the meaning of a referent is made present) is necessary for Schellingian symbolic language. Both absolute and meaning are immediately there; no extra work is required.

This, however, raises a new question: does language essentially involve mediation or is an immediate language conceivable? That the experience of language is ineluctably mediated is certainly true for de Man and all theorists within the Saussurean tradition. Language operates in two ways: first, by assigning value to each signifier through its difference from all other signifiers; second, by means of the signifier referring to the signified. Both operations involve mediation: value is mediated by the value of all other signifiers and the signified is mediated by the signifier. This is also true within the hermeneutic tradition as well: hermeneutic activity is the mediated procedure of retrieving meaning concealed behind meaningless being. On this basis, Titzmann, for example, has criticized the valorization of immediacy in theories of the symbol during the *Goethezeit*: 'The meaning of the symbol requires no interpretative reconstruction...it is "immediate"...In the symbol therefore hermeneutics is annulled: the symbol neither allows for an explanation nor requires one' (1979, 656).

Schelling (as Titzmann implies) rejects all these forms of mediation. He denies that mediation is necessary to language. What are we to make of this? How can we answer the question whether language necessarily involves mediation or not? If it does, then Schelling's notion of an immediate language is a contradiction in terms; if it does not, Schelling's symbolic language becomes an alternative model for the functioning of language.

Rationalist heautonomy is again crucial to answering this question, since Schelling here positions himself in a constructive tradition, in which immediacy is a defining characteristic of all knowledge. Take, for example, Kant's comments concerning mathematical construction: one of the main differences between knowledge constituted from mathematical construction and that constituted from typical *Vorstellung* is the immediacy of the relation between concept and intuition present in the former. Mathematical concepts can be fully and directly 'laid out' in intuition in a way other concepts cannot. For Schelling, the same is true, except of course that he extends the range of construction to all ideas.

Spinoza's third kind of knowledge provides a helpful comparison. Spinoza defines the most adequate mode of cognition in his system as intuitive, and so,

---

[10] See *SW* 5:631–2; 1989, 202–3; Coseriu 1977, 8; Adams 1983, 20.

in consequence, it is immediate (it exhibits what is known immediately to the knower).[11] Indeed, Spinoza speaks of the third kind of knowledge being obtained 'without going through any procedure' (1985, §24). Yet, simultaneously Spinoza insists that the third kind of knowledge is syllogistic—that is, it reaches what is known as the result of a discursive process. The third kind of knowledge therefore is both immediate and discursive.[12] Spinoza here forms part of the same constructive tradition as Kant and Schelling (as I argued in Chapter 6)—and this focus on immediacy marks a crucial difference between the *dialectical* tradition running through Fichte and Hegel and the *constructive* tradition of early modernity of which Schelling's *Identitätssystem* is the culmination. In the dialectical tradition, mediation is key: what is most expressive or true is what is reached by means of a process of mediation. This is not the case in the constructive tradition, where discursive knowledge can still be immediate.

(c) Identity

A similar story can be told about the contrast between Schelling's commitment to identity as a defining property of language and the twentieth-century obsession with difference. Obviously, there are good linguistic, ontological, and ethical reasons for the importance difference has attained in the twentieth century. However, what I have attempted to show in this book is that there are also plausible reasons for Schelling's commitment to identity. For de Man, the identification of meaning and being is an ideological strategy; it suppresses genuine difference in favour of a fictional utopia which is never to come. This ideology falsifies and conceals the 'essence' of language which resides in difference (1984, 6). De Man asserts, 'That sign and meaning can never coincide is what [should be] precisely taken for granted' (1983, 17). However, to assert that language essentially exhibits difference is (at least *prima facie*) just as plausible as asserting it essentially exhibits identity—both claims rely on particular metaphysical presuppositions that need to be understood before they are evaluated.[13] It has been the task of my argument to uncover Schelling's presuppositions.

(d) Production

Finally, there remains the question of reference. I have insisted that it is Schelling's rejection of this aspect of language which is potentially so fruitful.

---

[11] As my discussion of intuitive cognition made clear in Chapters 1 and 2.

[12] See Joachim 1940, 43; Gueroult 1974, 2:468.

[13] And indeed de Man's presuppositions have not escaped censure. See Eagleton 1990, 358; 1991, 200.

Rejection of reference frees Schelling from worrying about correctly or incorrectly representing an already existing entity; what is rather at stake is how intensely entities are generated through language. *Description is replaced with production.*

It is often thought that reference is essential to language. De Man's critique of the phenomenalization of meaning, for example, is partly an attack on denials of the referential function. The symbol suppresses 'the referential function of language—that is *always* there, irreducibly, whenever we talk about anything called "language"' (Warminski 1996, 14). In de Man's words, 'The referential function is a trap, but inevitable'[14]—and so theories of symbolic language which attempt to avoid this trap, he contends, always end in ideology.

Flying in the face of linguistic good sense, Schelling jettisons reference,[15] and I have already described at length the two relations with which he replaces it—indifference and production. Indifference is merely a way of flagging up the lack of a replacement for reference: since meaning is already fully present in being, there is no need for any kind of mechanism to make present an absent meaning. Production, however, is a mechanism which defines the workings of language (as well as of all *Darstellungen* in general). Production does not, however, define the relation between being and meaning; rather it defines the relation between language and the absolute. Language does not refer to the absolute; it produces the absolute.

The question then becomes: is production a legitimate category by which to envisage the operation of language? It is important here to note what distinguishes production from reference as a model for language. Referential language talks about reality more or less accurately; productive language is reality more or less intensely. Reference presupposes that word and reference are external to one another (at least partially) and only extrinsically related. This, as we have seen with signification, relies on a qualitative opposition between word and referent, as well as some form of causal or mediating relation between them. On Schelling's metaphysical presuppositions, these are merely reflective ways of theorizing language—they do not attain to the idea of language. Production, on the other hand, posits the essential identity between word and absolute. It is, in fact, one of the only consistent positions for a monist when it comes to language: words cannot refer to referents as separate, distinct entities, because words and referents are fundamentally the same thing. There is no room for reference, if one is a monist. Again, this is not to prove that production is a legitimate category for conceiving language; it is

---

[14] De Man, quoted in Warminski 1996, 1.
[15] He does not deny, however, that non-symbolic language (language that has degenerated into schematism) is partially referential, nor does he deny that to those who have not transcended reflection it seems referential.

merely to contend that, on Schelling's philosophical presuppositions, production seems a plausible candidate.

THE CRITIQUE OF THEOLOGY

Such then are the immediate linguistic consequences of Schelling's construction of symbolic language. The question I now turn to answer, however, is its consequences for scientific thinking in general and theological thinking in particular. As I made clear at the beginning of the chapter, theology here functions as a cipher for the entirety of scientific practice for Schelling, but it also occupies a privileged position in Schelling's reflection on this topic. As we shall see as the section progresses, Schelling uses his conception of the symbol as a tool to criticize the current practice of theology. He tests theology against the symbol and finds it lacking. This creates a new task for the thinker—the reformation of theology (and so science in general) along symbolic lines.

A Theology Without Reference

The Schellingian construction of symbolic language has three immediate consequences for theology.

First, God is not the object of discourse. He is not the referent of theological language. God is not infinite meaning. The absolute cannot, and so should not, be made into the object or meaning of propositions, for—and this is key—this would be to reduce the eternal to the infinite, to mistake the third for the second potency. God maximally manifests himself in the third potency, but only does so to a much lesser extent in the second potency. To think God through the second potency, rather than the third, is thus a form of reflective thinking, limiting the potential productivity of thought. Theology should not therefore treat God as an object of discourse; theology need not be about God.

In consequence, theology can be about anything at all. What matters is not the object of discourse (the second potency), but the extent to which the eternal is produced (the third potency). There is therefore no limitation on the meaning or content of theology: it can talk about whatever it wants. Theology need not be worried about adequately, fully or accurately representing an external entity, for such a procedure is, according to Schelling, reflective. Rather, the criterion for the success of theology is the degree to which it produces God, and this is directly dependent upon (or equivalent to) the extent of the indifference pertaining between being and meaning. This indifference is, moreover, a purely formal criterion and can be achieved no matter what the content of the theological discourse might be. Theology, in conclusion, has no specific subject matter it need talk about; it has no proper content or predetermined field. All that characterizes good theology is a purely structural requirement—the indifference of meaning and being.

Indifference of meaning and being is the formal criterion for successful theological practice. Therefore, theology is more divine the less it talks of God! In order for theology to produce God as the third potency to the maximum possible extent, it needs to suppress all its referentiality, including, most notably, its tendency to talk about God. Only when reference is completely eliminated does the requisite indifference of meaning and being obtain, so that theology's language—and consequently theology itself—becomes symbolic. In short, theology must be poietic, not referential—produce God, not refer to him.[16] Again, it needs to be remembered that such claims also hold true for the other sciences (including philosophy). Science in general must stop describing reality in order to produce it; it must suppress reference in the name of the intense indifference of meaning and being.

The God of the Third Potency

On the basis of the above, Schelling is able to criticize theology as it is currently practised. He sets the above ideal of a poietic theology over against past and present theologies, so as to reveal the latter's inadequacies. At the centre of his critique lies Christian theology's mistaken identification of God with the infinite object of thought. Much theology past and present has failed to realize that God is not infinite, but eternal. As such, this theology has practised a reflective (i.e. less intense) form of thinking in which God is not produced to the maximum possible extent. Theology has not been poietic enough.

Thus, Schelling rails against those who try to make God the object or meaning of discourse, those who 'are not able to fashion any other notion of the absolute but that of a *thing*' (*SW* 7:158; 1984b, 256). It is in epistemology, rather than linguistics, that Schelling is most articulate on this point (although the correspondence holds firm). God is not the object of knowledge:

> Reason does not *have* the idea of God, it *is* this idea and nothing else ... In no kind of knowledge can God occur as the *known* (the object). As known he ceases to be *God*. We are never outside of God so that we could set him in front of us as an object. (149–50; 250–1)[17]

Just as there is no referent, there is no object of knowledge. Hence, Schelling insists definitively at the beginning of the 1804 *System*:

---

[16] It is worth remembering that essence (even when that essence is called God) does not pre-exist form, but is generated by form.

[17] See further *SW* 6:172; 1994c, 164—*SW* 5:215–17; 1966, 10.

In our first reflection on knowledge, we believe to have distinguished in it a subject of knowledge and the object of knowledge . . . I purposely say: we *believe* to have discriminated, for precisely the reality of this distinction is at issue here, and it will become readily apparent that this very distinction between a subject and an object in knowledge constitutes the fundamental error in all knowledge . . . We now abandon forever that sphere of reflection that discriminates between the subject and the object. (*SW* 6:137–40; 1994c, 141–3)

In the same way, therefore, as previous philosophy's attempt to separate out an object of knowledge has been a serious error retarding the progress of the discipline, so too Christianity's confusion of God with infinity is for Schelling the very essence of 'dogmatism' (152; 152). Dogmatism relegates God to the second potency; it makes of him an infinite object. Put another way, dogmatic theology concentrates on the first relation of Schellingian language at the expense of the second—that is, Christian thought is obsessed by the question of how the first two potencies relate (how being can signify and refer to meaning); it therefore remains ignorant of the resources offered by the third potency, i.e. how the elimination of any discrepancy between finite and infinite generates the eternal. Dogmatic theology is oblivious to the poietic potential of indifference, and remains bound to a reflective and representational thinking concerned with how the finite can adequately capture the infinite.

Schelling is insistent again and again: dogmatic theology is wrong. God is not an object to be thought, but the third potency itself. God, as we saw at the start of Chapter 4, is another name for reality and not an infinite element in reality. God is reality itself. As the 1804 *System* puts it, 'God is not the supreme but the unconditionally One, not the endpoint of the last link in a sequence but the centre. There is no world outside him to which he relates in the manner of cause and effect' (152; 152). God is everything, and it is, according to Schelling, atheism to claim otherwise. Atheism is the failure to identify God and the third potency; it reduces God to either a finite, sensible object (the first potency) or to an infinite, ideal object (the second potency).[18] Both are forms of idolization. Christian theology—insofar as it is and has been *dogmatic*—is *atheist*. On the contrary, only eternity is divine and worthy of theological contemplation.[19] Schelling's task with respect to theology is therefore to reform it—to rectify its fundamental mistake by elevating God back to his proper place as eternal.

At stake once more is a speculative transformation, this time of theology. Just as with aesthetics, theories of the symbol, or philosophies of language,

---

[18] 'For him whom the soul is actual, God is not external but is a God within. All others relate to God as to their ground . . . he lies in the infinite distance, as mere object . . . For him whose soul is itself grasped by the divine, God is no externality . . . God is in him and he is in God. The true atheists are those who invoke atheism when one claims that God is not external to us and we are not external to him' (*SW* 6:562).

[19] See *SB* 2:351; Fichte and Schelling 1997, 87.

Schelling is here intent on taking pre-existing theologies and appropriating them for his own end. In short, it is a matter of redirecting theology towards the absolute: theology must be turned away from representation and reference towards indifference. Christian theology is not and has not been sufficiently speculative—not absolute enough. In consequence, it has 'sunk to its lowest ebb' in recent times, attained 'the farthest pole from concern for its idea' and so become 'a theology totally divorced from speculative thought' (*SW* 5:303; 1966, 99).[20] Its obsession with the infinite has obscured what is properly scientific—the eternal. According to Schelling, it is now a case of renovating what is unproductive in the theological tradition to make it more speculative, intensifying its absoluteness.

A Genealogy of Christianity

This task to reform theology needs to be set in a wider context, however, because Christian theology's divinization of the infinite considered in the previous section is a symptom of a much more fundamental problem. In short, Christianity as such is a religion of the second potency—of the ideal, the infinite, and the subjective. In all Christian thought, it is the second potency which predominates. Christianity obsesses over the infinite and ignores the eternal—this for Schelling constitutes its very definition. Again, it is a question of Christianity ignoring the second relation of Schellingian language in favour of the first. For Christianity, the ideal (or the infinite) is what is ultimate, and it is obsessed with how this ideal can be adequately signified or represented by the real. The relation of both to the eternal is consequently forgotten. The ideal is privileged at the expense of the eternal. There is no aspiration to indifference. On this account it is obvious why Schelling would want to criticize Christianity, and criticize it he does. Between 1801 and 1805, this criticism takes many forms, but is most evident in the detailed genealogy of the Christian religion Schelling charts in both the *Philosophie der Kunst* and *Über die Methode*.

'With Christianity begins a new world', writes Robinson in his lecture notes to the *Philosophie der Kunst* (1976, 173). The turning point of world-history is the life of Christ; through it the ancient world is turned upside down. Modernity is the 'reversal' of antiquity and in a series of propositions in the *Philosophie der Kunst*, Schelling schematically lists the oppositions that divide the two eras: in antiquity art is the product of nature, in modernity of freedom (§44); the finite predominates in the former, the infinite in the latter (§45); in the former, the universe is intuited as nature, in the latter as providence or history (§47);

---

[20] See further 296–303; 92–100.

sublimity is the 'basic character' of the former, beauty of the latter (§47); the collective is fundamental to the former, the individual to the latter (§48); the former exhibits unchanging eternity and being, the latter transience and becoming (§49); space dominates in the former, time in the latter (§50); nature is revealed and the ideal world concealed during antiquity, whereas the ideal is revealed and 'nature retreats into mystery' during modernity (§51); the former gives rise to a 'nature religion' founded on mythology, the latter to a revealed religion based on tradition (§52); finally, in the former ideas are concretized in being, in the latter in action (§53). From this list, it should already be evident that modernity (and so Christianity—the two are synonyms for Schelling) is defined by the second potency, in opposition to antiquity which is defined by the first. History, action, subjectivity—the hallmarks of Christianity—are all phenomena in which the second potency, the ideal, predominates. Thus for Christianity to be characterized by such phenomena already suggests it privileges the second potency, and Schelling goes on to stress this fact repeatedly in his history of the development of the religion.

Christianity begins with Jesus Christ and, according to Schelling, Christ can be considered in two ways. He is a liminal figure: he is not quite modern, but also not quite Classical. 'He stands as the boundary between the two worlds' (*SW* 5:292; 1966, 89).[21] On the one hand, Christ marks the end of the series of Classical deities as both their termination and also their culmination: he perpetuates and even perfects many of the principles by which the Greek gods were understood.[22] Yet, on the other hand, Christ is not merely Greek, but the god who breaks down Hellenistic paradigms to establish the modern world. Schelling thus insists on the inadequacy of understanding Christ through Hellenic terms alone; the influx of 'Oriental ideas', he counters, is integral to such understanding. While Greek religious thought is dominated by the finite, Oriental religious thought is completely in thrall to the infinite. 'In the Orient, the finite is completely overbalanced by the infinite' (Robinson 1976, 173). It is schematic and is 'never able to elevate itself to the symbolic level' (*SW* 5:422–4; 1989, 56–7). The influx of the Orient had a crucial influence on Christ's fate. Rather than remaining content with the Greek ideals of finitude and nature, Christ succumbed to the infinite, to the ideal, to the second potency:

> How utterly differently does this incarnation of God within Christianity manifest itself when compared with the concept within paganism of the divine that has become finite. In Christianity the finite is not the most important element. (*SW* 5:431–2; 1989, 63)[23]

[21] See Marquet 1973, 266–7.
[22] 'Christianity's leading idea is . . . Christ as culmination, the closing out of the ancient world of the gods. In Him, as in the ancient gods, the divine principle becomes finite' (*SW* 5:292; 1966, 89). He is 'the peak . . . of the polytheistic universe' (Tilliette 1994, 9).
[23] See Marquet 1965, 65–6.

Christ abandoned the real for the ideal, and henceforth 'lead[s] all of the finite into and to the infinite' (432; 64). This shift is represented by the events that lead from the Crucifixion to the Ascension: they represent Christ's abandonment of his finite, real body and his escape into the infinite—'the nullification of the finite' (432; 64). They inaugurate a new era of a religion of the transcendent, of the infinite existing beyond (not within) the finite. Tilliette writes:

> The fundamental contrast between paganism and Christianity prevents one from making Jesus into the finite icon of the infinite, the infinite enclosed in the finite, like a Greek deity; on the contrary, he is in fact a fugitive image, expanding the finite into the infinite, destroying the finite in the infinite and ideality. This indicates how much his life is seen in terms of his death. (1994, 7–8)

In death, Christ fails to be symbolic. His finitude cannot remain indifferent to the new power of the infinite that arrives from the Orient. The infinite surges forth in excess and surplus. The death of Christ 'closes the world of the finite and opens the world of the infinite' (*SW* 5:294; 1966, 91). Moreover, this ultimate failure of the symbolic through an upsurge of the ideal will be a recurrent motif throughout the whole history of Christianity. Christ sets the pattern that modernity is doomed to repeat: whenever moments in Christian theology approach the symbol, an excess of the infinite always drives them back into transcendence and ideality.[24]

Despite any hesitation one might have over the categories Schelling here employs ('the Classical' versus 'the Orient'), Schelling's basic point seems sound: if one is a monist or even just committed to a philosophy of immanence, the affirmation of the transcendent and consequent negation of this world (tendencies which one could interpret as the significance of Christ's death and subsequent ascension) seem problematic. They seem to valorize a 'two-world' metaphysics which Schelling rejects, and so it is on this basis he designates these aspects of Christian religion less productive of reality—events in which the second, rather than the third, potency dominates.

Moreover, from this account, one can already begin to see the task Schelling will set for thought: to come to terms with this new, excessive infinity present in Christianity; to cultivate the real and the finite so it can enter back into a relationship of indifference with the infinite, so that God will be produced more intensely.[25]

---

[24] Christ's death is thus 'the original sin' of Christianity which it is doomed to repeat over and over (5:290; 1966, 86). See Tilliette 1970, 1:448; Brito 2000, 69.

[25] See further Marquet 1965.

Christianity and Modern Thought

Christianity fails to be symbolic. Yet, Schelling is equally insistent that contemporary thought cannot just discard it and start again with a more symbolic religion. And this is because, he claims, Christianity has thoroughly determined modern thought to the point that all philosophy, natural science, and art since Descartes has been irremediably infected with the ideality of Christianity. It is for this reason Schelling devotes so much space to charting the deficiencies of Christianity in both the *Philosophie der Kunst* and *Über die Methode*. While other disciplines (like politics or natural science) are just as catastrophically reflective as theology, just as marked by the excess of the second potency, Schelling provides no parallel genealogy. For such genealogies would be redundant; they would not get to the root of the problem. Only a genealogy of theology tackles how and why reflection has come to dominate modern thought, because Christian theology is the *cause* of all reflective thinking in modernity. It is not just that theology exhibits the dualisms, the lifelessness, and the causal categories inherent in all modern thinking better than any other form of thought, it is that Christ's Ascension and the theology that arose from it gave rise in the first place to all the dualisms on which modern science is based. Theology is the root of unproductive thinking.

Reflection has its roots in Christianity; nowhere does Schelling make this clearer than in the opening to *Über das Verhältnis der Naturphilosophie zur Philosophie überhaupt*. He begins by calling attention to 'the fundamental error that has lurked unchallenged at the base of almost all recent philosophical efforts' and goes on to make two further claims: first, that 'the error is in a certain way the focal point of our whole modern culture' and, second, that Christianity is its origin (*SW* 5:108–9; 1985, 368). When Descartes opposed mind and body, he was merely bringing 'to conscious and scientific expression . . . the dichotomy that had long been present': he was making explicit a Christian problem. Indeed, Schelling continues, 'It can be shown that all the more recent innovations in philosophy . . . are just different forms of a single opposition, thus far unsurmounted and indeed insurmountable by our culture' (116–17; 373–4). Christian oppositional thinking defines how we philosophize and theologize. Schelling makes the same point with Hegel in the *Einleitung* to the *Kritische Journal*:

> The Cartesian philosophy expounded in philosophical form the universally comprehensive dualism in the culture of the recent history of our north-westerly world—a *dualism* of which both the quiet transformation of the public life of men after the decline of all ancient life, and the noisy political and religious revolutions are equally just different-coloured outward manifestations . . . All the sciences have been founded upon this death. (*SW* 5:15–16; Hegel and Schelling 1985, 284)

Only once the source of all modern failures in thinking has been identified can the healing process begin; moreover, it follows naturally that this healing process must first and foremost be a matter of renovating this source—reforming theological thinking. Hence, the possibility of a future symbolic science which employs symbolic language requires the reformation of theology.

AN ABSOLUTE THEOLOGY

Thought's most pressing task is therefore the reformation of theology. And the rest of this chapter—indeed the rest of this book—is devoted to outlining Schelling's response to it. What, I ask, must thought do to establish indifference between the finite and the infinite, and so become maximally poietic? How does science overcome its Christian inheritance to become symbolic? Only once this task has been achieved will science in general and theology in particular manifest reality properly.

Symbolic Practices

It is a question therefore of (what I dub) *symbolic practices*—practices of thought which potentiate science. My focus in what follows is on these symbolic practices which Schelling believes will intensify the productivity of thought in modernity. Through them, Schelling hopes to transform all discourse, including theology, into a symbol.

This is another way of talking about the process of *Bildung* I outlined at the end of Chapter 5: 'the gradual intensification of all forms' (*SW* 5:147; 2008, 285) is the aim of all being—a cultivation of the third potency until it predominates. This 'striving of the individual after absolute being' (Troxler 1988, 36) is the Schellingian version of the *imitatio Dei* where, rather than imitating or in any way approximating to a pre-existing deity, *Bildung* is concerned with the production of the divine.[26] Symbolic practices repeat this process of *Bildung* within the domain of science; they designate the means by which science cultivates its own idea until it becomes symbolic. Provisionally, in the present section, I provide some initial examples of the symbolic practices Schelling recommends. In the next chapter, I turn far more specifically to how Schelling intends to make scientific language symbolic.

---

[26] See *SW* 6:561–2; Bär 1999, 168.

(a) Heroism

Schelling's account of *Bildung* describes how each *Darstellung* is obligated to intensify its production of indifference, to become identity and so the idea of itself (which as we have seen is identical to becoming one's own name). What emerges here is an *ethics of productivity*—and this is precisely what Schelling outlines in the closing pages of the 1804 *System* under the figure of the hero. Heroism, 'the free, beautiful courage of man to act as God directs' (*SW* 6:559), is a specific symbolic practice Schelling recommends: the individual should cultivate the capacity to 'infinitely affirm' the absolute (542). One must act according to identity. Heroism is therefore defined as follows:

> What flows from [acting in accordance with] God is not mere ethics (which always involves a relation of submission), it is more than ethics. I will tell you what I posit in place of this concept...It is religion, it is heroism, it is faith, it is fidelity to oneself and to God. (558)

This reference to religion is significant, for it is further evidence for Schelling's critique of a Christianity which subordinates God to the second potency. Schelling criticizes 'feeling for the divine or devotion' (558) in the name of divine production. He continues (implicitly criticizing Schleiermacher and Jacobi, among others), 'True religion is heroism, not idle brooding or over-sensitive contemplation or feeling' (559). Religion itself needs to be reformed for the sake of a heroic production of identity.

(b) Art

Artistic creation is another crucial example for Schelling of how to intensify *Darstellungen*. Art is not a contemplative or passive mode of knowing reality; it is an action which produces reality. It is thus for Schelling the highest indifference of knowing and action or necessity and freedom—the phenomenon in the ideal world in which the third potency predominates.[27] Art is an ideal symbol, and in consequence is a helpful aid in becoming symbolic: it is one strategy that increases productivity. Schelling writes:

> In art the mystery of creation becomes objective, and art is for this reason absolutely creative or productive. For the absolute in-formation, which becomes objective in the production of art, is the source of all, and the production of art is thus a symbol of divine production. (Robinson 1976, 158)[28]

This is also why Schelling defines artistic genius as 'the immediately productive element or force of the work of art' (*SW* 5:459–60; 1989, 83)—in other

---

[27] See *SW* 6:569–74.
[28] See also *SW* 5:631–2; 1989, 202.

words, in genius indifference is total, and so, Schelling puts it bluntly, 'The poet himself... becomes a god and the most perfect image of divine nature' (652; 216). In the 1804 *System*, Schelling closely ties this conception of the artistic genius to the hero (*SW* 6:570): both exemplify the ethics of productivity. The genius, like the hero, produces the absolute to the maximum extent, hence is poietic.[29]

(c) *Church*

Another strategy Schelling recommends as a symbolic practice is joining a church. That is, through participating in a community ('truly public action' (5:736; 1989, 280)) the symbolic intensity of thought is also strengthened. The Church is privileged by Schelling in this way because he sees it as the only 'live' social body in modernity that exhibits the requisite organic wholeness or heautonomy for 'group symbolism': 'The body of the Church is constructed as an open, infinite unity which gathers all men into a spiritual unity' (Maesschalck 1989, 109). In Schelling's own words, it is 'a kind of spiritual drama in which each member ha[s] a part' (5:434; 1989, 65). Just as in an organism, here too there is a reciprocity of causation between the parts which does away with the need for a transcendent *archē*. The Church forms a heautonomous symbol and, as such, increases the poiesis of its members. Schelling sees this ecclesiastical potential particularly within the Catholic Church. He claims, 'The true Church is necessarily Catholic' (Robinson 1976, 164), and it alone exhibits the heautonomy and syntheticism of a symbolic phenomenon (*SW* 5:435; 1989 67). He concludes, 'Only the Church itself is symbolic in Christianity' (436; 68).[30] In other words, the third potency predominates in the Church, so that participating in it is another aid in the pursuit of symbolic thought.

(d) *Naturphilosophie*

Schelling also recommends *Naturphilosophie* as a symbolic practice. This is because *Naturphilosophie*'s concern with nature (and the real in general) is the perfect antidote to the surplus of the ideal inherited from Christianity. Its tendency to the real is 'quite the opposite of the tendency within Christianity' (*SW* 5:447–8; 1989, 75–6). Schelling continues:

> One must not seek to force the realistic mythology of the Greeks onto Christian culture; one must rather, in quite the reverse fashion, seek to plant its idealistic

---

[29] Genius is 'the indwelling element of divinity in human beings. It is, so to speak, a piece of the absoluteness of God. Each artist can thus produce only as much as is united or allied with the eternal concept of his own essence in God' (*SW* 5:460; 1989, 84).

[30] See also 434; 65—455; 81.

deities into nature itself, just as the Greeks place their realistic gods into history. This seems to me to be the final destiny of all modern poesy . . . Neither do I hide my conviction that in *Naturphilosophie*, as it has developed from the idealistic principle, the first, distant foundation has been laid for that future symbolism and mythology that will be created not by an individual but rather by the entire age. It is not *we* who want to give the idealist culture its gods through *physics*. We rather await its gods, gods for which we are already holding the symbols, ready perhaps even before they have developed in the culture itself independently from physics. (448–9; 76)

Naturphilosophie brings thought back down to earth, grounding history in nature, cultivating the real so that it is once more able to enter into a relation of indifference with the ideal. *Naturphilosophie* leads to the rebalancing of the first two potencies. This is evidently one motive behind Schelling's notorious call for the development of a new mythology through *Naturphilosophie*—a call often repeated within the *Identitätssystem* (as well as outside of this period). This new mythology consists in the creation of new deities—new personifications of indifference which only a real supplement to Christianity (*Naturphilosophie*) can achieve. The philosopher 'regenerate[s] religion by the exaltation of *Naturphilosophie*' (Tilliette 1970, 1:387). Again, therefore, *Naturphilosophie* is a key way to cultivate the third potency in thought—it is another symbolic practice.[31]

Naturphilosophie, the Church, artistic creation, and heroism are four key elements in the thinker's armoury for the reformation of Christian theology and the recreation of indifference. Only through such symbolic practices can discourse become symbolic. These are not the only four possible symbolic practices of course, nor is the above a full account of their potential; however, the preceding is meant as an introduction to Schelling's response to the problem of the surplus of the ideal in Christian modernity.

'The Gospel of the Absolute'

Through symbolic practices, Christian theology can be renovated: the ideal can enter into indifference with the real; discourse can thus become maximally productive of God. In short, theology can become symbolic. Philosophy, Schelling writes (although what he writes should be extended to all science):

with its truly speculative standpoint, has restored the true meaning of religion, has done away with empiricism and the latter's natural ally, naturalism, and thereby paved the way for a rebirth of esoteric Christianity and the Gospel of the absolute. (*SW* 5:305; 1966, 102)

---

[31] See Marquet 1965; Dietzsch 1975, 398.

'The Gospel of the absolute' designates the era in which thought has become symbolic.

However, Schelling's texts remain extremely ambiguous (in a manner reminiscent of Hegel's) on the question of whether this 'Gospel of the absolute' still deserves the name Christianity—that is, he remains seemingly undecided whether Christianity is irremediably tethered to the second potency or whether there are forms of Christianity which can indeed be symbolic. Thus, on the one hand, Schelling speaks of an 'esoteric' core of Christian thought that needs to be renewed (as above), but, on the other hand, he does also call Christianity 'a transition' (*SW* 5:448; 1989, 76).[32] This ambivalence is summed up in the following quotation which speaks of a 'new religion' which is simultaneously the 'fulfilment' of Christianity:

> Whether the present moment in time, which has become such a remarkable turning point for everything shaped by time, and for the sciences and the works of man, will not also be a turning point for religion; and whether the time of the true gospel of the reconciliation of the world with God is drawing near to the stage where the temporal and merely outward forms of Christianity disintegrate and disappear—this is a question that must be left for each and everyone who understands the signs of the future, to answer for himself. The new religion, which already announces itself in revelations to single individuals, is a return to the first mystery of Christianity and a fulfilment of it. It will be discerned in the rebirth of nature as the symbol of eternal unity. The first reconciliation and resolution of the age old discord must be celebrated in the philosophy whose sense and significance is only grasped by those who recognize in it the life of the divinity newly arisen from the dead. (5:120; 1985, 376–7)

Whether what is to come is Christian or not, however, the import of Schelling's comments is clear: we are on the cusp of a new type of thinking and so a new religious experience. The *Identitätssystem* is a programme for a revolution in thinking which will overcome the reflexive, unpoietic nature of our theological inheritance, so as to attain a new symbolic form of discourse through which God will be manifest to the maximum possible extent.

Through symbolic practices, science can become symbolic; yet—as I have insisted again and again in this book—a necessary condition of this becoming symbolic of science is the becoming symbolic of language. Only if language too becomes symbolic can science obtain symbolic status. Therefore, the whole programme of the *Identitätssystem* and the fate of Schelling's 'Gospel of the absolute' ultimately rests on the elimination of any residual referentiality in language.

What is more, as Schelling indicates in §73 of the *Philosophie der Kunst*, language is the paradigmatic symbol. Nothing can be as symbolic as language;

---

[32] See also *SW* 5:120; 1985, 376—*SW* 5:456; 1989, 82—Robinson 1976, 165.

therefore nothing is better placed to combat the surplus of the ideal in Christianity and return thought to a state of equilibrium. Language is the sensualization of ideal meaning: by embodying the ideal in sounds and graphic marks, the ideal is brought into the real without thereby losing any of its ideality (I discussed this at length in the previous chapter). Indifference is the result. Language is therefore well-placed to combat Christian theology's excess of the ideal—and, as the only symbolic phenomenon to fully indifferentiate real and ideal, it is the only form which is quite so well-placed for this task.

Indeed, this is ultimately an implicit polemic against the apophatic currents of Christian thought. Apophaticism, crudely put, is an admission that God as an infinite object exceeds language. Theology's preference for the apophatic has, on Schelling's terms, consigned it to the second potency, and in consequence this has been extremely detrimental to its capacity to generate God. Apophaticism obstructs theological poiesis by failing to use language as a means of bringing the ideal into the real. Such tendencies have made Christianity more reflective. Schelling insists, on the contrary, that theology cannot give up on language, for only by articulating its truths and insights can it combat its own propensity to the ideal, and so approach indifference. As I mentioned in the previous chapter, entities only become genuinely real for Schelling by being named—and this is also true of theological entities. All science, especially theology, must cultivate language, not renounce it.

How, though, the question remains, do thinkers so cultivate language; how do they intensify their speech until it finally obtains symbolic status? This is a question I have yet to answer, and it is to this question in particular I turn in the final chapter. So far I have sketched four general strategies for the potentiation of scientific thought; what I describe in the final chapter is a more specific symbolic practice for the potentiation of scientific language. At stake, then, is the relationship of metaphilosophy and language: as this chapter has demonstrated, Schelling criticizes those thinkers who fail to produce reality intensely and he provides recommendations for the production of more intense sciences; what is now at issue is the role language plays in this process.

11

Systematic Eclecticism

Absolute theology is theology that has become symbolic—it exhibits God in the most productive possible way. In other words, theology's form here approximates to formal identity, so that essential identity is thereby generated intensely. Moreover, this is partly because absolute theology employs symbolic language (as do all absolute sciences): this ensures the symbolic nature of its form. In general, science becomes symbolic through its use of symbolic language.

Such were my conclusions in the previous chapter. However, my argument does not end here, because on its own these claims remain rather removed from concrete scientific practice. In this chapter therefore, I delve further into the nuts and bolts of how the absolute scientific system can actually be attained. That is, I answer the question: how does science become absolute? Moreover, I answer it by returning once more to both the example of theology and §73 of the *Philosophie der Kunst*, for I contend that enacted in the very text of this section is one way in which theological concepts and vocabularies are made absolute.

In the previous chapter, I considered four preliminary symbolic practices Schelling recommends to aid the becoming absolute of science: heroism, art, church, and *Naturphilosophie*. Taken in isolation, however, these practices too appear disengaged from actual scientific practice. Thus, they are in need of supplementation, and so in this chapter I concentrate on one more symbolic practice advocated by Schelling that returns us to the concrete production of scientific texts. In short, he recommends the eclectic appropriation of forms as materials for the expression of reality or God. Absolute theology (for example) can only be established, he contends, once theological terms and concepts are no longer conceived as normative constraints on thinking, but as one more set of tools for constructing a system that is productive of God to the maximum possible extent.

This chapter takes the form of a case study of §73 of the *Philosophie der Kunst*, focusing in particular on what we here discover about Schelling's own scientific practice. It is sometimes claimed that in §73 Schelling uses theology in a sustained manner for the first time. Even if this is only partially true, it still means that §73 is a privileged site on which to see the becoming absolute of theology played out. On the basis of this case study, I draw some further conclusions concerning the role of theology in particular and systematic practice in general in Schelling's *Identitätssystem* with reference to his idea of the interrelation of the faculties in *Über die Methode*. Finally, I return once more to the Schellingian practice of speculative transformation which has permeated so much of my discussion.

THE INTRODUCTION OF THEOLOGY IN §73

In Chapter 9, I discussed Schelling's insistence in §73 of the *Philosophie der Kunst* that language and reason are identical. This identity of reason and language is also a central tenet for the *Logosmystiker*, especially Hamann (as I explored in Chapter 2). What is more, following this initial identification, Schelling goes on to present views that are even more obviously drawn from acquaintance with this theological tradition. He writes:

> In most philosophical and religious systems, particularly those of the Orient, the eternal and absolute act of self-affirmation in God—his eternal act of creating—is designated as the *speaking* word of God, the *logos*, which is simultaneously God himself. One views the word or speaking of God as the outflow of the divine science, as the creating, multifarious, and yet congruous harmony of the divine act of creation. (*SW* 5:483; 1989, 100)

He then goes on to interrogate the formative arts (music, sculpture, and painting) on the basis of this claim, concluding (in a manner that the actual discussions of these art forms would not have prepared one for):

> Just as knowledge still grasps itself symbolically in language, so also does the divine knowledge apprehend itself symbolically in the world such that also the *whole* of that real world is itself a primal act of speaking. Yet, the *real* world is no longer the living word, the speech of God himself, but rather only the spoken—or expended—word. In this way, the formative arts are only the dead word, and yet nonetheless *word*, the act of speaking. (483–4; 100–1)

The *Identitätssystem* is here reinterpreted into traditional theological terms. The self-affirmation of the absolute is God's speech-act; the construction of matter is the hearing of God's spoken word; reason's pre-eminence is due to its status as Logos. Schelling openly deploys concepts from theological traditions as a means to understand the workings of symbolic language. Therefore, in order to grasp the full significance of §73 one must not only consider Schelling's actual construction of symbolic language, but also his use of theology to do so.

Central to these passages is the idea of the Logos in its triple signification as divine revelation, human reason, and language. God's creation and revelation are 'primal acts of speaking'; in consequence, the entirety of the real world (especially music, painting, sculpture, and the matter out of which they are constructed) needs to be interpreted linguistically. Matter—as the product of the divine speech-act of revelation—is the spoken word of God; it is a form of divine language. Further, it is precisely on the basis of this move that Schelling is able to bestow priority on the verbal arts over the formative arts. This is because, while nature has become reified so that it is extremely difficult to recover its linguistic origins, products of human language remain patently characterized by such origins. Nature has concealed the Logos behind a dead surface of meaningless being, whereas human language and the verbal arts still persist as language and so perpetuate the divine speech-act more effectively. In Schelling's terms, matter is the 'spoken' word of God, while language is the 'speaking' word.

The foregoing should sound remarkably similar to my presentation of themes from the *Logosmystik* tradition in Chapter 2. Reason is language, creation is language, nature is congealed language—an isomorphism is set up here in Schelling's work (just as it is in the writings of Hamann and Böhme) between human language, nature, and the divine. They must all be viewed through the same linguistic lens. Logos is the ultimate paradigm for reality.

In 1928, Heinrich Knittermeyer proposed that §73 of the *Philosophie der Kunst* (and the above passages in particular) marked a decisive and irrevocable shift in Schelling's philosophical development. No longer is nature the basis of Schellingian philosophy, it is now language:

> In [his] reference to the 'speaking Word of God'—the divine Logos—a blow is struck to the disinterestedness of Schelling's philosophy. Here the absoluteness of the word is openly victorious over the absoluteness of matter. *Philosophie und Religion*, the piece which soon followed, adopts this idea to develop a new viewpoint. (1928, 346–7)

According to Knittermeyer, §73 announces Schelling's (as yet unconscious) intentions of moving from *Naturphilosophie* to a philosophy of mythology and revelation. The trajectory of Schelling's philosophy is here played out in miniature. Moreover, Knittermeyer goes on to conjecture, theological ideas drawn from the *Logosmystik* tradition are what bring about this epochal shift. The influence of Böhme, Hamann, and even Eckhardt first becomes perceptible at this moment in Schelling's writings, and these ideas precipitate a transition away from a paradigm of natural science towards images drawn from mystic strands in Christian theology. In short, Logos rather than organism now becomes the privileged descriptive tool in Schelling's philosophy.[1]

---

[1] See Henningfeld 1984, 21, for further discussion.

There is much that is problematic in Knittermeyer's understanding of Schelling's development. The idea that while writing the *Philosophie der Kunst* between 1802 and 1804 Schelling's interest in *Naturphilosophie* waned is patently false—some of Schelling's most significant writings on *Naturphilosophie* date from 1806 (for instance). However, in general, Knittermeyer's contention that §73 reveals many of Schelling's theological interests openly for the first time is still plausible.[2] Some of the images used in §73 (especially nature as the spoken word of God and reason as Logos) do indeed, as I have just suggested, seem to be drawn from the *Logosmystik* tradition far more directly than anything present in Schelling's earlier writings. §73 does mark a moment at which Schelling seems much happier to openly deploy theological language. It is for this reason Bär insists,

> Schelling can be seen as the most prominent proponent of *Logosmystik* discourse in early romantic reflection on language. At the centre of his philosophical consideration of language stands the creative Word of God, as it was known to all Baroque theorists of language and in particular Böhme. (1999, 144–5)[3]

He concludes, 'Schelling places himself in a line passing through Böhme and Hamann . . . a long and influential German tradition . . . of *Logosmystik*' (158).[4]

We must be wary of taking this line of thought too far. I argued in Chapter 8 that Schelling's construction of symbolic language in §73 is not an unexpected development, but *necessitated* by the claims of the *Identitätssystem* as a whole. Schelling needs to construct a theory of symbolic language for his philosophy to have any claim to be rational and symbolic whatsoever. To this extent, §73 of the *Philosophie der Kunst* does not point to the future, but is an integral part of the project Schelling had been outlining since 1801. One of the purposes of the first half of this book, in which I contextualized Schellingian symbolic language first in terms of the debates of his time and then in terms of his *Identitätssystem*, was to argue that §73 of the *Philosophie der Kunst* does not come out of nowhere: its conclusions and details are both responses to debates around the symbol in the 1790s and also products of the specific and unique metaphysical and epistemological claims he makes from the 1801 *Darstellung* onwards. What Schelling says in §73 is no departure from the norm, but exactly the conclusions we would expect from a philosopher intent on rigorously thinking through his philosophical presuppositions in the realm of linguistics. It is merely *how he says it* which is new and unexpected.

[2] For example, more generally, the *Philosophie der Kunst* is the first of Schelling's works to consistently use the term 'God' as a name for reality.

[3] See also Coseriu 1977, 1.

[4] This is not to say, it must be emphasized, that there is anything in the text which conclusively proves Schelling had read Böhme (or any other *Logosmystiker*) first-hand before 1805.

Therefore, while the imagery may have altered, the fundamental thought-structures are the same. §73 of the *Philosophie der Kunst* does not in any way mark the end, disintegration, or deconstruction of the *Identitätssystem*; rather, it marks the culmination of the *Identitätssystem*. The theology employed in the section does not undermine the fundamental tenets of the *Identitätssystem*; it articulates them in a slightly different vocabulary. What Schelling says in §73 is no theological turn. Schelling uses theological imagery as an aid to clarify and strengthen his stable, systematic position. It is for these very reasons that I am interested in these passages here: their theological form, embedded as they are in the context of the *Identitätssystem*, is a particularly significant way-in to Schelling's views on the practice of theology.

The question therefore arises: why does Schelling resort to this surprising vocabulary? To repeat, the decision seems to have nothing to do with the content (or essence) of his conclusions, but merely the style (or form) in which they are articulated. This implies that the interplay between the essence of the *Identitätssystem* and the theological form it temporarily assumes aids Schelling's thought. In short, theological forms are employed to intensify the claims of the *Identitätssystem*—the rest of this chapter is devoted to unpacking and making plausible such a contention.

THE QUESTION OF FORM

Initially, it is important to indicate the extent to which this interplay between the form and essence of the *Identitätssystem* is commensurate with Schelling's elucidation of the form/essence distinction in the *Identitätssystem*.

Schelling is a monist with regard to essence. There is one essence to all of reality, and this essence is identity. In consequence, all sciences have essentially the same subject matter—identity. All language (theological, philosophical, mathematical, or poetic) talks about the same thing—essential identity. Schelling exclaims, 'What do I boast of?—[Of having] proclaimed . . . the potential sameness of all knowledge no matter of what topic' (*SW* 7:143–4; 1984b, 246). All future scientific endeavour must be intent on one thing alone, repeating the same essence over and over. Scientific progress does not therefore consist in what is said, but how it is said. In other words, it is a question of form, not essence.[5] The form of science becomes the crucial issue: if all science has the same essence, what matters is the intensity with which this essence is produced, and this, as I have emphasized repeatedly in this book, is a question

---

[5] See Troxler 1988, 28; Brito 2000, 61. Schelling's first ever publication was of course entitled, *Über die Möglichkeit einer Form der Philosophie überhaupt*.

of form. The production of essence is directly and solely dependent on the nature of the form in which it is produced. Essence is a product of form.

The Schellingian ideal is a maximally poietic science, a science which produces essential identity with the maximum possible intensity. And poiesis is conditioned by form. For Schelling, form decides the fate of science.[6] Therefore, what is needed is 'the gradual intensification of all forms' (*SW* 5:147; 2008, 285)—a process of *Bildung* by which form becomes increasingly productive of essential identity. Moreover, the criterion for such maximally poietic form is indifference (or formal identity). The more scientific discourse manifests indifference—both in terms of the number of indifferences it manifests and the intensity with which it manifests them—the more it is poietic. The task facing science is therefore to intensify its form, to manifest indifference more patently.

In short, Schelling is a philosopher of form: his philosophy turns on the manipulation and mutation of forms for the production of identity. In fact, as we shall see as this chapter progresses, to call him a 'philosopher' of form is still too imprecise, since philosophy is merely one more form to be exploited in the name of the system and 'the formation of the speculative' (*SB* 2:436). Moreover, Hegel was absolutely correct to identify Schelling as a formalist (1977b, §15–16, 50–1). Just as he accurately draws attention to the prominent role of construction in the *Identitätssystem* or its starting point in the absolute, so too with the identification of formalism as a defining feature of Schelling's philosophy. However, as with all Hegel's criticisms, it must be added: just because Schelling's philosophy begins in the absolute or belongs to the constructive tradition or is primarily concerned with form does not make him wrong; much more is needed from Hegel and Hegelians alike to justify the tone of such observations and so to demonstrate that it is necessarily better to be a philosopher of content rather than a philosopher of form. An image from Vater's commentary on *Bruno* illustrates perfectly (although, perhaps, despite himself) that this is a question of two competing modes of philosophizing:

> To turn one's mind from the [Schellingian] version of absolute philosophy to the *Phenomenology*'s is like turning one's gaze in a gallery from a Mondrian to a Seurat, both purporting to be portraits of the same subject, the former an exercise in pure geometry, with representation all but effaced and colour muted, the latter a sheet explosion of minute packets of experience, a multitude of coloured points which only gradually, and with much effort, organise themselves into a meaningful pattern. (1984, 93)

Just as Mondrian is not obviously a worse painter than Seurat, so too it is not obvious why Schellingian formalism should be dismissed.

---

[6] See *SW* 7:142–3; 1984b, 245–6—*SW* 5:241; 1966, 34.

The above model for the potentiation of scientific forms applies self-reflexively to the *Identitätssystem*. The force of Schelling's argument means that the *Identitätssystem* says nothing new and does not even try to. It merely repeats the same essence as all other philosophies. This notion of the fundamental sameness of all philosophy is one of the reasons that Schelling is led to speak of the one true system of philosophy (*SW* 4:352), as well as to appeal to a perennial philosophy recurring through all of Western history from Pythagoras through to Fichte (400–1). In essence, all philosophy is the same. It is when it comes to form that the *Identitätssystem* is to be distinguished from all previous attempts at producing essential identity. And this is not only because Schelling realizes the importance of the intensity of all forms while formulating the *Identitätssystem*, but also more importantly because Schelling believes he has discovered the methodological practice needed to intensify all forms to the maximum possible extent.

As such, the *Identitätssystem* is self-consciously constructed around this insight into the centrality of form to the philosophical endeavour. Style, vocabulary, structure, and even grammar stand at the heart of the *Identitätssystem*'s precedence over all previous attempts at philosophy. Form, Schelling tells us again and again, is what matters. This point has been seriously neglected in the scholarship, yet it is ultimately the reason why Schelling experiments with the dialogue form and with the *more geometricus*; it is the reason why he adopts Spinozist vocabulary, then Platonic vocabulary, then theological vocabulary; it is the reason why he draws the magnetic line or talks in mathematical formulae. All these experiments in form—and I will return to them in more detail in what follows—are attempts to articulate essential identity as intensely as possible. They are all trials in philosophical *Bildung*. In short, the *Identitätssystem* speaks so clearly and persistently of identity precisely because Schelling tries in a creative and sustained manner to form identity most intensely.

Furthermore, it is my contention that all these various experiments in form which stand at the heart of the *Identitätssystem* are variations on one fundamental practice which Schelling thinks will make his system the most poietic possible. This is another symbolic practice, one more way to cultivate indifference and so produce the absolute to the maximum possible extent. For this particular symbolic practice, all previous scientific discourse is reduced to the status of *materials* that can be appropriated to aid the production of identity. This is, I contend, something like what Schelling means when he writes to Fichte, 'I have been able to make use of idealism as a tool' (*SB* 2:351; Fichte and Schelling 1997, 87). Idealism (and in particular the ways in which idealism is articulated in the *Wissenschaftslehre*) is a 'tool' Schelling picks up to help him in his project of intensifying the form of his system as much as possible, so that it can ultimately become maximally poietic. I designate this practice 'systematic eclecticism'—that is, the magpie-like appropriation of individual concepts and styles from various scientific discourses for the sake of producing the absolute. Schelling takes 'the best bits' from the rest of science to make his system the best.

ÜBER DIE METHODE: THE EQUALITY OF THE SCIENCES

At the moment, some of the above (especially my appeal to systematic eclecticism) may appear somewhat conjectural. It is the task of the next three sections to flesh out this symbolic practice concretely through Schelling's texts. In the next section, I will give a number of examples of systematic eclecticism in practice, but in the present section I examine in detail the text in which Schelling lays out the theoretical basis of systematic eclecticism—*Über die Methode*.

At the heart of *Über die Methode* stands the claim:

> As for philosophy, I maintain that there is no such faculty, nor can there be, for that which is all things cannot for that very reason be anything in particular. It is philosophy itself which becomes objective in the three positive sciences [theology, *Naturphilosophie* and history], but it does not become objective in its totality in any single one of them. (*SW* 5:284; 1966, 79)

Courtine glosses this passage thus:

> There is no faculty of philosophy; philosophy is not a part of the general organism of knowledge or an element in the institution of the university, it is the soul of all, the life or spirit which gives to the body of sciences precisely its organic status. (1990, 144)

Philosophy, Schelling claims, is not a typical discipline; it is not a discourse which articulates objectively the one essence of all reality. Instead, it plays the role of 'the life or spirit' of such discourse—essential identity itself in its purity prior to becoming objective. 'Only philosophy accedes to the essential self-sameness of absolute identity' (Courtine 1990, 134). For this reason, philosophy acts as the glue which unifies all other disciplines ('the sciences are one in and through philosophy' (*SW* 5:261; 1966, 56)). Every discipline is ultimately concerned with essential identity or philosophy, so philosophy names that which unifies all elements of the university.

Every discourse therefore tries to repeat philosophy, so as to articulate the absolute (or identity or indifference or God) maximally. Yet, Schelling is equally clear no one academic discipline on its own can achieve this.[7] What

---

[7] Philosophy 'does not become objective in its totality in any single one [science]' (283; 79). See also Courtine 1990, 144.

is thus required is that all disciplines cooperate with one another, entering into a larger organic whole, called 'the university'. The university is Schelling's name for the assembling of the sciences for the sake of the production of identity. No one science achieves this; only together as the whole or universe of knowledge does scientific discourse come close. It is only as an assemblage of all possible forms of scientific discourse (where each science plays an equal part in one organism) that identity—or what Schelling here calls philosophy— is maximally produced.

However, Schelling's identification of philosophy and essential identity in *Über die Methode* might appear problematic. As we have seen repeatedly in this book, there is no such thing as 'pure' essential identity 'uncontaminated' by form. It does not exist. Essence is only produced in form; it does not pre-exist form. Thus, if Schelling's characterization of philosophy is read as 'pure' essential identity that does not become objective (which seems a possible reading here), this falsifies many of the principles of the *Identitätssystem*. Moreover, such an identification of philosophy and essential identity gainsays much of what Schelling writes elsewhere concerning the nature of philosophy. Elsewhere Schelling is not shy of asserting the discursiveness of philosophy: philosophy uses language and so articulates essence in a determinate form. Everything is formed and philosophy is no exception. There are forms of philosophy, just as there are theological forms and mathematical forms—and the thinker can make use of any or all of these forms to produce the absolute maximally.

Schelling insists most forcefully on the ineluctability of formation even in philosophy at the close of *Bruno*. The character Bruno ends his exposition of the Schellingian philosophy with the following comment,

> I have always sketched for you the figure of the one sole object of philosophy. How to proceed to build from these foundations, how to bring the sacred seed of philosophy to its fullest flower, how to cast such a doctrine into a form appropriate to it—you may pursue these questions on your own. (*SW* 4:307; 1984a, 203)

However, this is immediately deemed insufficient by the other participants: the philosopher is not somehow able to elucidate the 'one sole' essence of reality prior to and independent of form. 'How to cast such a doctrine into a form appropriate to it' is not a superfluous question that can be dealt with once the real, serious business of philosophy has been completed. On the contrary, this 'serious business' (the articulation of essence) is immediately and entirely dependent on the form in which it is couched. The intensity with which the essence is produced depends on form. Form is prior. For such reasons, Anselm (as convenor of the dialogue) immediately rebukes Bruno for his oversight:

But, my good man, it seems to me that we very much have to trouble ourselves about the detail of the forms of philosophy. For philosophy is not simply the endeavour to understand the supreme reality by means of universals alone; it attempts to portray this reality in strong, enduring lines, and with unwavering steadiness and lucidity, the way nature does. This is what elevates art to the status of art, and science to that of science . . . As long as it lacks enduring form and shape, it will not escape corruption. And though perhaps the least perfect forms have perished and the noble matter once bound to them has been set free, that matter must still be alloyed . . . for philosophy is forever challenged to assume more enduring and less changeable shapes. (307–8; 203)

Anselm continues:

The grand and true forms of philosophy have disappeared, more or less. Philosophy's subject matter is by nature perfectly simple and indivisible, and only to the extent that a given form of philosophy embodies this simplicity will its contents be true and correct. (309; 205)

Much could (and should!) be written about this remarkable passage, but ultimately Anselm's correction is simple: formation is the first and most important task for philosophy, since the better the form, the more intense the essence. Truth, Anselm goes so far as to claim, is dependent on the form of philosophy.

Each of the four participants in the dialogue then draws on the history of philosophy to elucidate such a philosophical form and I will make some comments about these further discussions in the next section. For now, what is important is Schelling's insistence on the ineluctable formation of philosophy in *Bruno*. Schelling here contradicts his problematic characterization of philosophy in *Über die Methode*: philosophy is one more scientific discourse among others, attempting to articulate identity. In this respect at least, philosophy is not special.

Philosophy does not therefore hold some privileged position which allows it to avoid objectivity and express identity perfectly and purely. Despite Schelling's claims in *Über die Methode*, this is not at all the position of the *Identitätssystem* as a whole. On the contrary, philosophy is completely equal to theology, mathematics, and the natural sciences as one more way essential identity can be potentiated through form. Hence, Schelling's position in *Über die Methode* should be: there is no faculty of identity, and all the faculties there are (theology, history, the natural sciences, *and* philosophy) produce identity as intensely as possible through the mediation of their own specific forms.

This indicates the distance separating Schelling from Hegel: for Hegel, the philosophical *Begriff* is capable of articulating the absolute without ultimately needing to draw on the various languages of *Vorstellung* employed by the other sciences. Philosophy exists on a higher plane and enjoys a superior medium—the *spekulative Satz*. It breaks with the *Vorstellungen* in which other sciences remain entrapped. From a Schellingian point of view, however, there is a fundamental equality between all the sciences, including philosophy. Each takes place in determinate *Darstellungen* and each tries to produce identity through the resources provided by these *Darstellungen* to the best of their abilities. Of course, some disciplines may have more and better resources than others, but, Schelling insists, no single science working in isolation can be maximally poietic. Therefore, one could distinguish the two in the following manner: for the Hegelian, philosophical language expresses reality *properly* (that is, there is only one proper discourse for reality); for the Schellingian, all scientific languages (including philosophy) do so *improperly*.[8] However, if one did so distinguish Hegel and Schelling in this manner, one would have to be very careful about the resonance of the term 'improper'. Schelling certainly does not conceive of this as a deficiency. The spectre of apophaticism hovers close at this point. Even to speak (as I have been speaking) of the different sciences all trying to articulate identity is dangerous. And the danger of all this is *representation*—envisioning essential identity as something which pre-exists science and towards which science strives. The danger is suggesting that somehow each science inadequately captures identity or that all science is doomed to vainly hint at something that exists above and beyond it. All this would falsify the *Identitätssystem*: there is no failure in the Schellingian cosmos, because there is no representation.

To repeat, essence does not pre-exist form; form produces essence. So, the impropriety of scientific discourse does not subtract from a benchmark of identity; it produces that identity in the first place. All forms potentiate identity, and some do it better than others. The task of the thinker is to locate the most productive aspects of each science and assemble them into a system; the result is a system of identity, an *Identitätssystem*.[9] All sciences are equal, and thus in principle there is no reason to prefer one science to another. Instead therefore of an unfounded total commitment to one science practised in isolation, the impartial thinker should cultivate an even-handed indifference to all science, so as to bring potentially productive elements together into a systematic whole that is maximally poietic. This is the symbolic practice of systematic eclecticism invoked in the previous section. The thinker must choose anything and everything that will intensify the form of discourse and so potentiate identity. *Bildung* occurs through plundering forms.

In consequence, 'impropriety' becomes the very ideal of science, and the *Identitätssystem* in particular is built on the virtue of impropriety. The improper science is one indifferent to borders and barriers between fields, but which plunders every science *equally* in order to intensify its poiesis. This is

---

[8] On this distinction, see Whistler 2012a.
[9] Rather than (it should be added) an '*Identitätsphilosophie*', a name which incorrectly privileges philosophy as the paradigmatic discipline for the production of identity.

genuine interdisciplinarity, treating all disciplines equally as the material out of which one constructs a symbol.

THE TRUE SIGNIFICANCE OF SPECULATIVE TRANSFORMATION

This is, moreover, precisely the meaning and role of the notion of 'speculative transformation' which I have invoked throughout the book. We have seen how Schelling appropriates material from aesthetics for the sake of a metaphysics of art. Concepts, vocabularies, and styles of thinking are plundered in aid of the production of identity in the domain of philosophy of art. The symbol itself is of course the paradigmatic example here: Schelling takes this concept from Kant, Goethe, and A. W. Schlegel, but in so borrowing it, he alters it (as we have seen, Schelling's second-order interpretation of the symbol is unique). He redeploys it so as to articulate the basic principles of the *Identitätssystem* more effectively. The symbol is imported into the armoury of the *Identitätssystem* as a term whose potential productivity in the right context is immense.

This kind of speculative transformation in the name of a systematic eclecticism is to be found throughout the *Identitätssystem*. A similar story can be told about mythology, about the magnetic line which appears in the 1801 *Darstellung*, the mathematical terminology of the potencies, even the tropes of reflection and refraction. Speculative transformation is the ultimate symbolic practice for Schelling: it permeates, as we have seen, his whole philosophy. Mythology, physics, theology, mathematics, and the history of philosophy are all languages which together make the absolute to the utmost extent. Systematic form takes shape through the speculative transformation of the forms of all sciences.

Schelling's distance from Hegel is again illuminating, since Hegel too subscribes to a philosophical practice which could be dubbed 'speculative transformation'. For the Hegelian, there is a qualitative break between philosophical form and the forms of the other sciences—the break between *Vorstellung* and *spekulative Satz*. The forms of the other sciences are sublated and translated into philosophy. From the Schellingian viewpoint, however, philosophy does not break with the other sciences: all sciences are equal because they are all forms of *Darstellung*. As one would expect, there are no qualitative distinctions here, just quantitative differences in intensity. Every science produces the absolute to a certain intensity through *Darstellungen*. Thus, the system does not sublate or translate the forms of other sciences; it redeploys them, assembles them, and potentiates them.

At this point I want to hone in on the philosophy/theology relation in particular, for these are the two sciences most deployed in the *Identitätssystem*. Both are equally legitimate material for the production of identity, and it is this equality which characterizes the relation between philosophy and theology more than anything else. Builders of a system of identity must select their materials from all and any of the sciences, independently of any unjustified prejudice for either philosophy or theology. It has of course to be admitted that Schelling chooses philosophy more often than theology; however, there is no a priori reason why this is the case (it is just that Schelling found the theology of his day in a far worse state than philosophy, which had at least undergone a Copernican revolution). What matters is the poietic potential of the form, whether that form is philosophical or theological. Anything from philosophy and anything from theology that can be assembled into a system which produces essential identity to the maximum possible extent should be.

This relation between philosophy and theology is especially noteworthy, because certainly since Kant (if not for much longer) theology and philosophy have measured themselves against each other. Philosophy has played the role of theology's twin and rival, against which the latter has tested its strength and through which it has uncovered its own weaknesses—and vice versa. Theology and philosophy have cultivated a 'special relationship', an intimacy that has made their squabbles all the more fierce. While this is obviously true of the twentieth century (from Heidegger's *Phänomenologie und Theologie* through to Milbank's *Theology and Social Theory*),[10] it is also very much true of the *Goethezeit*. On the one hand, there was the Jacobian, counter-modern claim that philosophy is nihilistic and can only be saved by theology; on the other hand, there was the common philosophical position (shared in different ways by Kant and Hegel—at least on standard readings) that theological language should be translated into conceptual language. Philosophy here completes theology: the confused and mythic discourse of theology needs to be reformulated into philosophical vocabulary in order to make its insights explicit and secure.

These positions share a hierarchical mode of thinking. The relation between philosophy and theology is modelled on a hierarchy through which one discipline is made superior to the other. Talk of the relation between theology and philosophy remains mired in the categories of superiority and inferiority. A pressing question thus becomes: is the equality of theology and philosophy conceivable? The answer I am developing here is that it is. Schelling's *Identitätssystem* makes possible (even if it does not explicitly articulate) the equal treatment of theology and philosophy. In short, visible here is the fact that philosophy and theology (along with all other scientific disciplines) are

---

[10] See Barber 2011, 11–20.

equivalent materials to be plundered to express reality as intensely as possible. Schelling appropriates concepts from philosophy and from theology as resources for intensifying the manner in which his system articulates reality. Theology and philosophy are conceived non-hierarchically, because they are both employed in the same way *for the sake of something else* (the system).

I will draw this point out further using two illustrations: a speculative transformation of philosophy and then a speculative transformation of theology. As we shall see, in terms of structure and in terms of purpose the two procedures are identical.

At the end of *Bruno* (as I discussed in the previous section), Anselm upbraids Bruno for neglecting the question of form, since philosophy's ability to express the absolute is entirely dependent on it. In order to remedy this fault, Anselm goes on to propose that each of the participants in the dialogue consider one set of concepts from the history of philosophy to test out their productivity. Alexander begins by experimenting with a materialist vocabulary, then Anselm does the same with a kind of Platonized Leibnizianism. Both of them are concerned with locating and selecting those aspects of materialism or intellectualism which are most conducive to poiesis. Schelling here acts out the process of systematic eclecticism, dramatizing the task of the philosopher before our eyes. The philosopher must undergo an apprenticeship in the history of philosophy, rigorously probing the potential productivity of past systems for the sake of constructing a symbolic *Darstellung*. Philosophers must return to the history of their discipline to creatively appropriate what is of use to them.[11] Thus, Schelling begins the *Identitätssystem* in the 1801 *Darstellung* by assembling what he has borrowed from Spinozist and Fichtean forms of thought, then during the subsequent years he adds concepts and styles borrowed from the Platonic corpus as well as many others. Some of these forms are very quickly dropped (such as the dialogue structure of *Bruno*), whilst others become embedded into the *Identitätssystem* (like the *Ideenlehre*): they pass the test of productivity and are adopted as a part of the systematic form that produces identity.

A very similar speculative transformation can be discerned with respect to theology. I examined such a transformation at length at the beginning of the chapter: Schelling adopts the language of the *Logosmystiker* so as to articulate his construction of symbolic language more intensely. This is an experiment: Schelling toys with a theological terminology as a means to potentiate the form of the *Identitätssystem*. Not all of the concepts deployed in §73 of the *Philosophie der Kunst* survive this test (the idea of reason as logos, for example, plays little role in Schelling's philosophy of the next few years); however, some do, and to this extent at least Schelling's experiment with *Logosmystik* is

---

[11] This apprenticeship also takes place in terms of contemporary thought: Schelling and Hegel's *Kritische Journal* sets itself the task of testing recent attempts at philosophy. See *SW* 5:3–7; Hegel and Schelling 1985, 275–9.

successful. These new forms aid Schelling in the production of essential identity. In §73 of the *Philosophie der Kunst*, Schelling succeeds in articulating the identity at the heart of language more intensely due to his speculative transformation of *Logosmystik*.

Moreover, such a process of speculative transformation with respect to theology is visible more generally too. I have already noted the deployment of 'God' in a late phase of the *Identitätssystem* as a new name for the absolute, and once again it is fair to assume that 'God' is integrated into the system precisely because it intensifies the form of Schelling's philosophy. Another significant example is the Trinity. In a post-Hegelian age, we are very accustomed to philosophical reinterpretations of the Trinity; however, Hegel was following in Schelling's footsteps, and (except for Lessing) Schelling was the first philosopher of the *Goethezeit* to exploit its speculative significance. In other words, Schelling sets a precedent in his speculative transformation of the Trinity; he puts it to work for the sake of identity. Thus in 1802, first in *Bruno* and then in the *Fernere Darstellungen*, trinitarian rhetoric becomes noticeable in Schelling's writings. Basically—and this should be no surprise—the *Potenzlehre* begins to be articulated as a Trinity.[12] Again, this is not some kind of 'theologization' or 'theological turn' in Schelling's thought, but the deployment of theological forms *for the sake of identity*. Just like philosophy, theology is material to be deployed by the thinker in the construction of identity. And to this extent a claim such as the following, 'The *Identitätssystem* signifies the return to an essentially religious philosophy' (Maesschalk 1989, 94), should be resisted at all costs.

The following sentiment from *Über die Methode* sums up the practice of speculative transformation clearly:

> Some forms are transient and perishable, and the forms in which the spirit of science is clothed are but the eternally different modes of the manifestation of genius forever renewing itself. In particular forms, however, there dwells a universal and absolute form of which the particular forms are but symbols, and [science] is the greater the more it succeeds in revealing this single universal form. (*SW* 5:241; 1966, 34)

SYSTEMATIC ECLECTICISM IN THE *IDENTITÄTSSYSTEM*

The practice of systematic eclecticism is therefore central to Schelling's thought between 1801 and 1804, even if Schelling himself never speaks in these terms. Nevertheless, there are three reasons why I contend that 'eclecticism' remains a

[12] See *SW* 4:390–423—*SW* 4:252; 1984a, 152—293; 190—328; 221.

helpful and appropriate label. First, as should be clear from the foregoing, the concept of eclecticism illuminates much of what goes on in the *Identitätssystem*. Second, there is a historical tradition of eclecticism in eighteenth- and nine-teenth-century thought to which Schelling is connected. Third, many commentators on Schelling invoke the idea of eclecticism.

In terms of the second point, the modern tradition of eclectic philosophy begins with Diderot's article on eclecticism in the *Encyclopédie*, where he draws attention to its potential as a philosophical methodology:

> The eclectic is a philosopher who stamps out pieties, prejudices, tradition, ancientness, universal consent, authority—in a word, everything which subjects the masses; he dares to think for himself—even ascend to the clearest, general principles, examine them, discuss them, admit nothing except on the testimony of his own experience and reason. (2011, 270)

The eclectic rises above superstition, above tradition and embraces auton-omy—he 'knows no master' (270). Such eclecticism is also the paradigm for a kind of systematic philosophy: 'This is the eclectic method . . . to form a solid whole, which is genuinely one's own work, out of a great number of collected parts that belong to others' (271), thereby 'constructing out of the ruins [of earlier science] . . . a durable, eternal city capable of resisting the attacks which had destroyed all others' (283).

This tradition, moreover, lives on in Hamann's practice of cobbling together an eclectic mix of quotations, references, and allusions and also in Goethe's theoretical writings which draw on a wide range of influences (from Plotinus to Hemsterhuis) to articulate the same basic point again and again in different vocabulary. Moreover, it also feeds directly into the work of Victor Cousin, a disciple (in part) of Schelling and the beneficiary of Schelling's only publica-tion after 1809. Cousin, for example, insists, 'What I recommend is an enlightened eclecticism which, judging all doctrines equally and hospitably, borrows from them what is common and true and ignores anything opposed and false' (1846, 12).[13]

As well as being suggested by this historical tradition, 'eclecticism' is an appropriate term to describe Schelling's philosophical practice during the *Identitätssystem* because it names a characteristic of his philosophy to which critics often draw attention. To take two examples: Shaw begins his 2010 work, *Freedom and Nature in Schelling's Philosophy of Art* with the following claim, 'The philosophy of Friedrich Schelling has a remarkable depth and breadth. It can move, often rapidly, from Plato to Spinoza, from physics to mythology, from art to astronomy, from medicine to theology' (2010, 1). A similar

---

[13] Significantly in his *Vorrede* to one of Cousin's works, Schelling refers to this concept as 'truly and splendidly presented by Cousin', even if, he also adds, eclecticism 'is perhaps not the right word' (*SW* 10:215).

observation is made in a completely different tone by Hegel in one of the earliest 'appreciations' of Schelling's philosophy: Schelling 'has ever pressed on to seek a new form, and thus he has tried various forms and terminologies in succession without ever setting forth one complete and consistent whole' (1896, 3:515). In other words, Schelling perpetually experiments with forms in the name of his system, regardless of whether such forms are properly conceptual or 'merely sensuous expressions' (538). In so doing, Schelling makes 'the mistake of applying forms which are taken from one sphere of nature to another sphere' (543). Hegel here resurrects the Aristotelian fallacy of metabasis: concepts and modes of argumentation developed in one science cannot be transposed into others. In contrast, the procedure by which Schelling forms his system of identity is, as Hegel once again correctly identifies, entirely orientated around the productivity of metabatic practice.

There are other concepts, similar to eclecticism, that Schelling does indeed employ in the *Identitätssystem* which shed further light on this practice; foremost among them is 'mixing'. Lacoue-Labarthe and Nancy bring out the centrality of mixing to German aesthetics of the time:

> The process of [creating artworks], or the process of assemblage, obviously supposes interpenetration and confusion. Or in other words, *mixture*. It could be said that this is precisely what the romantics envisage as the very essence of literature: the union, in satire (another name for mixture) or in the novel of poetry and philosophy, the confusion of all the genres arbitrarily delimited by ancient poetics, the interpenetration of the ancient and modern etc. (1988, 91)

Significant for my purposes is Schelling's reading of the most symbolic modern artwork: the *Divine Comedy* (already invoked in Chapter 3). What makes Dante's poem such an intense production is simply the following: 'It is the most indissoluble mixture, the most complete interpenetration of everything' (*SW* 5:153; 1989, 239). Dante mixed together all he could get his hands on, including poetic genres ('It is not an epic, it is not a didactic poem, it is not a novel in the real sense, is not even a comedy or drama . . . It is a quite unique and as it were organic fusion of all the elements of these genres' (154; 1988b, 240)) and scientific discourses (physics, astronomy, philosophy, and theology). As Schelling points out, 'To present Dante's philosophy, physics and astronomy purely in and for themselves would only be of minor interest, since his true uniqueness lies solely in the manner of their merging with the poetry' (155; 242). The forms themselves are not important; it is the fact that they mix which potentiates the poem.

Schelling indeed insists that this imperative to mix discourses is central to the regeneration of modern thought as a whole, and so the reformation of the sciences: 'For the culture of the contemporary world, however, science, religion and even art itself possess no less universal reference and significance than does history, and the true epic of the modern age would have to consist in the indissoluble mixture of just those elements' (151; 1989, 238). The 'Gospel of the absolute' is constituted by means of mixing or eclecticism. Dante's *Divine Comedy* is therefore not merely 'an archetype for the whole of modern poetry' (153; 1988b, 240), but the model for the absolute system—the precedent for the *Identitätssystem* itself. The absolute system eclectically mixes together as many forms as possible.

The position I am developing here is a metaphilosophical version of the extensity test recently identified by Grant as a key component of Schelling's *Naturphilosophie*. 'Every philosophical construction,' Grant states, 'undergoes the test of the *extensity* of its concepts' (2006, 194). And he elaborates as follows:

> [Philosophy] is 'the infinite science', and cannot therefore be 'conditioned' by eliminating anything a priori from its remit . . . The infinite science must test itself against the All, which lacks neither nature nor Idea. It is the *extensity* therefore, the *range* and *capacity* of philosophical systems that is being tested . . . [Schelling] challenges systems to reveal what they eliminate. Insofar as philosophy still leaves nature to the sciences, it continues to fail Schelling's test, and becomes a conditioned, that is, a compromised antiphysics. (2006, 19–21)[14]

For Grant, this test checks whether the various possible subject matters of philosophy (ideas, nature, religion, ethics) have all been included in the system. The absolute system talks about everything; it is maximally extensive. During the *Identitätssystem*, I contend, such absolute extensity is enacted on a metaphilosophical plane as well.[15] The more scientific forms, the more concepts, terms, and arguments which are eclectically appropriated from other discourses, the greater the range and capacity of the Schellingian system, and so the more intense or productive it becomes.[16] 'The becoming absolute of thinking' (Zeltner 1975, 81) is defined by the continual assemblage of eclectic forms.

As one final proof of the significance of systematic eclecticism or mixing to Schelling's philosophical methodology between 1801 and 1805, I will use it to provide some kind of answer to three outstanding, hermeneutical questions that I have posed concerning Schelling's *Identitätssystem* in earlier chapters, but am yet to satisfactorily answer. First, there is the problem set out at the end of the previous chapter concerning the becoming symbolic of language—what symbolic practice does Schelling recommend in order to cultivate the indifference of being and meaning necessary for maximally poietic language? Second, my contention that Schelling's interpretation of heautonomy is rationalistic

---

[14] Grant is quoting *SW* 2:56; see also Whistler 2010.
[15] Indeed, it does not really matter what the system talks *about* between 1801 and 1805, since the productiveness of the system is premised on its indifference to subject matter.
[16] Once again (see Chapter 5), we see the identity of intensity and extensity in the *Identitätssystem*.

remains underdeveloped—what do I (and Schelling) mean, for example, when I talk of the Schellingian organism as something constructed and not perceived? Finally, there is the problem raised at the end of Chapter 6 concerning how philosophers can guarantee the absoluteness of their constructions—that is, what can philosophers do or think to ensure their constructions are genuinely poietic of the absolute?

(a) The Becoming Symbolic of Language

In the previous chapter, I considered a number of symbolic practices which Schelling recommends as means of making science more productive, and so rescuing it from the tendency to reflection bequeathed by Christianity. Yet, none of these practices seemed particularly geared towards the language of science and how this could become symbolic—even though, as we have repeatedly seen, symbolic language is an absolutely necessary precondition of a maximally poietic science. Systematic eclecticism remedies this lack; it is a strategy specifically geared towards increasing the productivity of scientific language. Thinkers who employ it are not concerned with maintaining the integrity of the vocabulary they appropriate and certainly not with retaining its specific reference; rather, they select language from the sciences which has most potential for productivity—that is, which exhibits (or might exhibit in the right context) the indifference of being and meaning requisite for maximally poietic science. Systematic eclecticism is therefore a symbolic practice aimed at the becoming symbolic of scientific language; it is a concrete means of potentiating one's language.

(b) Rationalist Heautonomy

The self-sufficient wholeness of the Schellingian symbol is not something to be perceived straight-off, but the result of a constructive process—such is the claim I have repeatedly made throughout this book, and we are now in a position to see why. The answer, in short, is symbolic practices. This is because in recommending such practices, it is clear that Schelling does not think heautonomy is something that pre-exists ready-made in nature to be passively encountered by the subject; rather, heautonomy is *made*. Systematic eclecticism is a key example: only through a methodological strategy of the type outlined in this chapter can language be potentiated to the extent that it becomes symbolic (and thus heautonomous). Heautonomy is dependent on labour, on the practices of the thinker; it is rationally constructed, not empirically perceived.

(c) Guaranteeing the Absoluteness of Construction

At the end of Chapter 6 I asked how Schelling can be so sure that his (or any philosopher's) constructions can be absolute. That is, I wondered how he can be so certain that the 1801 *Darstellung*, for example, is not a schematic or allegorical *Darstellung*, but symbolic. What guarantees that philosophy is philosophy? This, as I then noted, is to pose the question of 'how to begin' so often asked of Schelling: how can philosophers be so sure that they are beginning in the absolute? Once again, the short answer is symbolic practices. The philosopher is someone who has carried out and is in the process of carrying out symbolic practices. The philosopher practises systematic eclecticism, and only through so doing is the absoluteness of *Darstellungen* assured, for only through such practices does science become symbolic and so maximally poietic. Philosophy is made and it is made by symbolic practices. To speculatively appropriate the forms of other sciences is therefore one way to guarantee one's *Darstellungen* will be absolute.

Symbolic practices are to be found right at the heart of the *Identitätssystem*. Systematic eclecticism, in particular, not only illuminates the way in which Schelling practises philosophy, but also sheds light on the way he interprets the symbol and even the manner in which symbolic language should be constructed.

ABSOLUTE THEOLOGY AS THE DISSOLUTION OF THEOLOGY

Systematic absoluteness is obtained at the expense of the integrity of disciplines. In conclusion, I want to illustrate this process by returning to the example of theology. How, we might ask, does systematic eclecticism and the other symbolic practices aid in the construction of a new, reformed theology—a 'Gospel of the absolute'? Key to answering this question is the realization that it ultimately depends on how 'theology' is to be understood. For if theology is conceived as a stand-alone discipline with its own vocabularies, concepts, and ways of thinking, then Schellingian eclecticism in fact puts an end to theology (rather than making it absolute). If, however, theology is understood as discourse of whatever form that manifests God to the utmost, then systematic eclecticism is a key strategy in the becoming absolute of theology.

Thus, on the one hand, the symbolic practices I have considered at length in this chapter are aimed at destroying the integrity of all fields of thought, including theology. Schelling advocates the dissolution of any boundaries isolating theology from other sciences. No science, theology included, can be maximally poietic *in isolation*—only as an assemblage of sciences, a democracy of thought, or a university is the maximum production of essence possible.

This process could even be dubbed the *de*-absolutization of theology. Theology must be taken down from its pedestal and transformed into one more tool for poietic practice. Indeed, Schelling insists on the urgency of this debasement, because (as I outlined in the previous chapter) theology's privileged position, determining all other disciplines, has actually been the defining problem of modern thought: Christian reflection has thoroughly infected all the other sciences owing to its superiority. Only therefore by cutting theology down to size can all science, including theology itself, increase its productivity: theology's reformation is dependent on its simultaneous debasement. This is one answer to the question of the theological significance of symbolic practices.

However, on the other hand, if theology is defined formally as any discourse productive of the divine,[17] then it is only through symbolic practices (such as systematic eclecticism) that this theology can become absolute. It is engendered on the condition that it appropriates those forms which maximally produce what is—that is, it cultivates symbolic language by appropriating tropes, concepts, and vocabularies from all fields of thought indifferently. The result of this practice of eclecticism is therefore an absolute theology, a theology whose form produces God most, and which is thereby defined by its lack of integrity, by its eclectic forms.

In the previous chapter, I used the results of Schelling's construction of symbolic language to describe his conception of theology in very similar terms. Theology does not have a referent; it should not be about God. Indeed, it has no predetermined field of study. All that defines it is the purely structural criterion of the indifference of meaning and being or formal identity. Systematic eclecticism gives rise to exactly the same theological enterprise: the theologian who practises it shows no respect for predetermined fields of enquiry or for traditional subject matter; what is at stake, rather, is the assimilation of those languages which exhibit formal identity most, for only they will guarantee an absolute theology.

Symbolic practices are therefore aids in the becoming absolute of theology, but only if theology is understood as a science which has renounced reference, which is open to speculative transformations and mutations of its traditional content—only, that is, if it is understood as a science that embraces the eclecticism of forms. Theology—and by extension science in general—must become promiscuous to become absolute.

Ultimately, in conclusion, Schelling's *Identitätssystem* is itself the most obvious candidate for such an absolute science. It renounces reference, it

---

[17] And note: not 'about the divine'.

frequently practises speculative transformations, and it experiments with all sorts of forms. Moreover, §73 of the *Philosophie der Kunst* in particular serves as a particularly clear model for the absolute system: not only does it elucidate much of the theory out of which Schellingian absolute science is constructed, it also consists in an exemplary performance of this absolute system itself.

Thus, on the one hand, §73 of the *Philosophie der Kunst* touches on much of what is at stake in the *Identitätssystem*. It is here that Schelling responds to the theories of symbolic language proposed by his contemporaries; it is here that many of the concepts, theories, and principles of the *Identitätssystem* are repeated in the realm of linguistics; it is here, moreover, that the last sliver of representation, reference, and signification is eliminated from Schelling's thought; it is here that Schelling proposes a theory of language as radical as anything seen before or since in modern Western linguistics. However, on the other hand and perhaps more importantly, in §73 of the *Philosophie der Kunst* Schelling experiments with forms: he draws on the *Logosmystik* tradition as a means to express the above doctrinal insights more intensely. This section is one locus in Schelling's oeuvre where the practices of speculative transformation and systematic eclecticism are particularly clear: he creatively assimilates the forms of another tradition to cultivate his system's production of God. §73 both describes and performs the becoming absolute of the system.

Bibliography

(a) Schelling's Writings in German

SB. *Briefe und Dokumente*. 3 vols. Edited by Horst Fuhrmans. Bonn: Bouvier, 1962–75.
SW. *Werke*. 14 vols. Edited by K. F. A. Schelling. Stuttgart: Cotta, 1856–61.

(b) Schelling's Writings in Translation

1953. *Concerning the Relation of the Plastic Arts to Nature*. Translated by Michael Bullock. Appendix to Herbert Read, *The True Voice of Feeling: Studies in English Romantic Poetry*. London: Faber.
1966. *On University Studies*. Edited by Nobert Guterman. Translated by E. S. Morgan. Athens: Ohio University Press.
1978. *System of Transcendental Idealism*. Translated by Peter Heath. Charlottesville: University of Virginia Press.
1980a. *The Unconditional in Human Knowledge: Four Early Essays*. Edited and translated by Fritz Marti. Lewisburg: Bucknell University Press.
1980b. *Of the I as a Principle of Philosophy*, in Schelling 1980a, 63–128.
1980c. *Philosophical Letters on Dogmatism and Criticism*, in Schelling 1980a, 156–96.
1984a. *Bruno, or On the Natural and Divine Principle of Things*. Edited and translated by Michael G. Vater. Albany: SUNY Press.
1984b. *Aphorisms as an Introduction to Naturphilosophie*. Translated by Fritz Marti. *Idealistic Studies* 14.3: 244–58.
1985. *On the Relationship of the Philosophy of Nature to Philosophy in General*, in Di Giovanni and Harris 1985, 363–82.
1988a. *Ideas for a Philosophy of Nature*. Translated by Errol E. Harris and Peter Heath. Cambridge: Cambridge University Press.
1988b. *On Dante in Relation to Philosophy*. Translated by Elizabeth Rubenstein and David Simpson. In David Simpson (ed.), *The Origins of Modern Critical Thought: German Aesthetic and Literary Criticism*. Cambridge: Cambridge University Press, 239–49.
1989. *Philosophy of Art*. Translated by Douglas W. Stott. Minneapolis: Minnesota University Press.
1994a. *Idealism and the Endgame of Theory: Three Esssays*. Edited and translated by Thomas Pfau. Albany: SUNY Press.
1994b. *Treatise Explicatory of the Idealism in the Science of Knowledge*, in Schelling 1994a, 61–138.
1994c. *System of Philosophy in General and of the Philosophy of Nature in Particular*, in Schelling 1994a, 139–94 [partial translation].
1994d. *On the History of Modern Philosophy*. Translated by Andrew Bowie. Cambridge: Cambridge University Press.
2001a. *Presentation of My System of Philosophy*. Translated by Michael G. Vater. *Philosophical Forum* 32.4: 339–71 [partial translation].

2001b. *Further Presentations From the System of Philosophy*. Translated by Michael G. Vater. *Philosophical Forum* 32.4: 373–97 [partial translation].

2004. *First Outline of a System of the Philosophy of Nature*. Translated by Keith R. Peterson. Albany: SUNY Press.

2008. *On Construction in Philosophy*. Translated by Andrew A. Davis and Alexi I. Kukuljevic. *Epoché* 12.2: 269–88.

(c) **Other Works**

Aarsleff, Hans. 1982. *From Locke to Saussure*. London: Athlone.

———2006. 'Philosophy of Language', in Knut Haakonssen (ed.), *The Cambridge History of Eighteenth-Century Philosophy*. Volume 1. Cambridge: Cambridge University Press, 451–95.

Adams, Hazard. 1983. *The Philosophy of the Literary Symbolic*. Tallahassee: Florida University Press.

Adler, Jeremy. 1998. 'The Aesthetics of Magnetism: Science, Philosophy and Poetry in the Dialogue between Goethe and Schelling', in Elinor S. Shaffer (ed.), *The Third Culture: Literature and Science*. Berlin: de Gruyter, 66–102.

Apel, Karl Otto. 1963. *Die Idee der Sprache in der Tradition des Humanismus von Dante bis Vico*. Bonn: Bouvier.

Bär, Jochen A. 1999. *Sprachreflexion der deutschen Frühromantik: Konzepte zwischen Universalpoesie und grammatischem Kosmopolitismus*. Berlin: de Gruyter.

Barber, Daniel Colucciello. 2011. *On Diaspora: Christianity, Religion, Secularity*. Eugene, OR: Cascade.

Barth, Bernhard. 1991. *Schellings Philosophie der Kunst: Göttliche Imagination und ästhetische Einbildungskraft*. Freiburg: Alber.

Barthes, Roland. 1994. *Oeuvres completes*. 3 vols. Edited by Eric Marty. Paris: Seuil.

Bayer, Oswald. 1983. 'Schöpfung als "Rede an die Kreatur durch die Kreatur": Die Frage nach dem Schlüssel zum Buch der Natur und Geschichte', in Bernhard Gajek (ed.), *Johann Georg Hamann: Acta des zweiten Internationalen Hamann Colloquiums (1980)*. Marburg: Elwert, 57–75.

Beaufret, Jean. 1973. 'Kant et la notion de *Darstellung*', in *Dialogue avec Heidegger*. Volume 2. Paris: Minuit, 77–109.

Behler, Ernst. 1993. *German Romantic Literary Theory*. Cambridge: Cambridge University Press.

Beierwaltes, Werner. 1972. *Platonismus und Idealismus*. Frankfurt am Main: Klostermann.

———1983. 'Absolute Identity: Neoplatonic Implications in Schelling's *Bruno*'. Translated by Darrel E. Christensen and F. A. Uehlein. *Contemporary German Philosophy* 2: 73–99.

———2002. 'The Legacy of Neoplatonism in F. W. J. Schelling's Thought'. Translated by Peter Adamson. *International Journal of Philosophical Studies* 10.4: 393–428.

Beiser, Frederick C. 2002. *German Idealism: The Struggle against Subjectivism, 1781–1801*. Cambridge, MA: Harvard University Press.

———2003. *The Romantic Imperative: The Concept of Early German Romanticism*. Cambridge, MA: Harvard University Press.

Benjamin, Walter. 1998. *The Origin of German Tragic Drama*. Translated by John Osborne. London: Verso.

Benz, Ernst. 1968. *Les sources mystiques de la philosophie romantique allemande*. Paris: Vrin.

Berkeley, George. 1975. *Philosophical Works*. Edited by Michael Ayers. London: Dent.

Biddle, Ian. 1996. 'F. W. J. Schelling's *Philosophie der Kunst*: An Emergent Semiology of Music', in Ian Bent (ed.), *Music Theory in the Age of Romanticism*. Cambridge: Cambridge University Press, 25–36.

Blumenberg, Hans. 1983. *The Legitimacy of the Modern Age*. Second edition. Translated by Robert M. Wallace. Cambridge, MA: MIT Press.

Boenke, Michaela. 2003. 'Giordano Bruno dans la philosophie de l'identité de Schelling'. Translated by Tristan Dagron. In Tristan Dagron and Hélène Védrine (eds), *Mondes, formes et société selon Giordano Bruno*. Paris: Vrin, 197–208.

Böhme, Jacob. 2001. *Essential Readings*. Edited by Robin Waterfield. Berkeley: North Atlantic Books.

Bowie, Andrew. 1993. *Schelling and Modern European Philosophy: An Introduction*. London: Routledge.

——2007. *Music, Philosophy and Modernity*. Cambridge: Cambridge University Press.

Breazeale, Daniel. 2002. 'Fichte's Philosophical Fictions', in Daniel Breazeale and Tom Rockmore (eds), *New Essays on Fichte's Later Jena Wissenschaftslehre*. Evanston: Northwestern University Press, 175–208.

Brito, Emilio. 2000. *Philosophie et théologie dans l'oeuvre de Schelling*. Paris: Cerf.

Bruno, Giordano. 1988. *Cause, Principle and Unity*. Edited and translated by Robert de Lucca. Cambridge: Cambridge University Press.

Carlyle, Thomas. 1908. *Sartor Resartus*. London: Dent.

Cassirer, Ernst. 1963. 'Goethe and the Kantian Philosophy', in *Rousseau, Kant, Goethe: Two Essays*. Translated by James Gutmann et al. New York: Harper.

Challiol-Gillet, Marie-Christine. 1996. *Schelling*. Paris: PUF.

Coleridge, S. T. 1839. 'On the *Prometheus* of Aeschylus'. In *Literary Remains*. Volume 2. Edited by H. N. Coleridge. London: Pickering, 276–303.

——1993. *Aids to Reflection*. Edited by John Beer. Princeton: Princeton University Press.

Copleston, Frederick. 1975. *A History of Philosophy*. 9 vols. London: Burns and Oates.

Coseriu, Eugenio. 1977. 'Schellings Weg von der Sprachphilosophie zum Sprachmythos'. *Zeitschrift für Französische Sprache und Literatur Beiheft* 5: 1–16.

Courtine, Jean-François. 1990. *Extase de la raison. Essais sur Schelling*. Paris: Galilée.

Cousin, Victor. 1846. *Cours de l'histoire de la philosophie moderne*. Series I, volume 2. Paris: Fournier.

Culler, Jonathan. 1988. *Framing the Sign: Criticism and its Institutions*. Oxford: Blackwell.

Davies, Stephen. 1994. *Musical Meaning and Expression*. Ithaca: Cornell University Press.

De Man, Paul. 1983. *Blindness and Insight: Essays in the Rhetoric of Contemporary Criticism*. Second edition. London: Methuen.

——1984. *The Rhetoric of Romanticism*. New York: Columbia University Press.

De Man, Paul. 1986. *The Resistance to Theory*. Edited by Wlad Godzich. Minneapolis: University of Minnesota Press.

——1996. *Aesthetic Ideology*. Edited by Andrzej Warminski. Minneapolis: University of Minnesota Press.

Deleuze, Gilles. 1990. *Expressionism in Philosophy: Spinoza*. Translated by Martin Joughin. New York: Zone.

——1994. *Difference and Repetition*. Translated by Paul Patton. London: Continuum.

Di Giovanni, George. 1987. 'Grazing in the Sunlight: On H. S. Harris' "The Cows in the Dark Night"'. *Dialogue. Revue canadienne de philosophie* 26.4: 653–63.

Di Giovanni, George and H. S. Harris (eds). 1985. *Between Kant and Hegel: Texts in the Development of Post-Kantian Idealism*. Albany: SUNY Press.

Dickerson, A. B. 2004. *Kant on Representation and Objectivity*. Cambridge: Cambridge University Press.

Diderot, Denis. 2011. 'Eclectisme', in Denis Diderot and Jean d'Alembert (eds), *Encyclopédie, ou dictionnaire raisonné des sciences, des arts et des métiers, etc.* Volume 5. <http://encyclopedie.uchicago.edu/>. Accessed 19 February 2012, 270–93.

Dieckmann, Liselotte. 1959. 'Friedrich Schlegel and the Romantic Concepts of the Symbol'. *Germanic Review* 34.4: 276–83.

Dietzsch, Steffen. 1975. 'Le problème du mythe chez le jeune Schelling'. *Archives de Philosophie* 38.3: 395–400.

Eagleton, Terry. 1990. *The Ideology of the Aesthetic*. Oxford: Blackwell.

——1991. *Ideology: An Introduction*. London: Verso.

Ende, Helga. 1973. *Der Konstruktionsbegriff im Umkreis des Deutschen Idealismus*. Meisenheim: Haim.

Esposito, Joseph L. 1977. *Schelling's Idealism and Philosophy of Nature*. Lewisburg: Bucknell University Press.

Esterhammer, Angela. 2000. *The Romantic Performative: Language and Action in British and German Romanticism*. Stanford: Stanford University Press.

Fackenheim, Emil L. 1954. 'Schelling's Philosophy of the Literary Arts'. *Philosophical Quarterly* 17.4: 310–26.

Fichte, J. G. 1982. *Science of Knowing*. Edited and translated by Peter Heath and John Lachs. Cambridge: Cambridge University Press.

——1992. *Foundations of Transcendental Philosophy (Wissenschaftlehre) nova methodo, 1796/9*. Edited and translated by Daniel Breazeale. Ithaca: Cornell University Press.

——1996. 'On the Linguistic Capacity and the Origin of Language'. Translated by Jere Paul Surber. In Jere Paul Surber (ed.), *Language and German Idealism: Fichte's Linguistic Philosophy*. Atlantic Highlands, NJ: Humanities Press, 119–45.

Fichte, J. G. and F. W. J. Schelling. 1997. 'Selections from Fichte–Schelling Correspondence', in Schulte-Sasse et al. 1997, 73–90.

Fischbach, Franck. 1999. *Du commencement en philosophie: Étude sur Schelling et Hegel*. Paris: Vrin.

Flach, Werner. 1982. 'Zu Kants Lehre von der symbolischen Darstellung'. *Kant-Studien* 73.4: 452–62.

Frank, Manfred. 1985. *Eine Einführung in Schellings Philosophie*. Frankfurt am Main: Suhrkamp.

——1992. *Der unendliche Mangel an Sein: Schellings Hegelkritik und die Anfänge der Marxschen Dialektik*. Revised edition. München: Fink.

——2004. *The Philosophical Foundations of Early German Romanticism*. Translated by Elizabeth Millán-Zaibert. Albany: SUNY Press.

Frenzel, Elizabeth. 1963. *Stoff-, Motiv- und Symbolforschung*. Stuttgart: Metzler.

Funkenstein, Amos. 1986. *Theology and the Scientific Imagination: From the Middle Ages to the Seventeenth Century*. Princeton: Princeton University Press.

Gadamer, Hans-Georg. 2004. *Truth and Method*. Second edition. Translated by Joel Weinsheimer and Donald G. Marshall. London: Continuum.

Galland-Szymkowiak, Mildred. 2006. 'Le changement de sens du symbole entre Leibniz et Kant'. *Revue Germanique Internationale* 4: 73–91.

——2007. 'Symbol und Zeitlichkeit bei Schelling, Solger und Hegel'. *Philosophisches Jahrbuch* 114.2: 324–45.

Gangle, Rocco. 2010. 'Theology of the Chimera: Spinoza, Immanence, Practice', in Anthony Paul Smith and Daniel Whistler (eds), *After the Postmodern and the Postsecular: New Essays in Continental Philosophy of Religion*. Newcastle: Cambridge Scholars Press, 26–43.

Gasché, Rodolphe. 1990. 'Some Reflections on the Notion of *Hypotyposis* in Kant'. *Argumentation* 4: 85–100.

Genette, Gérard. 1976. *Mimologiques: Voyage en Cratylie*. Paris: Seuil.

Godzich, Wlad. 1983. 'Introduction' to de Man 1983, xv–xxx.

Goethe, Johann Wolfgang. 1887–1919. *Werke: Weimarer Ausgabe* [*WA*]. Edited by Sophie von Sachsen. 5 Reihen, 133 vols. Weimar: Böhlau.

——1983. 'On the Subjects of the Plastic Arts'. Translated by Hazard Adams. Appendix to Adams 1983, 395–7.

——1987. *Faust: Part One*. Translated by David Luke. Oxford: Oxford University Press.

——1988. *Scientific Studies*. Edited and translated by Douglas Miller. New York: Suhrkamp.

——1989. *Wilhelm Meister's Journeyman Years, or the Renunciants*. Edited by Jane K. Brown. Translated by Krishna Winston. New York: Suhrkamp.

——1998. *Maxims and Reflections*. Edited by Peter Hutchinson. Translated by Elisabeth Stopp. London: Penguin.

Goethe, Johann Wolfgang and Friedrich Schiller. 1914. *Correspondence Between Schiller and Goethe*. 2 vols. Translated by L. Dora Schmitz. London: Bell.

Grant, Iain Hamilton. 2006. *Philosophies of Nature after Schelling*. London: Continuum.

Griffith Dickson, Gwen. 1995. *J. G. Hamann's Relational Metacriticism*. Berlin: de Gruyter.

Groves, Christopher. 1999. 'Ecstasy of Reason, Crisis of Reason: Schelling and Absolute Difference'. *Pli* 8: 25–45.

Gueroult, Martial. 1974. *Spinoza*. 2 vols. Paris: Aubier.

Gutmann, James. 1936. 'Translator's Introduction' to F. W. J. Schelling, *Philosophical Inquiries into the Nature of Human Freedom*. La Salle: Open Court. xi–lii.

Guyer, Paul. 2006. 'Bridging the Gulf: Kant's Project in the Third *Critique*', in Graham Bird (ed.), *A Companion to Kant*. Oxford: Blackwell, 423–40.

Halmi, Nicholas. 2007. *The Genealogy of the Romantic Symbol*. Oxford: Oxford University Press.

Hamann, J. G. 2007. *Writings on Philosophy and Language*. Edited and translated by Kenneth Haynes. Cambridge: Cambridge University Press.

Harris, Errol E. 1995. *The Substance of Spinoza*. Atlantic Highlands, NJ: Humanities Press.

Hayes, Charles. 1969. 'Symbol and Allegory: A Problem in Literary Theory'. *Germanic Review* 44.4: 273–88.

Heath, Thomas L. 1926. 'Translator's Introduction' to Euclid, *Elements*. Volume 1. Cambridge: Cambridge University Press, 1–153.

Hegel, G. W. F. 1896. *Lectures on the History of Philosophy*. 3 vols. Translated by E. S. Haldane and Frances H. Simson. London: Routledge.

——1977a. *The Difference between Fichte's and Schelling's System of Philosophy*. Translated by H. S. Harris and Walter Cerf. Albany: SUNY Press.

——1977b. *Phenomenology of Spirit*. Translated by A. V. Miller. Oxford: Oxford University Press.

Hegel, G. W. F. and F. W. J. Schelling. 1985. 'The Critical Journal of Philosophy: Introduction on the Essence of Philosophical Criticism Generally and its Relationship to the Present State of Philosophy in Particular', in di Giovanni and Harris 1985, 272–91.

Helfer, Martha B. 1996. *The Retreat of Representation: The Concept of* Darstellung *in German Critical Discourse*. Albany: SUNY Press.

Henn, Marianne. 1994. '"*Individuum est ineffabile*": Goethe and the Tradition of Silence', in Henn and Christoph Lorey (eds), *Analogon Rationis: Festschrift für Gerwin Marahrens zum 65. Geburtstag*. Edmonton: University of Alberta Press, 251–72.

Hennigfeld, Jochem. 1973. *Mythos und Poesie: Interpretationen zu Schellings* Philosophie der Kunst *und* Philosophie der Mythologie. Meisenheim: Hain.

——1984. 'Schellings Philosophie der Sprache'. *Philosophisches Jahrbuch* 91.1: 16–29.

Hintikka, Jaakko. 1969. 'On Kant's Notion of Intuition (*Anschauung*)', in Terence Penelhum and J. J. MacIntosh (eds), *The First Critique: Reflections on Kant's Critique of Pure Reason*. Belmont: Wadsworth, 38–53.

Hobbes, Thomas. 1845. *The English Works*. 11 vols. Edited by William Molesworth. London: Longman and Bohn.

Hölderlin, Friedrich. 1985. *Sämtliche Werke: Großer Stuttgarter Ausgabe*. 8 vols. Edited by Friedrich Beissner. Stuttgart: Kohlhammer.

Ingegno, Alfonso. 1988. 'Introduction' to Bruno 1988, vii–xxix.

Ingen, Ferdinand van. 2001. 'Jacob Böhme und die Natursprache: Eine Idee und ihre Wirkung', in *Erkenntnis und Wissenschaft: Jacob Böhme. Internationales Jacob Böhme Symposium (2000)*. Görlitz: Oettel, 115–27.

Jacobi, F. H. 1994. *The Main Philosophical Writings*. Edited and translated by George di Giovanni. Montreal: McGill-Queen's University Press.

Jähnig, Dieter. 1969. *Schelling: Die Kunst in der Philosophie*. 2 vols. Pfullingen: Neske.

Joachim, Harold H. 1940. *Spinoza's* Tractatus de intellectus emendatione: *A Commentary*. Oxford: Clarendon Press.

Kant Immanuel. 1987. *Critique of Judgment*. Translated by Werner S. Pluhar. Indianapolis: Hackett.

——1992. *Theoretical Philosophy, 1755–1770*. Edited by David Walford. Cambridge: Cambridge University Press.

——2002. *Theoretical Philosophy after 1781*. Edited by Henry Allison and Peter Heath. Translated by Gary Hatfield et al. Cambridge: Cambridge University Press.

——2007. *Critique of Pure Reason*. Translated by Norman-Kemp Smith. Basingstoke: Palgrave Macmillan.

Keach, William. 1993. 'Romanticism and Language', in Stuart Curran (ed), *The Cambridge Companion to British Romanticism*. Cambridge: Cambridge University Press, 95–119.

Knittermeyer, Heinrich. 1928. *Schelling und die romantische Schule*. München: Reinhardt.

König, Helga. 1976. 'Konstruction', in Joachim Ritter and Karlfried Gründer (eds), *Historisches Wörterbuch der Philosophie*. Volume 4. Basel: Schwabe, 1009–19.

Krueger, S. Heidi. 1990. 'Allegory and Symbol in the Goethezeit: A Critical Reassessment', in Gertrud Pickar and Sabine Cramer (eds), *The Age of Goethe Today: A Critical Re-examination and Literary Reflection*. München: Fink, 50–68.

Lachterman, David Rapport. 1989. *The Ethics of Geometry: A Genealogy of Modernity*. London: Routledge.

Lacoue-Labarthe, Philippe and Jean-Luc Nancy. 1988. *The Literary Absolute: The Theory of Literature in German Romanticism*. Translated by Philip Bernard and Cheryl Lester. Albany: SUNY Press.

Leibniz, G. W. 1998. *Philosophical Texts*. Edited and translated by R. S. Woolhouse and Richard Francks. Oxford: Oxford University Press.

Lessing, G. E. 1985. 'Letter to Nicolai, 26th May 1769'. Translated by Joyce P. Crick. In H. B. Nisbet (ed.), *German Aesthetic and Literary Criticism: Wincklemann, Lessing, Hamann, Herder, Schiller, Goethe*. Cambridge: Cambridge University Press, 133–4.

Llewelyn, John. 1990. 'Imagination as a Connecting Middle in Schelling's Reconstruction of Kant', in George MacDonald Ross and Tony McWalter (eds), *Kant and His Influence*. Bristol: Thoemmes, 170–200.

Lloyd, Genevieve. 1996. *Spinoza and the* Ethics. London: Routledge.

Locke, John. 1993. *An Essay Concerning Human Understanding*. Edited by John Yolton. London: Dent.

Lovejoy, Arthur O. 1936. *The Great Chain of Being: A Study of the History of an Idea*. Cambridge, MA: Harvard University Press.

Lukács, Georg. 1975. *The Young Hegel*. Translated by Rodney Livingstone. London: Merlin.

——1980. *The Destruction of Reason*. Translated by Peter Palmer. London: Merlin.

Macherey, Pierre. 1996. 'The Encounter with Spinoza', in Paul Patton (ed.), *Deleuze: A Critical Reader*. Oxford: Blackwell, 139–61.

Maesschalck, Marc. 1989. *Philosophie et révélation dans l'itinéraire de Schelling*. Paris: Vrin.

Maimon, Salomon. 2010. *Essay on Transcendental Idealism*. Translated by Nick Midgley et al. London: Continuum.

Marache, Maurice. 1960. *Le symbole dans la pensée et l'oeuvre de Goethe*. Paris: Nizat.

Marquet, Jean-François. 1965. 'Schelling et les métamorphoses de l'histoire'. *Critique* 212: 63–72.

——1973. *Liberté et existence. Étude sur la formation de la philosophie de Schelling.* Paris: Gallimard.

Marty, François. 1980. *La naissance de la métaphysique chez Kant. Une étude sur la notion kantienne d'analogie.* Paris: Beauchesne.

Mayer, Paola. 1999. *Jena Romanticism and its Appropriation of Jakob Böhme: Theosophy, Hagiography, Literature.* Montreal: McGill-Queen's University Press.

Mendelssohn, Moses. 1997. *Philosophical Writings.* Edited and translated by Daniel O. Dahlstrom. Cambridge: Cambridge University Press.

Michel, Paul Henri. 1973. *The Cosmology of Giordano Bruno.* Translated by R. E. W. Maddison. London: Methuen.

Mueller, Ian. 1981. *Philosophy of Mathematics and Deductive Structures in Euclid's Elements.* Cambridge, MA: MIT Press.

Müller, Curt. 1937. *Die geschichtlichen Voraussetzungen des Symbolbegriffs in Goethes Kunstanschauung.* Leipzig: Mayer.

Musil, Robert. 1995. *The Man Without Qualities.* Translated by Sophie Wilkins and Burton Pike. London: Picador.

Nassar, Dalia. 2010. 'From a Philosophy of Self to a Philosophy of Nature: Goethe and the Development of Schelling's *Naturphilosophie'. Archiv fur die Geschichte der Philosophie* 92: 304–21.

Niklewski, Günter. 1979. *Versuch über Allegorie (Winckelmann—Moritz—Schelling).* Erlangen: Palm und Enke.

Novalis. 1997. *Philosophical Writings.* Edited and translated by Margaret Mahony Stoljar. Albany: SUNY Press.

——2003. *Fichte Studies.* Edited and translated by Jane Kneller. Cambridge: Cambridge University Press.

Nuzzo, Angelica. 2005. *Kant and the Unity of Reason.* West Lafayette: Purdue University Press.

Nygaard, Loisa. 1988. '"*Bild*" and "*Sinnbild*": The Problem of the Symbol in Goethe's *Wahlverwandtschaften'. Germanic Review* 63:2: 58–76.

O'Brien, William Arcander. 1995. *Novalis: Signs of Revolution.* Durham: Duke University Press.

Otto, Stephan. 2003. 'Le "symbole de la vraie philosophie". La *Nolana philosophia* et sa transmission à Schelling par Jacobi'. Translated by Franck Fischbach. In Tristan Dagron and Hélène Védrine (eds), *Mondes, formes et société selon Giordano Bruno.* Paris: Vrin, 177–95.

Plato. 1963. *Cratylus.* Translated by Benjamin Jowett. In *The Collected Dialogues.* Edited by Edith Hamilton and Huntington Cairns. Princeton: Princeton University Press, 421–74.

Plessner, Helmuth. 1954. 'Das Identitätssystem'. *Studia Philosophica* 14: 68–84.

Pseudo-Dionysius. 1987. *The Complete Works.* Translated by Colm Luibheid. New York: Paulist Press.

Reinhold, K. L. 1985. 'The Foundation of Philosophical Knowledge', in di Giovanni and Harris 1985, 51–103.

Richards, Robert J. 2002. *The Romantic Conception of Life: Science and Philosophy in the Age of Goethe*. Chicago: University of Chicago Press.

Ricoeur, Paul. 1967. *The Symbolism of Evil*. Translated by Emerson Buchanan. Boston: Beacon Press.

——1974. *The Conflict of Interpretations*. Translated by Don Ihde. Evanston: Northwestern University Press.

Ridley, Aaron. 2004. *The Philosophy of Music: Themes and Variations*. Edinburgh: Edinburgh University Press.

Robinson, Henry Crabb. 1976. 'Schellings Aesthetik', in Ernst Behler, 'Schellings Ästhetik in der Überlieferung von Henry Crabb Robinson'. *Philosophisches Jahrbuch* 83.1: 153–85.

Rockmore, Tom. 2002. 'Fichte, Representation and the Copernican Revolution', in Daniel Breazeale and Tom Rockmore (eds), *New Essays on Fichte's Later Jena Wissenschaftslehre*. Evanston: Northwestern University Press, 345–57.

Rosenau, Hartmut. 1990. 'Schellings metaphysikkritische Sprachphilosophie'. *Zeitschrift für philosophische Forschung* 44.3: 399–426.

Saussure, Ferdinand de. 1966. *Course in General Linguistics*. Edited by Charles Bally and Albert Riedlinger. Translated by Wade Baskin. New York: McGraw-Hill.

Schaper, Eva. 1979. 'Schiller's Kant: A Chapter in the History of Creative Misunderstanding', in *Studies in Kant's Aesthetics*. Edinburgh: Edinburgh University Press, 99–117.

Schiller, Friedrich. 2003. 'Kallias or Concerning Beauty: Letters to Gottfried Körner'. Translated by Stefan Bird-Pollan. In J. M. Bernstein (ed.), *Classic and Romantic German Aesthetics*. Cambridge: Cambridge University Press, 145–84.

Schlegel, A. W. 1989. *Vorlesungen über schöne Literatur und Kunst (Berlin 1801–1804)*, in *Kritische Ausgabe der Vorlesungen*. Volume 1. Edited by Ernst Behler. Paderborn: Schöningh, 179–781.

——1997. 'Theory of Art (Selections from 1798–1803)', in Schulte-Sasse et al. 1997, 194–226.

Schlegel, Friedrich. 1957. *Literary Notebooks, 1797–1801*. Edited by Hans Eichner. Toronto: University of Toronto Press.

——1971. 'Athenaeum Fragments', in Lucinde *and the Fragments*. Edited and translated by Peter Firchow. Minneapolis: University of Minnesota Press, 161–240.

——1997. 'Introduction to the Transcendental Philosophy'. In Schulte-Sasse et al. 1997, 240–68.

Schleiermacher, Friedrich. 1999. *The Christian Faith*. Translated by H. R. Mackintosh and J. S. Stewart. London: T. & T. Clark.

Schulte-Sasse, Jochen et al. (eds). 1997. *Theory as Practice: A Critical Anthology of Early German Romantic Writings*. Minneapolis: University of Minnesota Press.

Seidel, George J. 1976. *Activity and Ground: Fichte, Schelling and Hegel*. New York: Georg Olms.

Seyhan, Azade. 1992. *Representation and its Discontents: The Critical Legacy of German Romanticism*. Berkeley: University of California Press.

Shaw, Devin Zane. 2010. *Freedom and Nature in Schelling's Philosophy of Art*. London: Continuum.

Sheehan, Jonathan. 1998. 'Enlightenment Details: Theology, Natural History, and the Letter *h*'. *Representations* 61: 29–56.

Solger, Karl. 1984. 'Erwin or Four Dialogues on Beauty and Art'. Translated by Kathleen M. Wheeler. In Wheeler (ed.), *German Aesthetic and Literary Criticism: The Romantic Ironists and Goethe*. Cambridge, Cambridge University Press, 125–50.

Sørensen, Bengt Algot. 1963. *Symbol und Symbolismus in den ästhetischen Theorien des 18. Jahrhunderts und der deutschen Romantik*. Kopenhagen: Munksgaard.

——1972. *Allegorie und Symbol: Texte zur Theorie des dichterischen Bildes im 18. und frühen 19. Jahrhundert*. Frankfurt am Main: Athenäum.

——1979. '"Die zarte Differenz": Symbol und Allegorie in der ästhetischen Diskussion zwischen Schiller und Goethe', in Walter Haug (ed.), *Formen und Funktionen der Allegorie: Symposium Wolfenbüttel 1978*. Stuttgart: Metzlersche, 632–41.

Spinoza, Benedict de. 1985. 'Treatise on the Emendation of the Intellect', in *Collected Works*. Volume 1. Edited and translated by Edwin Curley. Princeton: Princeton University Press, 3–45.

——1994. *Ethics*, in *A Spinoza Reader*. Edited and translated by Edwin Curley. Princeton: Princeton University Press, 85–265.

Spitzer, Michael. 2004. *Metaphor and Musical Meaning*. Chicago: University of Chicago Press.

Stephenson, R. L. 1995. *Goethe's Conception of Knowledge and Science*. Edinburgh: Edinburgh University Press.

Surber, Jere Paul. 1996. *Language and German Idealism: Fichte's Linguistic Philosophy*. Atlantic Highlands, NJ: Humanities Press.

——2000. 'The Problems of Language in German Idealism: An Historical and Conceptual Overview', in O. K. Wiegand et al. (eds), *Phenomenology on Kant, German Idealism, Hermeneutics and Logic*. Dordrecht: Kluwer, 305–36.

Susini, Eugène. 1942. *Franz von Baader et le romantisme mystique*. 2 vols. Paris: Vrin.

Szondi, Peter. 1974. *Poetik und Geschichtsphilosophie*. 2 vols. Frankfurt am Main: Suhrkamp.

Tilliette, Xavier. 1970. *Schelling: Une philosophie en devenir*. 2 vols. Paris: Vrin.

——1987. *L'absolu et la philosophie. Essais sur Schelling*. Paris: PUF.

——1994. 'La christologie de Schelling', introduction to F. W. J. Schelling, *Philosophie de la revelation*. Volume 3. Edited and translated by J. F. Courtine et al. Paris: PUF, 5–20.

——1995. *Recherches sur l'intuition intellectuelle de Kant à Hegel*. Paris: Vrin.

——1999. *Schelling: Biographie*. Paris: Calmann-Lévy.

Titzmann, Michael. 1979. 'Allegorie und Symbol im Denksystem der Goethezeit', in Walter Haug (ed.), *Formen und Funktionen der Allegorie: Symposium Wolfenbüttel 1978*. Stuttgart: Metzlersche, 642–62.

Todorov, Tzvetan. 1982. *Theories of the Symbol*. Translated by Catherine Porter. Ithaca: Cornell University Press.

——1983. *Symbolism and Interpretation*. Translated by Catherine Porter. London: Routledge.

Toscano, Alberto. 1999. 'Fanaticism and Production: On Schelling's Philosophy of Indifference'. *Pli* 8: 46–70.

——2004. 'Philosophy and the Experience of Construction', in Jane Norman and Alistair Welchman (eds), *The New Schelling*. London: Continuum, 106–27.

Troxler, I. P. V. 1988. 'Hauptmomente aus Schellings Vortrage nach der Stunde aufgezeichnet, 1801', in Klaus Düsing, *Schellings und Hegels erste absolute Metaphysik (1801–2)*. Köln: Dinter, 27–62.

Uslar, Detlev von. 1968. 'Die innere Bewegung der absoluten Identität bei Schelling'. *Studium Generale* 21: 503–14.

Vater, Michael G. 1976. 'Schelling Neoplatonic System-Notion: '"*Ineinsbildung*" and Temporal Unfolding', in R. Baine Harris (ed.), *The Significance of Neoplatonism*. Norfolk, VA: International Society for Neoplatonic Studies, 275–99.

——1984. 'Translator's Introduction' to Schelling 1984a, 3–107.

——2000. 'Intellectual Intuition in Schelling's Philosophy of Identity, 1801–1804', in Christoph Asmuth et al. (eds), *Schelling: Zwischen Fichte und Hegel*. Amsterdam: Grüner, 213–34.

——2008. 'Fichte's Reaction to Schelling's Identity Philosophy in 1806', in Daniel Breazeale and Tom Rockmore (eds), *After Jena: New Essays on Fichte's Later Philosophy*. Evanston: Northwestern University Press, 81–90.

Védrine, Hélène. 1967. *La conception de la nature chez Giordano Bruno*. Paris: Vrin.

Verra, V. 1979. 'La "construction" dans la philosophie de Schelling', in G. Planty-Bonjour (ed.), *Actualité de Schelling*. Paris: Vrin, 27–47.

Vieillard-Baron, Jean-Louis. 1971. 'De la connaissance de Giordano Bruno à l'époque de l'idéalisme allemand'. *Revue de métaphysique et de morale* 76.4: 416–19.

Wanning, Berbeli. 1988. *Konstruktion und Geschichte: Das Identitätsphilosophie als Grundlage der Kunstphilosophie bei F. W. J. Schelling*. Frankfurt am Main: Haag und Herchen.

Warminski, Andrzej. 1996. 'Introduction: Allegories of Reference', in de Man 1996, 1–33.

Wellbery, David E. 1984. *Lessing's Laocoön: Semiotics and Aesthetics in the Age of Reason*. Cambridge: Cambridge University Press.

Whistler, Daniel. 2010. 'Language after Philosophy of Nature: Schelling's Geology of Divine Names' in Anthony Paul Smith and Daniel Whistler (eds), *After the Postmodern and the Postsecular: New Essays in Continental Philosophy of Religion*. Newcastle: Cambridge Scholars Press. 335–59.

——2012a. 'Improper Names for God: Religious Language and the "Spinoza Effect"'. *Speculations* 3: 99–134.

——2012b. 'Purely Practical Reason: Normative Epistemology from Leibniz to Maimon'. *Epoché* 17.2: forthcoming.

——2012c. 'Post-Established Harmony: Kant and Analogy Reconsidered'. *Sophia* 52.1: forthcoming.

White, Alan. 1983. *Schelling: An Introduction to the System of Freedom*. New Haven: Yale University Press.

Zammito, John H. 1992. *The Genesis of Kant's* Critique of Judgment. Chicago: University of Chicago Press.

Zeltner, Hermann. 1975. 'Das Identitätssystem', in Hans Michael Baumgartner (ed.), *Schelling: Einführung in seine Philosophie*. Freiburg: Alber, 75–94.

Zourabichvili, François. 2002. *Spinoza. Une physique de la pensée*. Paris: PUF.

Index

A = A 70, 78–81, 95–6, 102–4, 106, 176–8
  see also identity
absolute 15, 18, 25–6, 44, 61–2, 70–5, 77–81,
    83, 87–93, 95–6, 100–5, 107–9, 113–15,
    123, 127–32, 134–7, 141–3, 146, 148,
    150–2, 154–6, 159–60, 162–3, 166–8,
    170–1, 174, 176–9, 182, 186–8, 193,
    198–9, 201–2, 206, 208, 210, 216–23,
    227–30, 235–6, 240–3
absoluteness in limitation 75, 89, 155–6,
    178–9, 182, 188–9
abstraction 5, 79, 136–7, 152
Adams, Hazard 17, 25, 31, 33, 42, 159–60
additive model 27, 161
adequacy 43–4, 70, 76, 80–2, 89, 96, 155,
    177–8, 197
aesthetics 12–16, 34, 44, 52, 61–2, 77, 142,
    203, 205, 211, 233, 238
affirmation 59, 80, 90–3, 95, 101–2, 105,
    107–8, 115–16, 128, 159, 163, 174, 179,
    187–8, 223
allegory 4, 6, 9, 11–12, 15–16, 19, 32, 39, 41,
    50–2, 64–6, 142–52, 161–2, 167, 187, 189,
    200, 203, 241
analogy 7, 28–9, 63, 66, 106–7, 116, 162–3
anti-discursiveness 33, 43–6, 49–50, 52, 165,
    168–73, 176
antithesis 19, 98, 100–3, 108, 110, 116, 127
apophaticism 33, 70, 72, 85, 142, 176, 178,
    221, 232
arbitrary sign 12, 30–4, 37–8, 46, 49, 84,
    190–1, 197, 199, 202, 204
archetype 8, 26, 86–7, 95, 134–5, 160
arithmetic 5, 125–9, 137, 151, 167, 175, 186
  see also mathematics
art 6, 13, 52, 59–62, 77, 112, 114–15, 128–9,
    142–3, 152, 154–7, 159–60, 163, 167–8,
    182–5, 187–9, 205, 212, 215, 217–18, 223,
    233, 237–8
  see also drama; music; poetry; sculpture
Ast, Friedrich 14, 26
atheism 211
autoconstruction 123–4

Baader, Franz 4, 35–6
Bär, Jochen 181, 185
beauty 7, 11–13, 15–16, 24, 44, 155, 189, 213
Beiser, Frederick C. 57–8, 100, 135, 176–9

Benjamin, Walter 40, 52
Bildung 92, 99, 115–16, 188, 216–17, 227, 232
  see also formation
Böhme, Jacob 35–7, 224–5
Bowie, Andrew ix, 69, 202–3
Bruno, Giordano 76–8, 178

Carlyle, Thomas 42
causality 16, 72–3, 87, 109–11, 118–21,
    127, 149
Challiol-Gillet, Marie-Christine 69, 88
characteristics 48–9, 189
Christ 174, 213–14
Christianity 4–5, 28–9, 110, 153, 198, 210–16,
    218–21, 224, 240, 242
church 5, 218–19, 222
Coleridge, S. T. 8, 14, 19–20, 38
concealment 27, 42, 74, 144, 187–8, 192, 224
Condillac, Etienne Bonnot de 31, 190
construction 42–3, 46, 63, 111, 117–40,
    142–3, 147–8, 150–1, 153–6, 158–60,
    162, 166–7, 169, 186, 199–201, 204,
    206–7, 227, 236–7, 239–41
correspondence 81, 85, 89, 96, 114,
    155–6, 178
Courtine, Jean-François 71, 92, 229
Cousin, Victor 237
Cratylism 32–3, 37, 199–200
Creuzer, Friedrich 6, 11

Dante 60, 64–5, 160, 238–9
Darstellung 7, 45, 48, 65–8, 81, 89, 94, 96,
    98–100, 103–4, 116, 121, 130, 133, 136,
    141–5, 150, 154, 158, 162, 165–6, 170,
    175, 179, 183, 188, 192, 201, 206, 208,
    215, 225, 232, 241
Davies, Stephen 202–3
Deleuze, Gilles 82, 121
de Man, Paul 11, 17, 19–20, 30, 40–5, 50,
    53, 202–9
Descartes, René 93, 117–18, 215
dialectic 28, 67, 90–3, 102–3, 106–7, 113,
    116–17, 150, 161–2, 207
Diderot, Denis 237
dogmatism 170, 211
double intentionality 24–5
drama 34, 143, 218, 238
dualism 6–8, 85–6, 108, 110, 172, 215–16